FRONTISEPIECE

Author in Montane Rain Forest on Volcán San Martín Tuxtla. August 1962, 3,500 feet. Photograph by R. F. Andrle.

MY BUTTERFLY MUSES

An Anthology of Adventures on the Nature of Butterflies

Gary Noel Ross, Ph.D.

Copyright, 2025

by

Gary Noel Ross

ISBN:

Hardcover: 1-59804-994-1

Paperbound: 1-59804-993-3

All rights reserved.

Published and for sale by
Claitor's Publishing Division
PO BOX 261333
Baton Rouge, LA 70826
http://www.claitors.com

PREFACE

"Heaven help the scientist who, using butterflies for science alone, fails to appreciate their beauty and to take advantage of the wonderful places into which they lead us."

H.B.D. Kettlewell's 1963 presidential address to The Lepidopterists' Society: "Lepidoptera as scientific tools." *Journal of The Lepidopterists' Society,* Volume 17, No. 3, Pages 173-177.

I am a lepidopterist, a butterfly scientist. My mantra is "Butterflies are the essence of beauty and the paragon of the insect world." I state this with unabashed certainty. The majority of my life has centered on field research, not sitting behind a desk, not standing in front of a class, nor searching though museum collections. My unstoppable zest for learning about butterflies has taken me not only across the United States but to exotic—and sometimes even dangerous—venues within Canada, Puerto Rico, Dominican Republic, Mexico, Guatemala, Belize, Honduras, Costa Rica, Colombia, Brazil, Peru, Bolivia, Kenya, West Papua (Indonesia, New Guinea), and Madagascar. In most instances, my projects have involved elucidating the natural history of butterflies.

But I am an ethnobiologist, too. I have, for example, cultivated an avid and abiding interest in the mythology, symbolism, and art of the butterfly as expressed in the psychology of Indigenous cultures, particularly those of Mexico, Guatemala, and the southwestern United States. I have learned that the butterfly is a global symbol/metaphor for a literal and transcendental figure representing the afterlife. I have no doubt that the concept of a butterfly is ingrained in the DNA of *Homo sapiens,* the same as, for example, the innate love of trees and pets that manifests itself throughout human history. In between travels, I have delved into gardening for butterflies at my home in Baton Rouge—for both science and for their value to the human psyche. To me, the butterfly is seductive and ethereal. And I am one of its lifetime devotees.

My research to date has resulted in 705 published manuscripts with/without photographs. Of these, five are in a book format: *Gardening for Butterflies in Louisiana* (1994), *Everything You Ever Wanted to Know about Butterflies* (1995), Survey of the Butterflies of the Wah'Kon-Tah Prairie, Missouri (*Holarctic Lepidoptera, 2001/2005, Vol. 8:1-2*), Life History of the Seminole Crescent, *Anthanassa texana seminole* (Lepidoptera: Nymphalidae) (*Holarctic Lepidoptera, 2001-2005, Vol. 9:1-2*), and Louisiana's Avery Island and its Enigmatic Butterflies (*Southern Lepidopterists' News, June 2020, Vol. 42: Supplement*). Three illustrated essays published in periodicals have been honored with awards of recognition: two national ("John Burroughs Literary Award for Outstanding Nature Essay,"1996 and 2024) and one state ("Louisiana Wildlife Federation Award for Conservation Communicator of the Year," (2001); all are represented herein.

Having entered my "Golden Years," I have waxed reflective, sentimental, nostalgic. Candidly, I have lived what many may describe as a "charmed life," or what Peter Matthiessen in 1965 described as "At play in the Fields of the Lord." Ostensibly, my experiences have far exceeded my dreams of youth. And I am deeply appreciative. But I, also, am troubled. As a consummate naturalist, I know that Humankind has not behaved at its finest. Year after year, one new global threat compounds another. Our singular home, Planet Earth, has deteriorated into an increasingly pollutant-warped planet at a time when current technology can solve most woes. The beauty of the past, which could always be counted on to echo through the generations, is now severely compromised. Human ethics, spirituality, and—I dare say, even common sense—have all been replaced by ubiquitous avarice, pride, and an insatiable desire to acquire more and more—regardless of tangential long-term damage to our own species, *Homo sapiens*, and the environment in general. As a result, many of the exotic places that fueled my psyche with stunning vistas and adventures no longer exist, are too unsafe to visit, or have been declared by government officials as "off limits" to international researchers.

Then, there are the exponential advancements technology has made over the past decade or so. Although much of the new technology has proven positive, even epic on a global scale—environmentalists/conservationists have noticed an increasing and alarming negative backlash: a disconnect with and a lack of respect for Nature. Put another way, many contemporary citizens rely on viewing videos on screens in their private residences for access to education, work, recreation, and entertainment in lieu of personal one-on-one interactions outside their home turf. In fact, many, if not the majority, of the nation's current "techno-savvy" find "the great outdoors" alien and even fearsome. Even attendance at zoos, once the most popular genre for entertainment/recreation, has fallen sharply. Confounding.

Consequently, I embarked on a new project that I hope will inspire a renewed sense of wonderment in what has become my "lost world." The result is "*My Butterfly Muses: An Anthology of Adventures on the Nature of Butterflies.*" Within its pages are eighteen personal essays—tales, if you will—from my lengthy past. Each presents butterflies at their grandest in their reasonably intact habitats. All except one of the essays was published previously in a more technical format in a scientific periodical and/or in a commercial nature-centered magazine. Here, each is presented in a new format, I hope, to engage both professional and non-specialists, who espouse an interest in nature, and who will chance a break from the ubiquitous video screen. The style is a synthesis between technical *and* popular writing accented with dramatic photographs—in other words, serious science presented in everyday, conversational language.

The eighteen essays vary in length to maximize variety. Although all are based on real life experiences, each is independent. The lead story is my personal odyssey with its genesis in 1953. It provides, albeit in a circuitous format, a relevant background for the essays that follow and span seven decades. Most of my research behind the essays was personally funded, although during my twenty-four years of university teaching, I was the recipient of three modest research grants: *National Science Foundation* (1977), *National Geographic Society* (1996), and *The Nature Conservancy, Missouri Office* (1998)].

I invite you to join me as I engage in raw adventure—with both its ups and downs—as I pry into the private lives of butterflies. The scope is broad: We will travel from a gas-production platform seventy miles offshore in the Gulf of Mexico to a wonderland beneath the arid New Mexican desert; from the mosquito-infested coastal lowlands of Louisiana and a barrier island off the coast of Mississippi to the grassy landscapes of the Southwest and Midwest; from the mountain tops in Arkansas and Colorado to the humid tropical rainforests of Mexico, Brazil, and Indonesia; from an unrecorded pine forest on the slopes of a poorly explored dormant volcano in tropical southeastern Mexico to the epicenter of centuries-old textile and dye production in the semi-arid highlands of southern Mexico; from a "close encounter of the third kind" with Indigenous peoples in New Mexico, Mexico, and New Guinea, to my home butterfly garden where Mother Nature reveals her whimsical side. Each venue is unique. Although the original publications on which these stories are based were lavishly illustrated, I have kept photographs (many of which are now vintage) here to a minimum to focus attention on the drama of the texts. Also, I have reduced the list of references cited for each chapter, noting only those I deem critical for readers who wish additional details for clarity, or perhaps, even for future personal study.

This romp, which sometimes may seem tauntingly magical, is a history of my life—in essence, my de facto memoir. But my ambition is more—much, much more. My fervent hope is that you will not only experience a "feel-good" moment but also be inspired to champion my passion for butterflies and "the wonderful places into which they lead us." Then, you will be enlightened with a new respect for the awesomeness of life and the human spirit, as far as we know, all unique to Planet Earth, a.k.a. "Mother Earth." That would make our world a profoundly more "human" place. I am keeping my fingers crossed!

In conclusion, I would like to express my heartfelt appreciation to all individuals who have played a key part in my life-long odyssey. And although several have passed away, they have left family with whom I have remained cordial. I feel privileged, and I extend my gratitude to all. That said, I am particularly indebted to those singled out below:

- James K. Adams, Editor of *The Lepidopterists' Society*, Dalton, GA
- John G. Anderson/Walter Anderson Museum of Art (WAMA), Ocean Springs, MS
- Peter Wade Anderson/Sherwater Pottery, LLC, Ocean Springs, MS
- Robert F. Andrle (deceased) and son, Christopher Andrle, Buffalo, NY
- Murray S. Blum (deceased), University of Georgia, Athens, GA
- Anthony P. Cassard, Claitor's Law Books and Publishing Division, Baton Rouge, LA
- Dale Clark, former editor of *The Lepidopterists' Society*, Glenn Heights, TX

- Boyce A. Drummond, Colorado State University, Fort Collins, CO
- Charles E. Harris, President/CEO, *Natural History* Magazine, Inc., Research Triangle Park, NC
- John E. Hartgerink, Baton Rouge, LA
- Bruce Howard, Mandeville, LA
- Daniel Jalanivich, Harbor Master, Ocean Springs, MS
- Brandon J. Johnson, Baton Rouge, LA
- Randy P. Lanctot, Baton Rouge, LA
- John and Royce Lind (deceased), Summer Institute of Linguistics, and children: Cindy, Mike, Laura, Juanita, and Christy (AZ)
- J. Barry Lombardini, Editor of *Southern Lepidopterists' Society*, Lubbock, TX
- Vittorio Maestro, Editor Emeritus of *Natural History* magazine, Brooklyn, NY
- Heather Martin, Ethotera Art Studio, Ocean Springs, MS
- McGuire Center for Lepidoptera and Biodiversity, Florida Museum of Natural History, University of Florida: Thomas C. Emmel (deceased), John B. Heppner, Douglas S, Jones, Darcie Macmahon, Deborah L. Matthews, Anupama Priyadarshini, James B. Schlachta, Andrei Sourakov, Andrew D. Warren—Gainesville, Fl
- McIlhenny Company and Avery Island, Inc.: Shane K Bernard, Garrie L. Landry, Pam McIlhenny, Harold "Took" Osborn, Lisa B. Osborn, Bernard Patout, Tony Simmons, Cathy Thomason—Avery Island, LA
- William (Bill) and Jan Neale, El Dorado Springs, MO
- Johnny D. Pourciau, Baton Rouge, LA
- Everett Powers (retired from Baton Rouge Arts and Humanities Council), Spartanburg, SC
- Sarah Rayner, Baton Rouge, LA
- Tom Schaal (deceased), former pilot, Petroleum Helicopters, Inc., Lafayette, LA
- Robert Sherman, Baton Rouge, LA
- Harald and Barbara Schmitz family, Caucalândia, Rondônia, Brazil
- Roger L. Still, Columbia, MO
- Ted and Sue Thoreson and daughter, Tannen Gurley, El Dorado Springs, MO
- Isaac Vásquez Garcia (deceased) and current family descendants, Teotitlán del Valle, Oaxaca, Mexico
- F. Randy Wright, Baton Rouge, LA
- Frank Zachariah, Baton Rouge, LA

Thank You!

Gary Noel Ross, Ph.D.
January 18, 2025

DEDICATION

I dedicate this work to two extraordinary people as described below.

STEPHEN M. RUSSELL, Ph.D.: Professor Emeritus of Ecology and Evolutionary Biology, The University of Arizona. The ornithologist was my freshman biology teacher in college and the instructor for my first course in Natural History. It was Steve's passion for nature that cemented my boyhood fantasy of becoming a naturalist specializing in tropical flora and fauna. His detailed doctoral research on the birds of British Honduras (currently, Belize) became common reference points throughout his courses. During each class, I hung onto every word. Steve was instrumental in my first road trip to Mexico in 1960 so that I could experience a tropical forest and the ornate blue morpho butterfly. At this same time, Steve introduced me to the National Audubon Society and its annual touring film series. Later, in 1961, Steve arranged for me and another junior-level student during a summer college break to visit Belize to collect butterflies and birds for museum preservation and exhibition. Such experiences proved pivotal in my desire to take my education to the graduate level (1962) at Louisiana State University, Baton Rouge, and to concentrate on tropical butterflies (see Chapters 2, 3, 4 and 5). Over the intervening years, Steve and his wife, (both longtime residents of Tucson, Arizona), and I have remained in contact.

VITTORIO T. MAESTRO: Editor Emeritus of *Natural History* magazine. In the spring of 1985, Vittorio, then senior editor of *NH*, was the editor who reviewed my first unsolicited essay and photographs submitted to a commercial popular science magazine. The story chronicled my youthful field experiences dating back to 1963 when I was researching an unknown myrmecophilous metalmark butterfly in southeastern Mexico (see Chapter 5). Sensing my passion for science and storytelling, Vittorio quickly recommended that my story, which I had submitted in early 1985, be scheduled for the upcoming November issue of *NH*. Ever since, Vittorio has championed many of my stories of adventure in the natural world for other issues of *NH*, several of which I have rearranged and included herein, two of which have been honored with national literary awards: The John Burroughs Association Nature Essay Award (1996 and 2024) (see Chapters 7 and 10). Over the years, Vittorio, and his wife, Laura (lifetime residents of New York City, New York), and I have developed an abiding friendship, including visits on several occasions to each other's home. Without Vittorio's early professional editorial insight, I probably would have remained a reclusive scientist.

TABLE OF CONTENTS

PREFACE	iii
DEDICATION	vii
TABLE OF CONTENTS	ix
CHAPTER 1: I WAS A TEENAGE CAVEMAN	1
CHAPTER 2: MY FIRST BLUE MORPHO BUTTERFLY AND A NATURAL CATASTROPHE	13
CHAPTER 3: MY SCARIEST MOMENT IN THE FIELD	21
CHAPTER 4: SAGA OF THE WHITE MORPHO BUTTERFLY AND EVIL WOMEN	27
CHAPTER 5: CASE OF THE KIDNAPPED CATERPILLARS	37
CHAPTER 6: "A CLOCK-WORK ORANGE"	53
CHAPTER 7: BUTTERFLY WRANGLING IN LOUISIANA	67
CHAPTER 8: BIRDWING BUTTERFLIES AND STONE AGE TRIBES	77
CHAPTER 9: DIANA IN AMERICA	87
CHAPTER 10: A PRAIRIE ROYAL	99
CHAPTER 11: AN AMERICAN BUTTERFLY WIZ	111
CHAPTER 12: BUTTERFLIES AND THE ZUNI TRIBE OF NEW MEXICO	115
CHAPTER 13: A LOUISIANA BUTTERFLY "HAPPY HOUR"	127
CHAPTER 14: AN ADVENTURE IN THE AMAZON AND A MOTHER'S FINAL WISH	131
CHAPTER 15: FLYING HIGH	143
CHAPTER 16: AN ELUSIVE SWAMP CREATURE	151
CHAPTER 17: THE ENIGMATIC BUTTERFLY ART OF WALTER INGLIS ANDERSON	159
CHAPTER 18: THE BUG IN THE RUG	171
CREDITS FOR PHOTOGRAPHS	185

CHAPTER 1: I WAS A TEENAGE CAVEMAN

A childhood family vacation inspires a lifelong passion and profession

December 27, 2010. Baton Rouge, Louisiana. The temperature is fortyish. A monotonous drizzle soaks the air and earth. This inclemency coupled with a specter of post-Christmas malaise has me moody. After spending the last hour or so thinking about what to do, I opt to tackle a long-delayed project: sorting through two moldy, medium-size cardboard boxes of family mementos that I had inherited in 1997 after an automobile accident claimed the lives of my father and stepmother (my mother had died earlier in 1991).

That the decades' old family traumas were continuing to affect me is not the sole reason for my lengthy procrastination. I believed that most of my family's easily disposable mementos (photos, holiday cards, and letters, for example) had been damaged or destroyed in early September 1965 by flood waters from a Category 3 hurricane. "Billion-Dollar Betsy," as the behemoth came to be quantified, had flooded my parents' home with over four feet of dirty trash-laden water, leaving behind a heavy layer of putrid sludge and unrecognizable refuse. Most keepsakes, which had been stored on closet floors, were destroyed. I, at the time, was away at Louisiana State University in Baton Rouge, having just returned from a six-month entomological expedition in southern Mexico. The bottom line is that I was under the impression that the boxes held nothing of personal value. And so, I relegated the boxes of mementos to a closet. But, born with exceptional curiosity, today I wonder: "Might any family mementos have been salvaged and put aside, now in boxes that have been languishing thirteen years in my closet?"

I am thrilled to discover that the containers are packed with vintage photographs: small black and white prints taken by my mother with what I remember as a Kodak *Brownie* and an Argus *Argoflex* camera (my mother was not a trained photographer, but a housewife with a fondness for taking pictures). The photos are low-key: family and school portraits, pets, holiday and birthday celebrations, and family vacations. I finger each photo as I would a sacred relic. I lose track of time. Soon, my wistfulness is suddenly altered. There amidst the motley lot are several film processing yellow envelopes labeled in my mother's pen: "California, 1953." With trembling fingers, I open the envelopes. Inside are sixty-eight 3 x 3 black and white, glossy photos. While several show slight water stains, most are in good condition. A handful taken at Carlsbad Caverns National Park in southern New Mexico graces the lot. Included are several photos of me, my brother, my father, and my mother posing near the administrative building near the entrance to the cave. Although the quality of the photographs is inferior to what is common for current digital images, and most show some water damage, the 1953 black-and-white photographs are revealing, nonetheless. My fingers tremble as I inspect the priceless family heirlooms.

Then, my "holy grail." At the bottom of the cache, hidden by the photos, are two large binders. One is black, ornate, and embossed with the words *Scrap Book*. The other is a pale green standard-size folder with a left-hand binding of tape and staples. On the cover, scrolled in red ink in the characteristic fanciful penmanship of my father are the words: *The Cave by Gary Ross*.

First, I tackle the scrapbook. There are twenty-two pages, each of heavy stock and suffering only minor disintegration. Transparent, discolored tape affixes a handwritten list of the 26 national parks, a list of the seventy-one known caves within the United States, and numerous pictures of national parks and monuments—seemingly culled from magazine and newspaper articles I had viewed.

Next, I inspect the greenish folder. Bound with heavy tape and staples, and showing only minor discoloration, the contents consist of standard three-hole, lined notebook paper with penciled writing—front and back. The format is that of a book: title page (*The Cave*), *Table of Contents* (list of seven chapters), a body of text numbered 1-52 with first page headed *The Cave,* and near the right edge, *By Gary Ross, July 1, 1953 to November 8, '53*. I experience a cascade of adrenaline. My mood brightens as I disregard the outside dreariness. A haunting question overpowers my mind: "How can this be?"

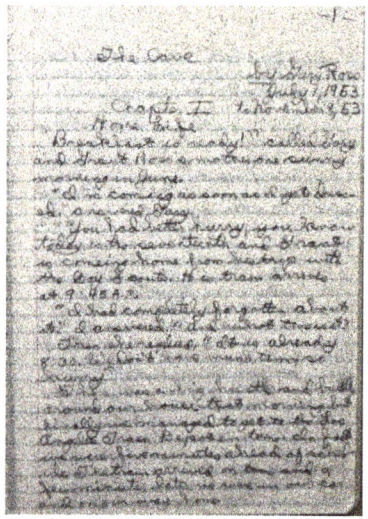

Prior to this day, I could recall only fragmented memories of the 1953 family vacation to California (including the visit to Carlsbad Caverns). My mind had grown sluggish, myopic. Uncovering my mother's photos and my fictional short story, however, corrected this. Today, I remembered that upon the family's return to New Orleans, I set about creating two primal projects. First, I fashioned a scrapbook of our overall adventures; and second, I composed a short fictional story—an abstraction of reality—based on my visit to Carlsbad Caverns National Park.

As I turn the aged pages of the scrapbook and read my fictional saga, my mind's vault of memories continues to unlock, triggering one flashback after another. Details emerge, resonate, time telescopes in. The nostalgia is visceral, palpable. The mental gymnastics, however, is exhausting. I rest the documents in my lap and stare out of a window into the gloom. I imagine all the circumstances over the past decades that had to coalesce to bring me to this point: my mother's initial sequestering of family photographs, my mother's respect for my schoolboy hobbies, my mother's desire to salvage these items following a devastating hurricane, my inheritance of the salvaged cache, and finally, my decision not to discard, but to investigate the contents of the aged "mystery" boxes I had inherited.

Then, an epiphany. The photographs assured me that my childhood family trip to California was thrilling, indeed. But it was more—much, much more. Now for the first time I understood that my exposure to Carlsbad Caverns National Park was so profound and transformative that it had set into motion a pathway of education and decision-making that channeled me into a career in the natural sciences. Furthermore, my fictional story, *The Cave*, had proven prophetic for my future literary pursuits and achievements. Plainly, my childhood road trip was the birth of Gary Noel Ross.

June 10, 1953. New Orleans. Summer usually epitomizes unbridled time for kids to play, to discover. Having recently turned thirteen, my younger brother of two years, Grant, and I, eagerly anticipated the family's annual week-long vacations to Waveland on the nearby Mississippi Gulf Coast. Our days were spent swimming (usually at dusk so that we could observe the spellbinding luminescent comb jellies (ctenophores), abundant in these coastal waters). During daylight, we set net traps for blue crabs, played volleyball with neighbors and before bedtime, played the popular board game *Pokeno* in this era of pre-television. With a penchant for butterflies from the age of five, I would spend some time using my home-crafted insect net to search for species I didn't possess.

But 1953 was different. In late spring Father had purchased a new family vehicle—a "Luna Gray Plymouth Cambridge Sedan"—to replace our jalopy ("hooptie"). New vehicles, at the time, required a lengthy "break-in" period. This consisted of driving at different speeds for different periods of time for the first 500 miles or so. To actualize this, my parents quashed the idea for the year's vacation to the Mississippi Gulf Coast. Instead, Father suggested that we embark on a three-week road trip from New Orleans to Los Angeles and Chula Vista to visit family friends who had recently relocated there.

Because the one-way distance was roughly 2,000 miles, that objective was audacious. Remember, in 1953 there was no interstate system for rapid travel. No GPS for navigation. No credit cards. No convenience stores for fast food and self-serve gasoline. No economical chain motels at convenient highway intersections. Too, most passenger vehicles in the '50s were not equipped with air-conditioning or even FM radios. And so on, and so on. We did, fortunately, receive some personal advice from our California friends. We were advised, for example, to seek out motels with attached cafés or restaurants where we could secure dinner and breakfast; for a quick lunch, we should patronize large truck stops. (What in today's economy would be considered debilitating hardships, were in 1953 simply "business as usual.")

Mother was apprehensive. She chided that we had never traveled more than 100 miles. Father remained dauntless. Grant and I pleaded as our minds envisioned fantastic, unworldly images. In the end, our collective petitions won out. And so, at three o'clock on the morning of June 10 we loaded our luggage into the trunk and onto the roof of our shiny new Plymouth sedan. Fittingly, I constructed a cursory sign out of cardboard that I taped on the back window: "CALIFORNIA OR BUST"!

En route we entertained ourselves by playing a game: competing to see who could first identify the model of a car and/or the state logo on a license plate of a vehicle in front of us. It seems silly today, but in the '50s the activity worked wonders for passing time. Because my father was a novice at driving, he had purchased a membership in the American Automobile Association (AAA). They mapped out our itinerary with different routes for going and returning with major scenic venues highlighted.

CHAPTER 1: I WAS A TEENAGE CAVEMAN

Our first AAA designated point of interest was Carlsbad Caverns National Park in the Chihuahua Desert of southeastern New Mexico. Since the park had no public lodge, we rented a quaint cabin for two nights in nearby Whites City. For travelers who had lived their entire lives in balmy south Louisiana, the hot, dry air and flora of the desert were exhilarating, exotic. After unpacking, my mother entertained herself by indulging her passion for photography. We high-spirited guys bolted to the rock-strewn hillside behind the cabin. We romped about in search of textbook desert critters such as tarantulas, scorpions, centipedes—and best of all, horned toads, and rattlesnakes. In no time at all we unearthed several beetles, one scorpion, and a single tarantula. Regrettably, not the stellar prizes I had envisioned, but "goodies," nonetheless.

With sunset at hand, we drove to the entrance of the cave. There, in an outdoor amphitheater that had been constructed from elaborate asphalt switchback ramps, we sat and listened as an affable ranger delivered a short lecture on the imminent spectacle. As the story goes, the caverns were discovered in 1901 when a local young cowboy named Jim White noticed what looked like smoke billowing from a large hole in the ground and disappearing into the setting sun. After investigating he found the "smoke" to be a stream of bats—untold numbers of flying mammals.

"That phenomenon remains to this day," the National Park Service (NPS) ranger declared. "Each evening between late spring and autumn, upwards of a million or so Mexican (Brazilian) free-tailed bats (technically known as *Tadarida brasiliensis*)—the most abundant mammal in North America—begin their nocturnal foray for insects in the surrounding desert. By dawn, the satiated bats return to their "Bat Cave," a side hollow not far within the entrance to Carlsbad. There they roost in clusters in an inverted position from the rock ceiling. Their excretory droppings accumulate as guano on the cave floor. In earlier times, this organic material was collected and sold for fertilizer. With the approach of winter, the winged mammals migrate south to warmer climes in Mexico, returning the following spring," the ranger concluded. I was bubbly!

Meanwhile, on this evening, the winged mammals were on point. A melee of frenetic black wings began to exit the gaping mouth of Carlsbad, streaming towards the departed sun. The ranger indicated that the movement was not helter-skelter. The bats used their specialized sense of echolocation (the use of sound waves to identify the position of objects) to set their course. After no more than thirty minutes, and with the western afterglow having transformed from cobalt to black, the number of bats waned quickly. And that was that.

The following morning, we purchased tickets for the first walking tour at 9:00 o'clock. Scheduled to last three and three-quarter hours, the trek would take us along three miles of trails through the underground labyrinth. The salesperson cautioned that while most of the excursion would be easy, the hike to the bottom was arduous: a mile-and-a-quarter descent along precipitous paved switchbacks beginning at the gaping natural entrance. We would return, however, to the surface via a modern elevator. About fifty participants convened in the rocky amphitheater. One of the two guides, park rangers attired in spiffy green uniforms accented by wide-brimmed hats bearing official NPS logos, advised that because the cave remains at 56 degrees year-round, we should don our wraps. Now, we were off.

As we began descending, we instinctively arranged ourselves into a queue with one ranger in front, the other in the rear. The light streaming through the entrance contracted quickly into a bluish shaft that softened upon each turn in the trail. Eventually we were awash in ghostly grayness. Up to now, adulatory chitchat was common throughout our group. But with darkness beginning to engulf, we hushed. My mind's eye began to conjure up storybook monsters lurching from the bowels of the earth, to whisk me away to their lairs. Before I could become too spooked, though, the lead ranger switched on electric lights, single white bulbs hidden strategically behind chunks of rocks that had fallen in the distant past. (The ranger assured us that since the discovery of the caverns, not a single newly fallen rock had been detected.) The trail had been discreetly partitioned into sectors for sequential lighting: The lead ranger could turn on lights in the sector before us while the backup ranger could turn off lights behind us. And thus, we progressed, lights on, lights off. Convenient. Dramatic. Exhilarating.

In places the trail was so narrow that it had been augmented with iron railings as a precaution against mishap. I instinctively grasped the cold, damp pipe for support. Finally, at 754 feet the trail leveled off. We paused. Here the lead ranger treated us to a technical, but easily comprehensible lecture about cave formation.

The geological construct goes something like this: The caverns are a product of ancient primal powers, specifically, inexorable interactions between limestone rock and groundwater. Approximately 250 million years ago the area, which is the modern national park, was then a vast and warm inland sea. The gradual decomposition and compaction of small marine life eventually produced a limestone reef. Known as Capitan Reef, the formation was uplifted by tectonic forces to form what is now the backbone of the Guadalupe Mountains and the extended cave system below. During this uplift, groundwater continually mixed with sulfur from subterranean oil reserves producing sulfuric acid, a substance that can aggressively dissolve limestone. The erosion resulted in the erosion of the rock to form the hollows that we see today. With continuing elevation, water eventually drained paramount for the creation of tunnels and rooms. Erosion from above caused one of the channels to collapse, creating what is now the natural entrance to the main cave (at least 100 smaller caves have been discovered within the national park). Dry air entering the chambers through this natural entrance evaporated any remaining water.

Meanwhile, water from rain and snow combined with carbon dioxide to form a mild acid known as carbolic acid. Because the solution carried minerals such as calcium carbonate, tiny crystals were deposited at an infinitesimal annual rate of about 0.005 inches (0.13 mm). In time, these crystals created a diversified array of sculptural/decorative formations within the hollowed-out caverns. Termed speleothems, these embellishments are sometimes colored from dissolved chromatic minerals such as iron. Speleothems are what attract most visitors to caves. Many such features bear technical names: the icicle-like formations hanging from the ceiling are named stalactites; their more robust counterparts created when water droplets impact the floor are called stalagmites. If the two eventually meet, a column is formed.

As we strolled through the subterranean wonderland, we were properly educated to a spectrum of other exemplary and enchanting formations: fluted cascades and drapery, cave pearls, grapes, soda straws, popcorn, and my personal favorite, helictites (delicate and translucent formations that cling to walls in seemingly gravity-defying poses). Gifted with vivid imagination, I could identify several whimsical animals—including my all-time favorite, butterflies.

I learned that formations that appear glossy and wet were growing; absent water, formations dry and become stable (about 95 percent in Carlsbad). While it is impossible to date the formations in the Carlsbad system, geologists theorize that none is older than the early Pleistocene, or about 1,000,000 years.

At his conclusion, the ranger made a startling announcement: "I am going to switch off all lights so that you can experience absolute darkness and absolute silence—except for the occasional sound of dripping water." We were requested to remain motionless and quiet as the lights were extinguished—one at a time. Finally, eerie emptiness except for the occasional drop of water that was amplified by the vastness of the surroundings. As a mini-experiment, I positioned my hands directly in front of my eyes. I saw nothing. I wiggled my fingers. Nothing. I felt as if the world had vanished, and I was simply a spirit. I winced; I fidgeted. I tacitly grabbed one of my mother's hands. With the return of light, I could hear everyone breathe a sigh of relief.

One visitor asked why there were no colored lights accenting the formations. The ranger responded: "The National Park Service wants visitors to experience the cave's naturalness. The single color in the cave comes from natural minerals." Another person wondered if we were in any danger. Answer: "The stable temperature and humidity in the cave minimize any type of rock movement. Earthquakes in the region are another matter. None has been recorded in historical times." Bolstered by the ranger's confidence, I smiled at my mother. The interlude provided me a few moments to concentrate on the ranger who labeled himself a "spelunker" or "caver." For me, the ranger seemed to be in his element, a profession based on love and passion. I felt a non-verbal connection. I thought: "Could I ever be fortunate enough to land such a job?" However, at 13, I could only gawk and pine.

The highlight of the tour was a section known as the "Big Room" featuring "Hall of the Giants." No superlatives can do this mega-expanse justice. With more than 30,000 square feet, or 14 acres, the domed hollow can hold six football fields and has a ceiling ranging from thirty to 285 feet; at the maximum, the copper Statue of Liberty (151 feet) would be easily contained—and the statue plus pedestal (305 feet) would almost fit. The room was touted as the second largest natural underground expanse in the world (today, the room is logged in as fifth largest in the United States and twenty-eighth for the world).

There were other splendors in this cordoned colossus: "Doll's Theater," Queen's Chamber," "Rock of Ages," and "King's Palace." In a few places, pools of still, clear water had been created from overhead drippings. With the water transparent, I could not judge depth, or what was rock and what was mirror image, the pools impressed me as beguiling, surreal. The ranger indicated that although the deepest levels of the cave extend down to over 1,000 feet, no running water has ever been located. Fittingly, Carlsbad lacks aquatic life such as blind fish and amphibians—small animals that are sometimes found in other caves throughout the world.

After 30 minutes or so, the loop trail returned us to a section of the "Big Room" that had recently been augmented with a small café marketing box lunches. Nearby picnic tables provided a place to rest, eat, and revel in what we had just observed. And because my mother had taken no photographs within the cave (lighting was far too limited), the break provided the opportunity for us to purchase postcards for souvenirs.

At the end of the tour, we were directed to the nearby elevators that would return us to the surface. The ascent was lickety-split. I thought how lucky we were to ride rather than back-hike the steep 750 feet of switchbacks. When the elevator slowed and the door opened, a brilliant light flooded the compartment. My eyes closed, reflexively. I quizzed: "Am I about to awake from a dream?"

Endowed with the indefatigable enthusiasm of pilgrims from a foreign land, we elected to participate in a mid-afternoon Nature Walk to learn about Carlsbad's desert environment. A group of about 15 participants assembled near the flag near the administrative building. A young ranger/naturalist escorted us along an asphalt trail that meandered through a rolling landscape of sand, rocks, and boulders. I was relieved that the trail had been engineered to accommodate even lowlanders from Louisiana. We learned that the sun-drenched landscape is classified as the Chihuahua Desert. Spanning parts of three states (New Mexico, Texas, Arizona) and extending southward into northern Mexico, the Chihuahua is the largest true desert (an area with ten or fewer inches of rain each year) in North America. Except for a few areas dominated by naked dunes, the Chihuahua is most acclaimed for its milieu of specialized vegetation.

Walking was uncomfortable. Lacking trees for shade, the heat and glare from the surrounding desert were pervasive—a turnabout from the labyrinth below. To our surprise, our clothing was not moistening with perspiration—another feature of desert environs. At one stopping place, we were afforded a panoramic view of the surrounding desert and the complex of rock-infrastructures, which blended well into the environment. What impressed me above all else, however, was my ability to see the horizon. Having resided all my life in a flat, verdant Louisiana, I had never been able to see the horizon in 360 degrees due to tall trees always blocking the view.

Here, with no obstructions, a domed sky formed a ubiquitous backdrop. Stunning, to say the very least!

Although there were no trees, there *was* greenery. The ranger, kinetic and astute, spieled exotic sounding names such as beargrass, candelilla, ocotillo, tarbush, palo verde, lechuguilla agave, century plant, creosote bush, soapweed yucca, sotol yucca, cholla cactus, prickly pear cactus, and mammillaria cactus with ease. I hung onto every word.

Halfway through the walk, Mother Nature upped the ante. As we rounded a bend, the ranger halted abruptly. In the middle of the trail before us was a three-foot, heavy-bodied snake, stretched and basking. "Western diamondback rattlesnake," the ranger quipped as he smiled and remained steadfast. "The striking diamond patterns on its back are a giveaway." Most participants were dumbstruck; my brother and I were ecstatic! The ranger then articulated the underlying philosophy of the National Park Service: "These lands are owned by the people and are for the people. The parks are sanctuaries that protect the nation's wildlife, flora, and geologic structures for future generations." Glancing at the resting snake, he said: "Even venomous rattlesnakes are important and must not be disturbed." Finally, the ranger used his walking stick to nudge the snake. The snake began to undulate slowly and silently. Within seconds the reptile was swallowed into anonymity afforded by the immensity of its haven. Drama ended, point well taken, and another life wish fulfilled.

During the succeeding days we visited other major attractions: White Sands, Grand Canyon, Petrified Forest, Painted Desert, Griffith Park and Observatory, Balboa Park and San Diego Zoo, and Knotts Berry Farm; we even took a day jaunt "south of the border" to Tijuana, Mexico. And butterflies? I was fortunate enough to observe at least a dozen species that were as alien to me as if I had traveled to another planet (and no, I didn't collect because my father said our vehicle could not accommodate my improvised handcrafted net of broomstick, coat-hanger, and bridal-veil netting).

In the end, nothing upended Carlsbad Caverns. The park's otherness (a subterranean wonderland, an exotic desert landscape and climate, numberless bats streaming through a gaping chasm at twilight), as well as it being the first tourist attraction of our road trip, were singular enough to imprint on a provincial Cajun kid from coastal, sultry Louisiana. The Southwest, for me, was a world unto itself—enchanted. And I loved every instant!

The twenty-one days on the road ended without mishap. Mother even conceded that she was happy that we had embarked on the adventure. Our major discomfort was the drives through the deserts of western Texas, southwestern Arizona, and southeastern California. But even those became tolerable if we began our day prior to dawn, settling into a motel shortly after lunch. (Also, acting on a tip from our California friends, hanging damp towels in one or more windows of the car raised the humidity and reduced the effect of the heat.)

Returning to New Orleans, my mind remained transfixed on the sights and sounds of our recent travels—a "world of magic." I was convinced that the study of nature was my true calling. In response, I immediately prepared a hardcover scrapbook to preserve all the brochures, postcards, magazine and newspaper articles I had collected since my father had proposed the vacation.

During the remaining summer and fall I devoted much spare time to composing a fictional adventure short story titled *The Cave*, based, of course, on my experiences in Carlsbad Caverns. [Summarily, in my story line there are two protagonists: my brother Grant, and I. We were young teenagers living in Los Angeles. Because we both enjoyed the outdoors, we often went hiking and collecting butterflies as well as other multi-legged critters in the nearby San Gabriel Mountains. On one such outing, we discovered the opening to what appeared to be a tunnel leading downward. After reporting this to a newspaper journalist, the tunnel turned out to be the entrance to a sizable cave. In short time the cave is explored by professionals, eventually developed into a popular state park that offers daily tours. My father becomes the superintendent; I serve as a ranger naturalist. Writing the story was a great pastime. I was able to incorporate many vivid memories from the family's first major sojourn. After completion of the manuscript, my father offered criticism, prepared a cover in his elegant penmanship, and suggested that I ask my eighth-grade teacher to proof the text for major grammatical errors. My teacher was so impressed that she asked me to read the story to the class. Despite a smidgen of embarrassment, I was proud.]

Time passed. I matriculated in undergraduate biology at a local, newly established university (Louisiana State University in New Orleans, currently the University of New Orleans. I devoted the next five years to graduate study in tropical entomology and ecology (specializing in butterflies) at Louisiana State University in Baton Rouge under Dr. Murray S. Blum. Upon completion of my education, I decided that my greatest value as a naturalist-educator-researcher would be realized if I remained in my home state where I had roamed about since childhood. That said, I selected Southern University in Baton Rouge for my vocation, using breaks to conduct field studies in and out of the country, and retiring at the age of 52 (1992) to immerse myself fully in research and publishing. To share my love of butterflies, I became heavily involved with creating popular events such as workshops and festivals, usually under the auspices of the North American Butterfly Association (NABA). When in 1972 I designed my only house in Baton Rouge, I created an urban wildlife landscape, especially to attract pollinators such as butterflies, bees, and bats. The cutting-edge design unleashed a rumpus in my conservative community and initiated a confrontation with city officials. Through it all, however, I didn't despair; today, I reside in "peace." With every new project away from home, I visited any nearby cave open to the public. On no less than four occasions, I revisited Carlsbad Caverns to relive memories; never was I disappointed. And throughout the decades, I have published in both technical and popular periodicals (cumulative total of publications of just over 700); of these, three have won prestigious literary awards.

And Carlsbad Caverns? Although discovered in 1901, the caverns were not adequately explored until 1924-1925 by the National Geographic Society. The 46,766 acres, which now

CHAPTER 1: I WAS A TEENAGE CAVEMAN

comprise Carlsbad and at least eighty smaller caves, officially became a national monument in 1923 under the presidency of Calvin Coolidge. The monument was upgraded to the nation's twenty-eighth national park on May 14, 1930, by an Act of Congress under President Herbert Hoover. In 1995 the park was designated a UNESCO World Heritage Site that currently brings in roughly one-half million visitors annually. And in 2016, the National Park Service designated the year as "The Centennial Year of America's National Parks." To commemorate, NPS unleashed a universal campaign with advertisements and special programming extolling the nation's premier system for preserving natural wonders. I was especially gratified when on June 17 the national news media headlined that President Barack Obama, and his family toured the underground colossus. The President is reported to have referred to Carlsbad as "cool" and "spectacular."

January 8, 2017. It is another one of those uncomfortable wintry days in south Louisiana—not unlike that fortuitous December 27 in 2010. Currently in my seventy-seventh year, my reality has spiraled in. With my life's odyssey nearing finality, I am less adventuresome and more contemplative. The outside dreariness again triggers reflection. I recall the reveal of my mother's memorabilia. I surrender to the mounting nostalgia. I retrieve *The Cave* and my mother's photos I have been storing in plastic bags in my home safe since December 2010, the date I first uncovered them. I position myself comfortably on a cushion on the floor. I do not turn on lights; four arched expanses of glass transmit a comforting grayness that is sufficient for my pensive mood.

I spread out my sixty-seven-year-old icons. My subconscious instinctively surfaces allowing me to experience the pleasure of my teenage adventure. Time stands still. I realize that what was, can be no more, of course. My psyche, though, is not troubled. The future of these documents is secure: A few years ago, I formalized a commitment with the McGuire Center for Lepidoptera and Biodiversity, Florida Museum of Natural History, University of Florida, to archive my lifelong collections—including these bits of childhood expressions. Having no close living family, these documents will constitute my legacy. My hope is that in the not-too-distant future, some young student whose innate curiosity about the natural world had not been dulled by modern technology, will discover *The Cave* and its accompanying photos, and be inspired to become a naturalist.

Perhaps. I bear testimony that stranger things have happened.

"Some days I would let the other rangers take over [the tours], and father and I would go explore more of the cave. We have explored approximately fifteen miles. But there are still miles upon miles that have never been seen by the human eye. Some people think that "The Cave" extends under the Los Angeles River—twenty five miles away from the entrance, but that has never been proven. I hope some day that I will finally conquer it. But until that day comes, I will never stop trying. The End."

Excerpted from Chapter VII (final chapter), *The Cave*, an unpublished manuscript by Gary Noel Ross, 1953.

SELECTED REFERENCES

Brinkley, D. 2009. *The Wilderness Warrior: Theodore Roosevelt and the Crusade for America*. Harper Collins Publishers. New York, NY. 940 pages.

Crane, C. 2000. *Carlsbad Caverns National Park: Worlds of Wonder*. Carlsbad Caverns/Guadalupe Mountains Association, Trade Paperback Edition. Carlsbad, NM. 55 pages.

Greene, E.J. 2006. *Carlsbad Caverns: The Story Behind the Scenery*. KC Publishers, Inc. Las Vegas, NV. 48 pages.

Klots, A.B. 1951. *A Field Guide to the Butterflies of North America, East of the Great Plains*. Houghton Mifflin Company, Boston, MS. 340 pages.

Opler, P.A. and V. Malikul. 1998. A *Field Guide to Eastern Butterflies*. The Peterson Field Guide Series. Houghton Mifflin Co., New York, NY. 488 pp.

Ross, G.N. 2010. How a national park influenced my life. *Wake-Robin* (Newsletter of the John Burroughs Association Inc., American Museum of Natural History), Winter (Vol. 42:2), pages 4-7.

Ross, G.N. 2013. My life-changing experience. *News of the Lepidopterists' Society*, Summer (Vol. 55:2), pages 71-74.

Ross, G.N. 2016. Lasting impressions. IN: Endpaper, *Natural History,* September (Vol. 124:8), page 48.

CHAPTER 2: MY FIRST BLUE MORPHO BUTTERFLY AND A NATURAL CATASTROPHE
A taste of Heaven—and Hell

With their extraordinary diversity of life, tropical forests are especially alluring to field biologists. As a sophomore in college in New Orleans with aspirations to becoming a lepidopterist, I took my first field trip to a tropical forest in August 1960. My passion for butterflies and the out-of-doors started early. Traveling from Louisiana with my younger brother (Grant) and a graduate student friend (Donald Sutton), both of whom were interested in reptiles, we crossed the Mexican border in Brownsville, Texas, and headed south toward the Tropic of Cancer. Our target was *El Salto* ("The Jump" or "The Waterfall"), a massive cascade located on the border between the states of Tamaulipas and San Luis Potosi, and near the town of El Naranjo and smaller community of El Meco (both in SLP). Physiographically, the region lies within the foothills of the fabled backbone of eastern Mexico, the Sierra Madre Oriental. Biogeographically, this is the northern limit of the Atlantic Tropical Deciduous Forest (simply, "jungle"); the majority of its flora and fauna are considered "tropical." Historically, the region is the homeland of the Huasteca people. The surrounding lowlands are dominated by sugarcane and citrus agriculture. *El Salto* is barely 400 miles south of the Texas border and 25 miles south of the Tropic of Cancer—the official geographic northern limit of the tropics.

The waterfall was grand. Turbulent water plunged 230 feet into a lower water course—narrow, shallow, and translucent blue green or turquoise. The force of the flow created billowing mist that nurtured a moist mini ecosystem. Ferns, mosses, liverworts, selaginellas, club mosses, and fungi carpeted everything exposed. Here and there within the water coarse natural mineral build-ups cordoned off concentric travertine pools that functioned as small catch basins—de facto aquaria and bathtubs. Several pools held caches of small, colorful fish—some of which I recognized to be the same as those in my freshwater tropical fish tank at home. The shoreline of the river—named Rio Salto (after the waterfall) but also referred to as Rio Valles—was shaded by stately moss-hung *ahuehuetes*, or Montezuma cypress trees (*Taxodium mucronatum*), a sister species to bald cypress (*Taxodium distichum*), common in my familiar southern swamps. A dirt road on the narrow floodplain bordering the river below the cataract accommodated occasional visitors and campers who enjoy frolicking in the larger travertine pools. In those days, most American tourists did not venture into Mexico's hinterlands due to poor roads and lack of facilities; and unlike present-day Mexico, did not have a high crime rate. This August, *El Salto* was deserted except for a few local *campesinos* (farmers) who were curious about my net-swinging activities. The tableau was otherworldly—the mystical *Xanadu* of the Silver Screen. My mind raced: "Could this be the home of the spectacular "blue morpho" butterfly that my biology professor had described to me?"

Butterflies filled the air. Sunlit mud puddles hosted large numbers of thirsty, brightly colored yellow and orange sulphurs (family Pieridae). Although I could identify a few species from my *Peterson's Field Guide* that described all butterflies recorded from eastern North America (including tropical strays), most of the varieties I observed were not included because they were exclusively tropical. (I identified most of my specimens upon my return to New Orleans by consulting academic tomes on tropical butterflies housed in the library of Tulane University). While collecting in the open sun was exhilarating, I yearned to explore the luxurious "jungle." Presenting as an emerald, highly textured and impenetrable wall, the vegetation was heavy, onerous. Luckily, there was a narrow trail to the right of the falls that appeared to lead into what my mind conjured as a shadowy "enchanted wood."

The trail was rocky, dank, and narrow—but manageable. While most plants were unfamiliar, I could occasionally recognize a sizable bottle-palm or ponytail palm (*Beaucarnea recuvata*)—a species commonly featured as an indoor ornamental in homes and offices. Too, the gumbo limbo tree (*Bursera simaruba*), a medium size species sporting a quirky shiny red bark that peels like the skin of a severely sun-burned beachgoer, was common (I recognized the tree from previous visits to southern Florida where the species is used in landscaping). After about 15 minutes, four large glitzy blue apparitions materialized a few yards ahead of me. The electric color—technically, iridescence—could belong to nothing other than what is popularly referred to as "blue morpho" (*Morpho helenor montezuma*). The butterfly is the most common and northern of the large taxa, *Morpho*, (family Nymphalidae, subfamily Morphinae); all make their home exclusively in the tropical forests of the Americas. Most species sport a lustrous (metallic) wing sheen known as iridescence—defined as "a play of color caused by differential refraction of light waves as in a soap bubble or oil slick." The shimmery color is a result not of chemical pigments but instead, by light interacting with the complex structure of the tiny scales covering the butterfly's wings—in essence, a structural color. The effect is dramatic, eye-popping—and not uncommon throughout both the organic and inorganic worlds: think some bird feathers, fish scales, and oil slicks.

CHAPTER 2: MY FIRST BLUE MORPHO BUTTERFLY AND A NATURAL CATASTROPHE

When it comes to butterflies, iridescence is best epitomized by species classified within the genus *Morpho*. Up to now, I had only seen photographs of a "morpho" in nature magazines in my local library. Here at *El Salto*, though, those opulent butterflies were common denizens in the remnant forests encircling the falls. [Since 1988, *M. helenor* has been receiving top billing in butterfly conservatoires, aka butterfly "houses." Consequently, M. *helenor* has become the poster species for the American tropics and conservation, being acknowledged by many professionals as the crown jewel of the insect world.] The butterflies' flight within the forest was invariably close to the ground along open trails. And their flight style was singular: a gallop similar to that of a horse (my mind conjured an image of the Pegasus of mythology). On occasion, I observed an individual or two feeding on fermenting sap oozing from the trunk of a tree beside the trail. To my surprise, the butterflies were not temperamental; they paid me no heed.

As lagniappe, in their resting position their underwings were exposed so that I could easily observe that there was no blue color there. Instead, the ground color was brown punctuated with numerous eyespots (ocelli). This type of body guise is known as camouflage, cryptic coloration, and mimicry.

Evolutionary theory posits that the deception created increases survival rate, and as such, is rife throughout both the animal and plant kingdoms.

Sighting the blue morphos was a life-long dream come true. I can affirm unabashedly that my 1960 introduction to the blue morpho when in my formative years, remains my purest sensorial and most profound butterfly memory. The memory is so indelibly implanted in my mind that my credo and everyday mantra have been honed as:

"The butterfly is the essence of beauty, the paragon of the natural world, and the single creature of creation that opens the very vaults of Heaven by inspiring us to dream anew."

My aspiring herpetologist companions had been rewarded, also. Their sightings included numerous reptiles such as iguanas, small lizards, and a two-foot Mexican vine snake (*Oxybelis aeneus*), a rear-fanged, mildly venomous tropical, arboreal species. Because all of us were struggling college students in a pre-digital age, none of us possessed a camera to capture these once-in-a-lifetime moments. Such is life!

Yet, my saga with El Salto and the blue morpho did not end. In August 1970, I revisited the cascade. The spectacle was as I remembered. With a state-of-the-art film camera, I was primed to chronicle some of the region's outstanding natural bounty. But, after day two, a catastrophe ensued in which I almost lost my vehicle and my life. Below is that narrative.

I was camping in my new vehicle: a four-wheel drive, nine-passenger Chevrolet Suburban Carryall on the narrow floodplain bordering the river. Torrential rains had pounded the area for the previous twelve hours. The rain ceased near dusk and so I retired into the bed of my Carryall, fully dressed, without trepidation. However, unbeknownst to me, the deluge had caused the small river above and below the cascade to rise dramatically. With the first glimmer of dawn, I was awakened by a tapping on my vehicle's rear window. A handful of *campesinos,* each carrying a flashlight, motioned for me to open the window. With gaunt faces, rapid-

CHAPTER 2: MY FIRST BLUE MORPHO BUTTERFLY AND A NATURAL CATASTROPHE

fire speech accompanied by manic gestures, the men warned that the river was overflowing into the parking area and that I should move my vehicle *immediately*!

Peering out, I was shocked: The river was reclaiming its flood plain—aka, my *camp site*. Flood waters were six to eight inches up the tires of my vehicle. With no forethought to safety, I opened the tailgate and jumped into the water, which was scarcely below the threshold of the doors. I quickly engaged the four-wheel drive mechanism (partially submerged) of the front wheels. The villagers then guided the vehicle along the submerged road as I slowly steered up onto the adjacent ridge. From this higher, dry vantage point, the morning light revealed the sheer horror of the moment. A swift current laden with muddy sediment was transporting dislodged logs, uprooted trees, and mats of assorted vegetation swiftly downstream. Now the gravity of the situation hit me. While asleep peacefully in my vehicle, a flash flood ensued. Had I not been awakened by villagers; the swift moving flood waters probably would have swept away the vehicle with me inside. The rescue team and I stood motionless beside my intact vehicle, which was dripping from its partial submergence. We all were too traumatized to speak as we imagined the "what if" scenario. For the

better part of the day, the river continued to rage, quickly engulfing the entire parking area with three to four feet of debris-laden water. By nightfall, the river receded into its normal bed. In its wake, the sun on the following morning showed through a cloudless sky, brightly. By mid-day, I was able to delight in chasing butterflies in my personal "Eden"—albeit one with an ominous caveat.

In July 1981 I re-visited *El Salto*. The cascade was no more. Several military personnel at the site informed me that in 1966, the federal government drafted plans to construct a hydroelectric plant on Rio Salto above the falls to provide power for nearby rural communities and sugarcane mills. The river upstream from the falls was re-directed into a gigantic conduit to power turbines for generating electricity. Afterward, the water was returned to the original riverbed about a mile below the precipice. To protect the facility, a small military outpost on the ridge accessing the hydroelectric facility was constructed. During my chat with one of the affable young soldiers, I learned that the "falls" currently are dry most of the time. But during the summer rainy season when excessive river water may overwhelm the turbines, overflow is shunted back to the bedrock of the original cascade. At other times, the smaller cascades and the ephemeral pools of turquoise water that remain below *El Salto*—and not to be forgotten, the tropical birds and insects—are sufficient oddities to attract a smattering of Mexican and American tourists and scientists. Gazing at the dry riverbed, I thought about the incalculable forms of aquatic life—plant, animal, microbial—that must have perished after the water's re-direction. An entire ecosystem was destroyed, clearly. When I asked the soldier about the spectacular forest-dwelling blue morpho, he smiled and nodded: "The government prohibits the cutting of trees—especially the *ahuehuetes*. The *mariposas azules* (blue butterflies) are here during the rainy season. We love to see them." Before returning to his duties, the soldier in a matter-of fact tone added: "We consider this place special because the Aztec Emperor Montezuma visited the area and bathed beneath the falls." Whether historic fact or idealized fiction, the account was another reason to bemoan the demise of the falls.

Later, I scouted for the trail that I had hiked in 1960. Thankfully, it remained; nothing catastrophic had occurred. As if teleported back in time, a blue morpho, with its characteristic color and gait, nearly brushed my pants on its flight downhill. My "blue muse" lived!

Currently, in my ninth decade of life, I frequently reflect on Mexico's lost cascade. I wonder if Man's advancement must always come before the well-being of plants, animals, or ecosystems? Isn't natural beauty important to our innate psyche? Simply put, does modernization have to trump Mother Nature?

At least for *El Salto*, hope rises. Citizens have rebelled against the demise of one of Mexico's paragons of nature. In response, the Mexican government began questioning its initial decision to re-direct water from the *El Salto* cascade. Consider: In 2018 legislators from the Municipality of El Naranjo along with Mexico's tourist commission petitioned the federal authorities to return the beleaguered *El Salto* to its natural flow. The result was a compromise in 2020. Today, except during periodic dry months (usually November-February), most of the water is re-directed to the bed of the cascade to ensure partial flow, so that in mid-summer through autumn, the falls roar in their primeval glory. Furthermore, the tourist commission embarked upon a campaign to advertise the natural and cultural beauty of the area now referred to as *La Huasteca Potosina*. There is minor infrastructure befitting a tourist attraction: a ticket booth (minimal charge per person with free parking), toilet, food stalls, and a shop for renting life jackets for swimming. And tourists have responded. Often commercial tour buses visit the area, allowing passengers a chance to cool down with a swim in the pools of enticing turquoise water. To date, damage to the surrounding vegetation has been minimal, and the tropical animal life—including the blue morpho—seems unaffected. The outcome, understandably, is not certain. But with stewardship, and perhaps a little luck, locals, tourists, and aspiring biologists can experience the glory of one of Mexico's most biologically diverse and picturesque natural wonders—all so, so close to the Texas border.

With fervent nostalgia, I cry: *"Viva El Salto y Viva las Mariposas Azules"* ("Long live *El Salto* and long live the blue morpho.").

[This is an integration of three previously published illustrated essays: "My First Blue Morpho and Mexico's El Salto Waterfall" in *Southern Lepidopterists' News*. September 30, 2009 (Vol. 31:3) pages 102-108; "The Price of Power" in *Natural History*, February 2022 (Vol. 130:2), pages 9-11; and "My Blue Muse: An Essay on Nostalgia, Disappointment and Hope." *News of the Lepidopterists' Society*, Summer 2022 (Vol. 64:2), pages 104-111. Partial texts reprinted with permission of the publishers and with minor edits.]

SELECTED REFERENCES

De la Maza Ramirez, R. 1987. *Mariposas Mexicanas*. Fondo de Cultura Economica, S.A. de C.V. Mexico, D.F., MX. 302 pages.

Glassberg, J. 2007. *A Swift Guide to the Butterflies of Mexico and Central America*. Sunstreak Books, Inc. Morristown, NJ. 266 pages.

Godman, F.C. & O. Salvin. 1879-1901. *Biologia Centrali-Americana. Insecta. Lepidoptera-Rhopalocera*. Two volumes. London. 487 pages, 782 pages.

Klots, A.B. 1951. *A Field Guide to the Butterflies of North America, East of the Great Plains*. The Peterson Field Guide Series. Houghton Mifflin Company. Boston, MA. 349 pages.

Lamas, G. 2004. *Atlas of Neotropical Lepidoptera. Volume 5A, Checklist Part 4A*. Association for Tropical Lepidoptera. Scientific Publications. Gainesville, FL. 439 pages.

Opler, P. and V. Malikul. 1992. *A Field Guide to Eastern Butterflies*. The Peterson Field Guide Series. Houghton Mifflin Company. Boston, MA. 396 pages.

Seitz, A. 1923. *Macrolepidoptera of the World. The American Rhopalocera*. Volume 5. Stuttgart, Germany. 1139 pages.

Young, A.M. 2018. Morphos and me. *Natural History*, February (Vol. 126:2), pages 14-17.

https://Sallysees.com/cascada-el-salto/
https://pulsoslip.com.mx/estado/reactivaran.cascada-de-el-salto/769106
https://en.wikipedia.org/wiki/El_Naranjo_San_Luis_Potosi

CHAPTER 3: MY SCARIEST MOMENT IN THE FIELD

The "Serpent" in Mexico's "Garden of Eden"

Snakes are not on my list of favorite animals. Some species are venomous, and therefore, can pose a real danger to me when I am alone in the field. Upping the ante, my lifelong home in southern Louisiana has no less than six potentially deadly species: cottonmouth (water moccasin), copperhead, coral, and three species of rattlesnakes. Understandably, I have considered snakes a bane during my entire life.

As Louisiana natives, my parents were not enamored with snakes, either. When I was a teenager who was constantly looking for an opportunity to trek into fields and woodlands in search of butterflies, my mother insisted that I always dress to safeguard myself from a possible snakebite. Fundamentally, my standard field attire *had* to consist of loose-fitting heavy trousers (never shorts!), long-sleeved shirt, and calf length, lace-up leather boots. Additionally, I carried a commercially available "snake-bite kit" that included a string tourniquet, small lancet, and rubber suction cups. Although I did encounter a sizable number of venomous reptiles (usually a cottonmouth), to my amazement, I never experienced a "close encounter." Just luck, I guess.

My penchant for butterflies, particularly those kaleidoscopic species that make their homes in the tropics, continued into my college years. When I began my graduate studies in the summer of 1962 at the age of 22, I was offered the opportunity to initiate research in southern Mexico as a partner of Robert F. Andrle, a fellow graduate student from Buffalo, New York, who was researching the biogeography of the Sierra de los Tuxtlas, or "Los Tuxtlas" (See Chapters 4 and 5.)

My work involved a six-month residency in a house that Andrle rented in Playa Azul on the shore of picturesque Lake Catemaco, the heart of Los Tuxtlas. Our Mexican neighbors were quick to warn us of a local snake that was common around habitations. The snake supposedly could kill a human within minutes. The reviled serpent was known as *sorda* ("deaf one"). The name refers to the snake's tendency to remain motionless when approached. So terrifying, the name was always spoken in muted tones, as if the very vocalization would bestow future bad luck. Truth is, the *sorda* was legend—evil incarnate!

And there was more. One day while netting butterflies in a small, shaded orange/coffee orchard across the road from my residence, I met an older gentleman. "Juan" walked with a decided right-legged limp. While sharing with me one of the oranges he was picking, Juan recounted that he had been bitten decades earlier in this very orchard by a small *sorda*. Because the specimen was a juvenile, and because the town with a physician was but a few miles away, Juan was able to secure medical attention quickly, and therefore, the bite proved non-lethal. "But as you can see," Juan quipped candidly: "I can't use my right leg." Juan pulled up the pant leg, revealing a terribly disfigured appendage. All muscle tissue had atrophied leaving discolored skin-covered bone. Juan smiled and resumed: "I do fine with only one leg."

[NOTE: The *sorda* is scientifically classified as fer-de-lance (*Bothrops asper*). The species is a ground-dwelling pit viper common throughout most of the forested tropics from Mexico south through Central America, and finally into northern South America. The name fer-de-lance is of French derivation, meaning "lance-head," and refers to the characteristic arrow-shaped head of most vipers. Other common names include *barba amarilla* (referring to the pale-yellow chin color) and *nauyaca* (referring to the two nostrils and two sensory pits below the eyes), and "yellow-jaw tommygoff." As with all pit vipers, the fer-de-lance has vertical eye pupils. Adults are heavy-bodied, commonly attaining a length of 5-6 feet, and capable of delivering 129-342 mgs. of venom in a single bite (50-62 mg. is usually lethal to an adult human). Body color is a basic grayish brown highlighted with large triangular blotches of black, brown, tan, and cream, a coloration that renders the viper amazingly camouflaged within ground litter. The snakes are ambush predators, haunting both forests and disturbed shaded areas such as coffee, banana, sugarcane plantations, and cornfields in search of small rodents, birds, and amphibians. The venom, potent and quick acting, targets blood and muscle tissues. Statistics indicate that *Bothrops asper* is responsible for more human deaths than any other reptile throughout the Western Hemisphere, a reputation due largely to the snakes' propensity to seek prey such as small rodents in agricultural lands and near dwellings where produce is stored. All in all, the fer-de-lance has been referred to by one herpetologist as a "biological land mine."]

The *sorda* became my new nemesis, my arch villain. Night after night the specter of this serpent became the stuff of my worst nightmares. To reduce my anxiety during butterfly forays, I carried on with my teenage dress protocol, even though such duds were uncomfortable in the hot syrupy days below the Tropic of Cancer. As an added precaution, I made it a point to walk only 15-20 feet at any given time before pausing to scan the ground ahead. That procedure served me well, except for one occasion, which now decades later, I can retrieve from my archive of memories still with heart-thumping clarity.

Late August 1962. Except for checkerboard patches of disturbed forest, the bulk of the lands surrounding the lake and bordering roadsides had been deforested to establish local pastures and *milpas* (corn fields). These open, conveniently accessible areas usually were ablaze with sun-loving flowering plants—and butterflies. From an academic view, however, the real "prizes" in the tropics are found in less disturbed environments such as secondary and virgin rainforests—relatively abundant in Los Tuxtlas. Such shaded habitats, though, are usually difficult to access, and Los Tuxtlas proved no exception. That said, there was one sizable swath of mature forest covering several ridges and hillocks a few miles north of the lake, and accessible from a pitted dirt road connecting Catemaco to Bahia Sontecomapan and the Gulf of Mexico.

CHAPTER 3: MY SCARIEST MOMENT IN THE FIELD

On a morning exhibiting no hint of clouds (even though August was the middle of the rainy season, the month occasionally witnessed brief periods with no rain) I hitched a ride in the back of an open truck transporting beverages. I chose as my drop-off point a roadside pasture associated with the tiny hamlet of Dos Amates ("two paper trees") approximately ten miles from my base. The pasture, approximately 15-20 acres in size and fenced with barbed wire, was nestled in a small pocket of land surrounded by hilly ground that had not been cleared, albeit not extensive, but nonetheless, the proverbial "forest primeval."

This forest was titillating. But to gain entrance, I first had to navigate the intervening pasture; and that posed a problem. On previous occasions, I had observed that local cattle did not take to a stranger with light skin, overdressed, a wide-brimmed hat, and carrying a large, collecting net—a one-of-a-kind visage for them, to be sure. In response, the animals always exhibited aggressive curiosity, something I could understand, but a hindrance, nonetheless. On this occasion, to avoid a potential confrontation, I hatched a new initiative: I would spend 15-20 minutes meandering outside the fenced pasture but in full view of the cattle. Once the animals calmed, I would ease under the fence, and while remaining close to the fence, slowly walk until I reached the forested high ground beyond the pasture.

Eureka! The bovines were duped. In no more than a half-hour, I was within my Mexican "Eden."

The forest appeared not to have been logged. Vegetation was stratified and taxonomically diverse, including a sampling of tall, buttressed trees piercing the canopy 70-80 feet above. Trunks and limbs of most trees were heavily carpeted in sprays of bromeliads and orchids, many of which were in bloom. Lianas dangled and looped throughout the greenery. Diminutive palms and ferns bearing delicate, feathery fronds latticed the ground, sufficiently spaced so as not to impede my walking despite the absence of a trail. Curiously, the brown leaf-litter was rife with small toads that hopped aside as I slowly advanced.

Butterfly diversity was high, also. Even some of the more exotic showstoppers—clear-winged ithomiines, longwing heliconians, and the indomitable metallic blue morpho (*Morpho helenor montezuma*), for examples—peppered the dim light. Yet, what trumped this paradisiacal tableau of winged jewels was a medium-sized butterfly with black and yellowish longitudinal bands on its upper wings. (The species appeared similar to the zebra longwing (*Heliconius charithonia*), common not only in tropical climes but in peninsula Florida and southern Texas.) During my tenure in Los Tuxtlas, I observed such an individual on but one other occasion. Unfortunately, my effort to net it had failed; ergo, I had no clue as to its identification. Here, however, the butterfly was both common and flying close enough to the ground for me to net a couple of individuals. At this same time, other butterflies of the same size and shape, but white in coloration, were flying above the vegetation. Occasionally, one would descend within a weak shaft of sunlight. Near the ground, these "whites" began pursuing the darker striped individuals close to ground level. Having netted specimens of both persuasions, I noticed that the two shared a common underwing pattern, usually a poignant indicator that individuals are of the same species. Furthermore, my inspection of the genitalia of both specimens revealed that any colorfully striped individual was a female, and the white individual, a male.

My prowess with butterfly taxonomy enabled me to peg these two different butterflies as members of a sexually dimorphic species belonging to the family Pieridae ("whites and sulphurs"). [Later, I was able to classify the species as *Pieriballia viardi*, commonly referred to as "painted white," an unusual forest pierid. Females are hypothesized to be involved in a mimicry complex along with the longwing *H. charithonia* and the clearwing, *Aeria pacifica*—both present on site. The theory is that *H. charithonia* and the clearwing, *A. pacifica*, are both distasteful to vertebrate predators such as birds, amphibians, and reptiles. Because *P. viardi* has a similar appearance, it can be confused with these distasteful species. Because of the deception, no individual is attacked.] Under no time constraint, I idled in the joy of my disclosure.

But all good things must come to an end, and as corollary, all "Edens" must have a proverbial "Serpent."

CHAPTER 3: MY SCARIEST MOMENT IN THE FIELD

Enter the dark side. I was approximately one hundred yards up a forested slope. As I removed a specimen from my net, I heard a dull but distinct, THUMP at my feet. Looking down, I detected nothing out of the ordinary. A bit unnerved, I concluded that one of the common toads had bumped into one of my boots during its whimsical antics. Ergo, I returned to the business at hand. Another THUMP! I cast my eyes downward; again, nothing. Perhaps by divine intervention, prudence, or simply chance, I turned my gaze onto a fern frond arching to the ground no more than 15 inches from my feet. Without changing my stance, I tilted my head to better view what might be hidden beneath the frond. There my eyes locked onto a three-to-four-foot-long serpent coiled with its upper body elevated into a characteristic "S" striking pose. The head was large and arrow-shaped; its eye pupils were slit-like; its jaws were yellow; its body color was dark and accented with diamond-shaped blotches. Equally important, the creature gave no hint of showing movement or sound. There was no room for skepticism. Unequivocally, I was face-to-face with my worst nightmare: FER-DE-LANCE, BARBA AMARILLA, NAUYACA—the legendary SORDA. And I was terrified!

I opined that those two previous thumps *had* to be the sounds of the unsavory snake striking one of my boots. I froze as the classic signs of abject angst—dilated eyes, rocketing blood pressure, beads of cold sweat on forehead, and uncontrollable body tremors—spiked. Only one thought looped through my mind: "Do something NOW, NOW, NOW!" But with an onerous "Satan" poised sinisterly, and with my position compromised, what *could* I do?

Thanks to a reflexive infusion of adrenaline, every muscle in my body tensed, my legs bent slightly, and I hurled myself backward. At the same instant, the *sorda* launched. But because I heard no thump, the snake failed to make contact. With this third strike thwarted, I adopted the behavior of *The Flash*, the American DC Comic Book superhero: I took off in a maniacal lickety-split. (In retrospect, I realize that this lack of vigilance was dangerous; I could have stumbled and hurt myself, or worse yet, treaded on another *sorda* attracted to the banquet of toads at the site. Upon reaching the pasture, my *Flash* mode persisted, outwitting the cattle. When I reached the road and safety, I sank, my energy depleted and my mind in a daze.

After a few minutes, I recovered my karma sufficiently to take stock of the situation. Absent pain, I theorized that I had escaped envenomation. Nevertheless, while seated, I inspected my boots. On the outer side of my right boot, I could make out two sets of tiny punctures practically side-by-side slightly below the boot's collar. Below, there was a slight stain from a previous rivulet of fluid. This was proof that the *sorda* had definitely struck my boot with its fangs, delivering venom. For one final affirmation, I removed the boot to check my leg. No redness. Catharsis!

My conclusion? I escaped the *sorda* because the serpent had been at the limit of its critical striking range. Although the fangs connected with my boot, they lacked the momentum to penetrate the thick leather, or perhaps, the leather had fulfilled its mission. Regardless, my mother's admonition of earlier years to wear protective boots had finally paid off.

I remained transfixed by the wonderment of Los Tuxtlas to complete my originally allotted six months. I had no other encounters with a "deaf one." But *never* did I return to the patch of forest that had proven both my metamorphic "Eden" and "Hell."

EPILOGUE: The original forests of Los Tuxtlas have been decimated during the later part of the twentieth century. An influx of new settlers has precipitated lumbering and clearing for new grazing and farming lands. In 1967 the Mexican government designated 155,122 hectares (598.93 square miles) as "Los Tuxtlas Biosphere Reserve." Nevertheless, little has been done to halt forest degradation. Today, conservationists estimate that only a scarce five-to-six percent of the original forest cover remains. In essence, my forest primeval of 1962 is no more.

[Published originally as "My Scariest Moment in the Field" in *Southern Lepidopterists' News*, March 31, 2009 (Vol. 31:1), pages 16-19. Reprinted with the permission of the editor, and with minor editing.]

SELECTED REFERENCES

Andrle, R.F. 2014 (1964). *A biogeographical investigation of the Sierra de Tuxtla in Veracruz, Mexico.* Robert F. Andrle with CenterSpace Independent Publishing Platform. Virginia Beach, VA. 219 pages.

Dirzo, R., and M.C. Garcia. 1992. Rates of deforestation in Los Tuxtlas, a Neotropical Area in southeast Mexico. *Conservation Biology* 6(1):84-90.

Glassberg, J. 2007. *A Swift Guide to the Butterflies of Mexico and Central America.* Sunstreak Books, Inc. Morristown, NJ. 266 pages.

Gomez-Pompa, A., Vazques-Yanez, C. and Guevara, S. 1972. The tropical rain forest: a non- renewable resource. *Science* 177, 762-764.

Lee, J. C. 2000. *A Field Guide to the Amphibians and Reptiles of the Maya World: The Lowlands of Mexico, northern Guatemala, and Belize.* Comstock/Cornell University Press, Ithaca, NY. 416 pages.

Ross, G.N. 1975-77. An ecological study of the butterflies of the Sierra de Tuxtla in Veracruz, Mexico. *Journal of Research on the Lepidoptera,* 14(2): 103-124; 14(3): 169-188; 14(4): 233-252; 15(1): 41-60; 15(2): 109-128; 15(3): 185-200; 15(4): 225-240; 16(1): 87-130.

Ross, G.N. 2010. Dark walk on the wild side. *Wake-Robin* (Newsletter of the John Burroughs Association Inc., American Museum of Natural History), Summer (Vol. 43:1), pages 13-15.

Soriano E.G., R. Dirzo, and R.C. Vogt. 1997. *Historia Natural de Los Tuxtlas.* Universidad Nacional Autónoma de México. México, D.F., MX. 647 pages.

Stafford, P.J. and J.R. Meyer. 2000. *A Guide to the Reptiles of Belize.* Academic Press. Cambridge, MA. 356 pages.

INTERNET: butterfliesofamerica.com

CHAPTER 4: SAGA OF THE WHITE MORPHO BUTTERFLY AND EVIL WOMEN

Gain and pain in a primeval Mexican rainforest

Although a staunch conservationist, Theodore Roosevelt was an ardent big game hunter who often secured specimens for personal trophies and museum displays by contrast, his friend John Burroughs, the nature essayist, was turned off by natural history museums:

"There lie the birds and animals stark and stiff, or else, what is worse, [they] stand up in ghastly mockery of life, and the people pass along and gaze at them through glass with the same cold and unprofitable curiosity that they gaze upon the face of their dead neighbor in his coffin."

Nevertheless, museums provide the public with an easy route to nature, and museum specimens have taught us much of what we know about anatomy, taxonomy, and evolution. As a career entomologist passionate about butterflies, I have engaged in my personal share of collecting specimens, that is, the killing of those things I love dearly. A long-hand, baggy net—characteristic of entomologists depicted in cartoon caricatures—has been my primary tool. On occasion, I have even resorted to collecting butterflies with a shotgun. The following was my first such unorthodox experience, more than six decades ago.

When a senior undergraduate student at Louisiana State University in Baton Rouge, during my fall semester of 1962, I met Robert F. Andrle. We were enrolled in an invertebrate zoology class. Bob, who was a doctoral candidate within the Department of Geography and Anthropology and thirteen years my senior and a wife and four young children back at home in Buffalo, New York. During a conversation with Bob I learned that he had recently received a research grant from the National Research Council of the National Academy of Sciences for a biogeographical study (with concentrations on birds) of the Sierra de los Tuxtlas ("Los Tuxtlas"). The venue was an isolated, poorly investigated volcanic range in southeastern Veracruz, Mexico near the agrarian communities of San Andrés Tuxtla, Santiago Tuxtla, and Catemaco. Two dormant volcanoes, Volcán San Martín (5,840 feet) and Volcán Santa Marta (5,446 feet), dominate the rolling landscape. Both masses arise from the Gulf of Mexico, near the Bay of Campeche, and the tropical coastal lowlands. Rainfall is one of the highest of all regions within Mexico. By 1962, much of the originally forested lands at the lower elevations had been dismantled. This resulted in a mosaic of *pueblos* (small settlements), pastures, and *milpas* (corn fields). Elevations above 2,000 feet were still blanketed in virgin (non-logged) rainforest, technically classified as "Tropical Evergreen Rainforest." Los Tuxtlas had the distinction of representing the northern-most extent of this ecosystem within the Western Hemisphere. Understandably, Los Tuxtlas represented an untapped paradise for scientists. Due to the region's remoteness, however, research in Los Tuxtlas had been scanty. Bob had initiated exploration of the region back in 1960. A reconnaissance in 1962 would expand his mission. Understandably, I jumped at the invitation to join Bob, and begin my seminal survey of the butterflies of the region.

The Andrle-Ross Expedition began in June and was to last through December 1962. Bob planned to drive his family—wife, Patricia, and four young children, Chris, Elizabeth, Tim, and Bobby—in February 1962 to Los Tuxtlas. There he would rent a house through December in "Playa Azul," a small upscale recreational development perched on the shores of Lago Catemaco. The lake was a sizable collapsed caldera at an elevation of 1,100 feet and noted for its black sand beaches. Therefore, with the approval of my new research advisor (Murray S. Blum), Bob and I agreed to join forces in June. I would hitch a ride to Playa Azul with Bob's major professor who was driving down to conduct field work in a coastal area in Tabasco. Then, I would reside with the Andrle family until the end of the year. Bob would conduct forays into the surrounding hinterlands with me as his sidekick. Bob would concentrate on identifying birds and mammals, I would net butterflies and note their ecology.

Our fieldwork settled into a pleasurable and productive routine. Each non-rainy morning Bob and I would arise in the darkened predawn hours. We then would drive—Bob's station wagon or rented jeep—or ride rented mules to a predetermined destination so that we could be in place as the first light washed the eastern horizon. (Birds are most active in the early morning.) Because butterflies are not early risers, I assisted Bob in spotting birds. Later when the light increased, I would wander off by myself attending to butterflies. Come noon, we returned to our comfortable base in Playa Azul. If the afternoons were clear, I would strike out alone to sample butterflies along flower-rich roadsides, in *milpas* (corn fields), hedgerows, small coffee and citrus *fincas* (groves), and even patches of remnant forest that encircled the lake.

But the more unsettled areas were our primary targets. Classified as "Primary Evergreen Montane Rainforest," the thick vegetation was pristine, virgin, unsullied—relatively undisturbed since the last volcanic eruption recorded in 1793. Rumor had it that the forest was the home to man-eating pumas, jaguars, and even evil spirits.

These virgin forests covered the mid to upper slopes of the major volcanoes (see FRONTISPIECE). But the volcanoes were difficult to access. Even dirt mule/horse trails were virtually non-existent. Luckily, on one of our forays in late July outside of the community of San Andrés Tuxtla, we located a newly cleared dirt road for logging. The road appeared to ascend into the virgin forests on Volcán San Martín, the highest peak in Los Tuxtlas. Now in the rainy season, the road was impassable. San Martín's mysterious netherworld would have to remain cloaked until another time.

One August morning, after three previously dry days, Bob, his seven-year-old son, and I took off in a jeep for Volcán San Martín. But the road was too wet, and so we resorted to "shank's mare" (our own two feet) to an elevation of about 2,200 feet. The forest canopy was at least 100 feet above the forest floor, and some titans rose even higher. High-pitched whines, much like those of buzz saws, filled the air. I suspected these were being produced by cicadas or katydids, not unlike what frequently occurs during summer days throughout eastern United States. On occasion, the whines were punctuated by the guttural grunts of howler monkeys (*Alouatta palliata mexicana*), reminiscent of the roars of lions. The howlers confined themselves to the high canopy, therefore, not easy to observe. On the other hand, cousins of the howlers, spider monkeys (*Ateles geoffroyi vellerosus*) were more common and more observable. In fact, the long-limbed, prehensile tailed primates genuinely disliked our intrusion. While non-vocal, they would descend to approximately 50 feet above us, breaking twigs to toss upon us. Worse yet, if they could position themselves directly above us, they would urinate and defecate. Understandably, we didn't dally. (As an aside, spider monkey meat was a common item on the menu in eateries in the town of Acayucan, the largest community in Los Tuxtlas; I was never tempted to sample!)

The forest, too, displayed a visual aberration: a large flying insect with transparent wings, each accented with a dark blue band near its apex. The flight was like nothing I had ever observed. The insect seemed to be struggling to remain aloft. From my ground perspective, the problem seemed to be the result of the four wings moving independently—out of sync, so to speak. The effect was uncanny. I was reminded of the blades of a helicopter beginning to rotate. Although the wings didn't have a circular motion, their individual movements created a disconcerting illusion. Regardless, the insects remained airborne, navigating slowly along the bordering forest, usually 15-30 feet above the ground. (Upon my return to Louisiana, I learned that the insect was a damselfly classified as *Megaloprepus caerulatus*, commonly referred to as the "helicopter damselfly," and the largest odonate (damselflies and dragonflies) in the world. The species is restricted to pristine rainforests from southern Mexico south through Central America and into northern South America. *M. caerulatus* is considered a keynote species (an indicator of virgin rainforests). Recalling my experiences in Los Tuxtlas, I can attest that the species was truly limited to patches of undisturbed rainforest.

Apart from these oddities, what eclipsed all for wonderment was the forest *per se*—a bastion of superlatives such as majestic, magnificent, staggering—a cathedral of greenery. The vegetation was not a smorgasbord. Instead, the vegetation was organized into layers, strata. Near the ground, low-light specialists were the rule. These included delicate ferns, dwarf feathery palms, saplings so spindly that their cache of oversized leaves seemed to defy the very laws of physics. All greenery was encrusted with grayish lichens and green fuzzy mosses. Above ground level, there were two strata of species that were recognizable as honest-to-goodness trees. First, a lower layer between 10 to 18 feet in height composed predominantly of palms, many of which possessed large spiny, menacing-looking trunks, and a smaller array of broadleaf/evergreen hardwoods. Next, a second layer soared to a height of 70 to 110 feet, a bit higher than the forests at lower elevations. Here, different broadleaf/evergreen species sported columnar trunks with interlocking upper branches that formed a dense canopy. Included within this upper layer—every few hundred square feet—was an occasional colossus anchored by a fluted buttress, the girth of which could easily accommodate a dozen people connected by outstretched arms. These behemoths pierced the forest canopy as "emergents." Because of layering, virtually no sunlight could reach the ground.

Finally, there were those trees that seemed as much animal as plant: strangler figs (*Ficus*). These parasites begin as seeds deposited in the crevice of a sturdy tree. The developing roots in tentacle-like fashion, eventually descend to the ground, smothering the host tree in the process. With most sunlight being commandeered by the parasite, the host eventually dies, leaving behind a vacuous cylindrical center. This unusual growth habit is considered a specific adaptation to competition for light in an otherwise dark forest.

Whether average or statuesque, all trees were festooned with epiphytes (air-plants) such as mosses, lichens, bromeliads, orchids, even cactuses; some were in bloom. In addition, most trunks supported an assortment of thin-stemmed climbers that were attempting to reach the canopy to secure more light than their stationary relatives. For example, some large, glossy-leaved species resemble the familiar aesthetic philodendron-like houseplants commonly used in the interiors of homes and offices. These ornamentals hugged the huge trunks as they snaked upward. Upstaging all, however, were thick, heavy rope-like vines called lianas. Leafless, such constituents resembled those free-swinging aerial "Tarzan-esque" ropes popularized by Hollywood and comic books. The virgin rainforest provided me with a touch of fantasy from my childhood dreams.

Absent flowers near the ground, butterflies did not congregate. Where sunlight drenched the road, however, a butterfly occasionally darted about or basked on an outstretched leaf. And surprisingly, even under the canopy's veil of darkness, there were some specialized butterflies. Classified as ithomiines (family Nymphalidae, subfamily Ithomiinae). These were slender-bodied, transparent-winged species that are commonly referred to as "clearwings" or "glasswings." This transparency of wings, combined with slow and shallow fluttering, creates an illusion that is otherworldly (see Chapter 14). Upon my first encounter with a "clearwing," I thought I was viewing something non-organic—perhaps a ghostly apparition enjoying the secrecy afforded by the dark forest. Upon approach, I realized that the visage was a living butterfly—one not endowed with typical colorful wing scales, but instead naked, rendering their underlying cellophane-like wing membranes, clear. Ever since, I have appreciated the graceful ithomiines as a whimsical touch—Mother Nature at play.

Suddenly, I spotted what appeared to be a snow-white bird above the towering world of greenery. But the flight was unusually slow, bobbing, weaving—interrupted with periods of gliding as if in slow motion. After a few seconds, I realized that the undulating specter could not be a bird, but a butterfly—a butterfly on steroids. My mind reflected on *"Macrolepidoptera of the World: The American Rhopalocera"* by A. Seitz, one of only two illustrated library references I could find on tropical butterflies during my preparation for the expedition. If memory served me correctly, the butterfly unequivocally could be none other than the "white morpho" (*Morpho polyphemus*). [NOTE: Morphos are the prized jewels of tropical American butterflies. Typically, individuals sport a brilliant, iridescent blue sheen on the upper surface of the wings (see Chapter 2). These butterflies are opulent and dazzling. The term "morpho" is purported to trace back to Greek mythology where the term refers to "form." The name is appropriate. The striking iridescence of the upper surface of the wings visible when individuals are flying, is in dramatic contrast with the underwings, which usually are brownish and accented with eyespots (ocelli). This dark color renders the butterflies cryptic when at rest—usually on ground litter. In fact, morphos spend a lot of time on the ground because they do not feed on flowers. The butterflies' favorite delicacies are rotting fruit, oozing tree sap, or even mineral/nitrogen rich products such as urine, mammalian feces, blood, tears, and carrion. (Recall the adage: *"One man's meat is another man's poison."*) Currently, butterfly taxonomists recognize 29 distinct species encompassing 126 subspecies (geographic races) within the genus *Morpho*. The vast majority of these species are metallic blue in color (see Chapter Two). Because of this glitz several species are bred today on butterfly farms and ranches for later exhibition in themed tourist attractions such as butterfly conservatories. As one might suspect, morphos are usually the most popular species in the exhibits. And for professional lepidopterists and amateur butterfly collectors, morphos are endearingly considered a "Holy Grail." By contrast, whereas most morphos are metallic blue, *M. polyphemus* is a striking exception: opalescent, pearly white."]

© 2010 Andrew D. Warren

From my vantage point along the road, I could see that the butterfly was particularly attracted to the emergent trees, presumably searching for a recognizable host to lay eggs. Seconds later, the butterfly resumed its navigation, flapping its gigantic wings with deep, deliberate, labored strokes in an effort to maintain itself above the lofty trees. I stood mesmerized, hoping that when the butterfly's flight trajectory intersected with the road, the insect would descend to within netting range. Regrettably, I had no such luck. The butterfly only dipped slightly in the sunlight before ascending once again to clear the wall of green on the opposite side.

Then, serendipity. Within seconds, two similar individuals that had been gliding high began descending as they intersected the sunny road. Still, they were beyond reach. More surprising: the pair began to circle each other slowly, as if pirouetting in a silent ballet. Surprisingly, their dance brought them lower and lower until they leveled off at no more than thirty to twenty-five feet above the sunny road. My ornithologist partner, intrigued by the birdlike size of the butterflies, hatched a plan: he could attempt to shoot down the insects with his 12-gauge shotgun equipped with an Improved Cylinder Barrel (ICB) and loaded with #9 lead shot. At first, I thought the idea preposterous. Bob explained: "Firing hundreds of tiny pellets is a proven method we ornithologists use for bringing down small birds like hummingbirds that are not too far away and that cannot be collected otherwise." Bob added: "Aim is not critical because the tiny pellets spread out." I stood in awe. Bob picked up: "Usually enough pellets hit the specimen to either kill it or immobilize it; either way, it falls to the ground, and you have your target." I was dubious, skeptical. A shotgun for collecting a butterfly? All I could envision from the unorthodox technique was a rain of white confetti. I waited a few seconds but soon concluded that the butterflies seemed not interested in descending any lower. I rationalized: "Specimens in any shape would constitute acceptable vouchers for formal documentation. What did I have to lose?" I gave Bob a halfhearted thumbs up.

My partner took aim at the butterflies that continued to wheel and reel approximately twenty-five/thirty feet above the road. I watched with bated breath. BANG! Amazingly, not one but *both* butterflies began a slow drift downward in the motionless air as if dried leaves, landing barely thirty feet before me. I sprinted, reflexively exclaiming "YES!" at a volume that so resounded that the troupe of spider monkeys nearby stopped their activity. To my amazement, the hapless specimens were still alive—barely, as evidenced by a slight quiver of their antennae. Their enormous wings had been peppered, for sure. Surprisingly, fully 90 percent of the underlying, supporting paper-thin membranes remained. Their appearance reminded me of "roadkill," that is, specimens impacted by vehicles along highways My spirit mused: "Not bad, not bad at all." Now I could closely examine the butterflies. Kneeling beside the hapless individuals, my hands trembled as I picked up one. Forewings and hind wings were equal in size, conveying an extensive wingspan of six to seven inches (explains why the "dust shot" had impacted its target); color was basically snowy white with an overlay of subtle opalescence—a sheen that bestowed an appearance of the "mother-of-pearl" that covers the inner lining of some shellfish. The tips of the forewings were black as were a few small ovals that accented the margins of the hindwings. The underlying wing membranes seemed unusually thin, so much so, that the ventral black/yellow-ringed eyespots (ocelli) and assorted black markings were discernible through the dorsal opalescence. And there was one other oddity: The thorax and abdomen, also powdery white, were inordinately small; perhaps this minimal muscle was the reason for such slow flight? Seems reasonable.

I validated that both specimens were males of the species known as *Morpho polyphemus*. I presume the two individuals were engaged in some ritualized aerial dogfight for dominance. [The name *polyphemus* is based on the name of a Greek cyclops. Apparently, the taxonomist who originally named the species was impressed by the numerous eye-like markings on the wings]. My subsequent identification proved the subspecies to be *M. p. luna* (referring to the white moon). It is the taxon represented by the largest-sized individuals, and native from southern Mexico southward into Central America. After a few minutes, all signs of life vanished in both specimens. I quickly placed the pair into my largest glassine storage envelopes. In turn, the envelopes went into a plastic container for protection in my field bag.

Following this unparalleled drama, we resumed our gnarly ascent of the volcano. As the morning progressed, we encountered other white morphos; all exhibited similar soaring behavior. About noon, one of those sublime moments that opens a window into the soul, came to pass. A single white morpho began descending toward a sizable patch of shrubbery growing in full sun along the roadside scarcely 100 feet ahead of me. I ran but halted abruptly just short of the greenery.

A flashback reminded me that the four-to-five-foot-high plants bearing large, maple shaped leaves and small clusters of white flowers were identified by locals as *mala mujer*. (Technically classified as *Cnidoscolus angustidens*, family Euphorbiaceae or "spurges"). The name translates to "bad, wicked, or evil woman." The plant is named because every leaf and stem are armed with a dense array of nettle-like hairs and spines that inflict severe/burning pain to any transgressing mammal. Moreover, I had

previously experienced the scourge of a *mala mujer*. When trekking along the border of a secondary forest, I had unknowingly brushed a leaf of the plant with my hand. My skin began to tingle instantly with fiery prickles. Shortly thereafter, the pain had rapidly intensified and remained for nearly an hour. Understandably, I took stock of the plant's appearance so as not to repeat the painful mistake.

My memory *now* was fully triggered. Making matters worse, here the *mala mujer* was not a random plant. No, at least a dozen or so chest-high plants formed a dense colony covering approximately 200 square feet, potentially a whole sea of pain. Exacerbating the situation, the morpho settled, posturing itself on a leaf near the center of the plot, as if recognizing that the plants provided a modicum of protection. There, with wings outstretched in the bright sunlight, it basked. The gleaming sun on the butterfly's lustrous white, the bright green foreground, the dark forest beyond, and the azure sky presented a surreal image—the proverbial "Sirens of the Deep." I moved quickly to the edge of the plant colony. I speculated that even my long-handle net could not reach the butterfly. If I were to be successful, I would again have to confront a diabolical *mala mujer*. "Can I tolerate what surely would be hundreds of stings? Would I ever have another such opportunity for netting a white morpho?" A daunting, risky conundrum.

In the end, zeal overruled common sense. With my testosterone driven psyche fully bolstered, my gut screamed "GO!" To minimize exposure, I adjusted my full-sleeved shirt to cover as much of my arms and neck as possible, leaving my face and hands exposed. When completed, I summoned all grit and dashed intrepidly into the "Green Hell." (I confess that at this same time, I muttered a sanctimonious "Lord Have Mercy!") When I judged the butterfly to be within netting range, I swung as vigorously as I could. And without checking for affirmation, I about-faced and bee-lined out of the greenery. Only when my feet were standing on the dirt road did I check the net. While fearing the worst, I was instead gratified. My quarry was within the net,

CHAPTER 4: SAGA OF THE WHITE MORPHO BUTTERFLY AND EVIL WOMEN

its over-sized wings creating an audible sound against the cloth as they were attempting to flap for escape. I shouted: "I got it! I got it!" I gently removed the butterfly, a female in mint condition, and even slightly larger than the previous two males that had been brought down by gunshot. I had collected my personal "Holy Grail"—and it was *unholey*!

As my adrenaline began to wane, I noticed that the skin covering the back of my hands, upper neck, and chin were blotched red, and burning—really burning. In an effort to cool the fiery sensation, I doused the afflicted areas with the only potential remedy I had—water from my canteen. No relief, if anything, the water exacerbated the pain. Trying to think positively, I focused on securing the specimen for transport in my collection gear. When completed, I contemplated my predicament. Mercifully, the pain, while intense, had plateaued; and there was no sign of anaphylaxis. My partner quipped: "You were lucky you were not wearing a short-sleeve shirt like you usually do." Yes, lucky, indeed!

The next day the pain had abated, although I retained bright red dots in the exposed areas—my "Red Badge of Courage," referring to a book by the same name that I had read in a high school English class. During subsequent excursions into the virgin forests in Los Tuxtlas, I frequently observed white morphos between August and October. The butterflies restricted themselves to the forest canopy except on those rare occasions when curiosity enticed them closer to the ground.

To sum up, at the end of my fifteen-month study in Los Tuxtlas, I amassed a cumulative total of 3,893 specimens representing 359 species, 133 genera, and eight families. Included in the total are 26 male and 6 female *Morpho polyphemus luna*—the subspecies with the largest individuals. [NOTE: During my research I excluded "skippers." These lepidopterans are unique in that their antennae have terminal hooks. Additionally, they are small, usually drab in color, and manifest quick, darting flights. Finally, when perched, skippers hold their wings horizontally, or else their hind wings in a horizontal position but the fore wings angled upward. At the time, skippers were considered by most lepidopterists to be not "true" butterflies (Papilionoidea), but rather a separate major taxon (Hesperioidea) that shares morphological characteristics of both butterflies and moths. However, times have changed. Currently, skippers are included in virtually all current butterfly field guides and surveys within their own family, Hesperiidae. Because skippers constitute a sizable component of tropical butterflies, had I included this taxon in my research, my total number of specimens and species would have been significantly higher. In 1997, based on the research of others, the number of "true" butterfly species is reported to be 531, and the number of skippers, 341. Together, the total is 872, the highest diversity for any geographic region in Mexico, and higher than the number of species throughout the entire continent of North America, north of Mexico (725, give or take a few).]

That said, my first capture of a female *Morpho polyphemus luna* in a bed of *mala mujer*, while bittersweet, remains my most salient and gratifying memory from Los Tuxtlas—my *tour de force*. As testimony to this intrepid experience, the tattered white morphos—as well as all of my other butterfly specimens—are now incorporated for posterity into the collections of the McGuire Center for Lepidoptera and Biodiversity, Florida Museum of Natural History, University of Florida. Unfortunately, during the later part of the twentieth century, the environment surrounding Lake Catemaco expanded to become a popular recreational destination for nationals as well as prime real estate for housing development. As a result, the forests were cleared on an industrial level. By 1986, an estimated 84 percent of the original forest cover had been lost. By the turn of the new millennium, conservationists estimated that no more than five-to-six percent remain, notwithstanding the establishment in 1967 of the "Los Tuxtlas Biosphere Reserve" comprising 155,122 hectares (598.92 square miles). In 1968, "Estación de Biología Tropical Los Tuxtlas" comprising 644 hectares (2.5 square miles) was established, and in 2006 there was global recognition as a "UNESCO Biosphere Reserve." Recent investigations indicate that even with this official protection, 56% of the land in the biosphere remains degraded pastureland.

[This is an integration of two of my previously published illustrated essays: "Holey Wings and a Holy Grail" IN: Naturalist at Large. *Natural History*, February 2012 (Vol. 120:2), pages 16-18, and "White Morphos, Shotguns, and 'Evil Women'" in *News of the Lepidopterists' Society* 2009 Winter (Vol. 51:2), pages 67, 70-71. Portions reprinted with the consent of the publishers and with minor editing.]

SELECTED REFERENCES

Andrle, R.F. 1966. North American migrants in the Sierra de Tuxtla of southern Veracruz, Mexico. *Condor* 68:177-184.

Andrle, R.F. 1967. Birds of the Sierra de Tuxtla in Veracruz, Mexico. *Wilson Bulletin* 79:163-187.

Andrle, R.F. 2014 (1964). *A biogeographical investigation of the Sierra de Tuxtla in Veracruz, Mexico*. Robert F. Andrle with CenterSpace Independent Publishing Platform. Virginia Beach, VA. 219 pages.

De la Maza Ramírez, R. 1987. *Mariposas Mexicanas*. Fondo de Cultura Económica, S.A. de C.V., México, D.F., MX. 302 pages.

Dirzo, R., and M.C. Garcia. 1992. Rates of deforestation in Los Tuxtlas, a Neotropical Area in southeast Mexico. *Conservation Biology* 6(1):84-90.

Fincke, O. 1992. Behavioral ecology of giant damselflies (Odonata: Zygoptera: Pseudostigmatidae) of Barro Colorado Island, Panama. IN: D. Quintero and A. Aiello (Eds.): *Insects of Panama and Mesoamerica, selected studies*. Oxford University Press. Oxford, GB. pages 95-113.

Glassberg, J. 2007. *A Swift Guide to the Butterflies of Mexico and Central America*. Sunstreak Books, Inc. Morristown, NJ. 266 pages.

Gomez-Pompa, A., Vazques-Yanez, C. and Guevara, S. 1972. The tropical rain forest: a non- renewable resource. *Science* 177, 762-764.

Leopold, A.S. 1950. Vegetation zones of Mexico. *Ecology* 31: 507-518.

Raguson. R.A. and J. Llorente-Bousquets. 1990-91. The butterflies (Lepidoptera of the Tuxtlas Mts., Veracruz, Mexico, revisited: Species-richness and habitat disturbance. *Journal of Research on the Lepidoptera* 29 (1-2): 105-133.

Ross, G.N. 1975-77. An ecological study of the butterflies of the Sierra de Tuxtla in Veracruz, Mexico. *Journal of Research on the Lepidoptera*, 14(2): 103-124; 14(3): 169-188; 14(4): 233-252; 15(1): 41-60; 15(2): 109-128; 15(3): 185-200; 15(4): 225-240; 16(1): 87-130.

Soriano E.G., R. Dirzo, and R.C. Vogt. 1997. *Historia Natural de Los Tuxtlas*. Universidad Nacional Autónoma de México. México, D.F., MX. 647 pages.

INTERNET: butterfliesofamerica.com:

CHAPTER 5: CASE OF THE KIDNAPPED CATERPILLARS

For a Mexican metalmark caterpillar and a wood ant, hijacking is a good thing

In 1962 I was a twenty-two-year-old nascent graduate student embarking upon a lengthy study of the butterflies in the Sierra de Tuxtla ("Los Tuxtlas") The upland is an isolated volcanic range that rises from the Gulf coastal plain of Mexico, one hundred miles southeast of the city of Veracruz (see Chapter 3). One remote habitat in the Sierra especially intrigued me because biologists had never noticed it. This was a small pine community found solely on several steep ridges radiating down the southeastern slope of Volcán Santa Marta, a dormant, 5,250-high volcano. The volcano was the domain of the Indigenous Sierra Popoluca culture, regarded as the probable descendants of the ancient Olmec culture that occupied the Gulf coast region of Mexico between 1200 and 400 BCE. During preliminary field work, I discovered what seemed to be an undescribed species of metalmark butterfly. Lepidopterist Harry Clench of the Carnegie Museum honored me in 1964 by formally naming the species *Anatole rossi*, or in the vernacular, "Ross' Metalmark."

I returned to the region for three months in 1963. When I first began unraveling the metalmark's life history, some of the particulars surfaced easily. I learned, for instance, that the butterflies live in colonies and that females lay their eggs exclusively on a particular species of croton (*Croton repens*), a ground-cover plant common in the region, and a distant relative to many varieties cultivated for their showy leaves and used as indoor decorations. I even turned up a few young larvae, or caterpillars. Then, my luck ran out. Even though I observed many severely damaged croton plants (they had apparently been eaten by mature caterpillars), I failed to locate a single large caterpillar (larva) or a chrysalis (pupa), the later, the developmental stage in which the caterpillar metamorphoses into a butterfly. Where were the culprits?

But I remained undeterred. The dynamics of each day went something like this: I spent most hours crawling about on hands and knees, often in rough terrain, searching for large caterpillars. Not finding any, I became very discouraged and resorted to hatching butterfly eggs and rearing the young larvae myself. My combination home/laboratory was a thatch-roofed, mud-floored hut, provided by my hosts, John and Royce Lind, American missionary-linguists who were studying the local Popoluca culture, which historically had no written language. The village, Ocotal Chico ("Little Piney Ridge") was isolated from the rest of the world, reachable only by a foot trail from a small Mexican settlement (Soteapan), itself accessed only by a mud road passable only during the dry season. Consequently, there was no electricity and no running water in the village.

CHAPTER 5: CASE OF THE KIDNAPPED CATERPILLARS

Acquired in the field, the young green caterpillars were kept in plastic sandwich-box nurseries. The larvae grew large and plump, shedding their skin five times in the process. Light green and relatively flat, each larva was equipped with short setae (hair-like appendages) protruding from its sides. All larvae thrived. But growth was relatively slow—70-79 days to reach maturation. During this time, each caterpillar underwent five molts to produce six distinct stages—technically, "instars." With each molt, size increased, so that the final instar was just under an inch in length, one-quarter inch in width; color was a mottled dark green. In addition, the first thoracic segment had two hornlike extensions, greenish with brown highlights protruding above the head; this guise reminded me of the "Horn Headdress," the *haute couture* for fifteenth century British "women-of-means." Following the second molt each caterpillar began to secrete droplets of clear fluid from two pores on its back, near the hind end. In the front, a pair of tentaclelike organs were periodically everted and withdrawn. Finally, a pair of hard, black bladelike structures, which constantly vibrated, projected over the caterpillar's head. At the time, I hadn't a clue as to the functions of these three

pairs of organs. The good news was that my in-house experiments proved that the tiny larvae did grow into larger versions. So, why couldn't I find any in the field?

One midday, as I sat on a log amid one of my metalmark colonies, nibbling a peanut butter and jelly sandwich (my lunch each day) and reflecting on the mysterious absence of caterpillars, my reverie was disturbed by activity on a croton plant barely three feet from where I sat. I dropped to the ground and drew closer. To my surprise, there was a fully mature caterpillar, which I recognized from my "nursery" research. Swarming over it were several large, reddish black ants. My visceral/parental impulse was to rescue the caterpillar from its impending doom by squashing the ants. I bound from my log to the plant. Before I could kill the supposed predator, I realized that there was no conflict between the ants and caterpillar. Instead, the larva continued to feed docilely, removing all soft tissue, creating a skeletonized, lacelike appearance. On the other hand, the ants were probing the caterpillar, seemingly "caressing" it with their antennae. The caterpillar, in response, everted its pair of tentacles near its head—an act that seemed to excite the ants even more. When an ant climbed aboard, the caterpillar reacted by releasing droplets of clear liquid from a pair of tiny openings at its hind end. This was quickly ingested by the frenetic ants.

Soon, the caterpillar began crawling down the plant. Within moments, it was within a shallow underground chamber at the shrub's base, something I had never seen before. The ants followed, hitching rides on the caterpillar's flat back as if they were allies. Once they were all inside the chamber, the ants sealed the entrance with dirt pellets. VOILA! All vestiges of insect infestation vanished. Invigorated by this revelation, I diligently searched the area for other similarly defoliated plants. My task was made easy since damaged plants stood out in stark contrast to those that were unscathed. Sure enough, without exception, each plant with skeletonized leaves was undermined by a subterranean niche—a metaphoric "corral"—that imprisoned between one to three large caterpillars and a handful of ants; several of the chambers even housed chrysalises attached to the roots of the croton.

Here was the solution to the mystery, and it had come serendipitously. In less than five minutes, my research had undergone a quantum leap. Empowered with enlightenment, I returned to my faux bench. Realizing that I was still hungry, I retrieved my partially eaten sandwich from the ground, chowing down on the best PB&J I had ever tasted! Although I spent many months observing the metalmark butterflies, caterpillars, and ants, I never again witnessed any of these ants and caterpillars above ground during the day, that is, the insects came out from their confined hiding places only at night. Had it not been for my chance encounter with what I like to think of as an errant, gluttonous caterpillar sneaking in an extra meal, I probably would have given up the project of completing the metalmark butterfly's complex life history. In hindsight, my vigilance overlaid with a little bit of luck paid off.

At last, things began to fall into place. I spent most of my hours during both daylight and early night on the pine ridges observing the caterpillars and their ant attendants. During the dark, I employed a flashlight covered with red cellophane, since my lantern, like any white light, would probably be interpreted as dawn, thereby disturbing the insects' behavior. Even my camera's electronic flash had to be used sparingly and on intermittent nights, to maintain normal field conditions and not bias data. To maximize the quality of my research, I employed both a 35 mm MIRANDA SLR camera loaded with Kodachrome 25 film and a BOLEX 16 mm movie camera loaded with single sprocket Kodachrome movie film to document many of my observations. (Incidentally, I also used my movie camera to document much of Popoluca culture to honor my missionary/linguist hosts. The final product was *"Saga of the Popoluca,"* a 55-minute documentary featuring an optical soundtrack composed of professional narration, background music, and relevant local sounds. Today, the historic movie is archived in the library at the office of WYCLIFFE BIBLE TRANSLATORS INTERNATIONAL INC, the western headquarters in Dallas, Texas.)

My nightly excursions into the forest with cameras, tripod, flashlight, and writing paraphernalia—sometimes even during torrential thunderstorms—didn't escape the interest of the Popolucas. Nicknamed *meme pixiñ* ("butterfly man") from almost the onset of my tenure in the village, I became the "talk of the town." You see, in Popolucan folklore, nocturnal outdoor activities are discouraged because of the presence of "evil spirits." To explain my mysterious behavior, the villagers concocted a systemic theory: The *meme pixiñ* was searching for legendary lost Spanish treasure. At first, this reaction elicited only a chuckle or two from me and my hosts. But soon, the situation became serious. One day I noticed that someone had been digging in one of my colonies and had destroyed several of my study plants with their underground inhabitants. Because the Popolucas were unaware of the clandestine insect partners at the bases of the croton plants (apparently the nexus between the caterpillars and ants was a well-kept secret from *all* diurnal residents of Ocotal Chico), the villagers paid no heed to the potential damage of digging around the plants. After all, their quest was to find any treasure I may have overlooked. For me, the collateral damage was a serious impediment to my work.

With urgency, my hosts and I met with several of the village leaders to try to curtail my casualties. We assured the men that I was only a "nature lover," interested in simple things like ants and grubs, and that if their digging continued, my project would be ruined, and I would have to leave the area disappointed. Afterward, I was not disturbed, although strange glances resumed from some Popolucas, especially the village witch doctor, who continued to spy on me from the nearby shadows.

During a six-month return to the Popolucan homeland in 1965, I worked out the details of the metalmark's life history, a paradigm that has proven to be one of the most complex for any known species of butterfly. As mentioned previously, the butterfly is locally common in its ideal realm—the pine ridges on Volcán Santa Marta. Like most other metalmarks, adults are relatively small. Coloration is a checkerboard of brown, orange, white, and black polygons. They spend most of their time flitting rapidly two to five feet above the ground or clinging to the tops or bottoms of leaves where they bask with outstretched wings—trademark behavior for most metalmarks. In clear weather, the butterflies are particularly visible in late afternoon when they dart about erratically, chasing each other for short distances in the last rays of the setting sun.

Adult butterflies feed exclusively on the nectar from the small white flowers of *Croton repens*, the host plant. The first indication that the butterfly's life cycle is unusual is that, while the croton plants are widely distributed, the butterflies congregate in small, isolated colonies. These enclaves, which contain eight to fifty butterflies, are found only on certain sunny ridge crests and upper slopes, and only in the vicinity of the few human settlements in the area—five small Popoluca Indian villages.

Within the butterfly colonies, females lay their eggs on the undersurfaces of croton leaves. Hidden on the underside, the very young inconspicuous green and relatively flat caterpillars spend their days and nights nibbling the plants' tissues. Young larvae are green, inconspicuous. The youngsters feed both during daylight and darkness. Eight to ten days after hatching a larva flaunts the specialized structures that I had noticed in my nursery. These enable it to attract ant associates. To reflect: A pair of glands near the larva's rear end produce a sugary secretion known as honeydew, which ants eat with the gusto of children devouring candy. A variety of insects—aphids, many scale insects, and to a lesser degree, certain butterfly, and moth caterpillars—produce similar honeydew secretions. The tentaclelike organs near the front of the caterpillar secrete a gaseous chemical pheromone, or scent, which also attracts the ants. And the caterpillar's vibrating, bladelike structures produce faint clicking sounds, inaudible to humans, but within the range of insect perception. (All of my conjectures were confirmed for a related metalmark in Costa Rica by Phillip De Vries in 1992). Technically, the structures are termed "myrmecophilous" (ant-associated), and the relationship between the caterpillars and attending ants comprise a category of symbiosis (the living together in harmony of two dissimilar organisms) categorized as "myrmecophily." Patently, metalmark larvae re-invent the traditional concept of "caterpillar."

Not long after these specialized organs become active in a newly molted larva, the caterpillar attracts ants of the species *Camponotus abdominalis,* commonly referred to as wood ants or carpenter ants because they nest in old logs, fence posts, and even house beams. This species can be found throughout most of tropical Mexico and Central America. At night, these ants scour the countryside (and villagers' houses, as well) looking for sweet things to eat. The *Anatole* caterpillars with their honeydew glands fit the bill very nicely.

When it first encounters a caterpillar during a nocturnal foray, the ant uses its antennae to stroke the caterpillar in the vicinity of the honeydew glands. The caterpillar responds by secreting tiny drops of moisture, which the ant imbibes. Usually within a few minutes, the ant worker is joined by several others of its kind, all of which consume the seemingly endless supply of treats. The wood ants do the caterpillar no harm, and after some thirty minutes of feasting, depart in relays to dig a small, shallow trench around the base of the croton. This excavation takes several hours but usually is complete by dawn or shortly thereafter. The resultant circular excavation is one to two inches deep with smooth sides—an extraordinary feat by nature's "good little architects and engineers." After completion, the ants return to the caterpillar and stroke it with their antennae. The constant stroking, which probably is an irritant, causes the caterpillar to crawl down until it finds itself within the underground chamber. The flatness of the caterpillar enables the ants to "ride" the caterpillar as it crawls downward, probably attempting to escape. Once within the shrouded chamber, the ants seal the entrance with small pellets of dirt from their previous excavating. Metaphorically, the ant "ranchers" have herded their "cow" into a protected "pen/corral," secured the "gate" so that "milking" becomes a private affair throughout the new day. And that's that!

At dusk, between 7:00 and 7:10, the pellets of dirt are removed from the ceiling of the pen and a few ants emerge, temporarily leaving their captive behind. Following the opening, these vanguards run back and forth over the leaves and stems of the plant, doubtlessly in search of potential enemies. To test if this were the case, on several occasions I placed small predatory arthropods such as bugs and spiders on the plants. The ants immediately seized these victims with their powerful mandibles, sprayed them from their abdomens with formic acid (an acrid liquid that smells something like vinegar) and carried them down the plant, depositing the virtually lifeless forms on the ground a few inches away. The Popolucan name for these ants translates as "the sour-smelling ones." Fact is, the villagers' language is rich with descriptive names for most common plants and animals. Nonetheless, because the Popoluca language does not contain a name for the elusive metalmark caterpillar, I conclude that the caterpillar and its relationship with two types of ants, were unknown to the villagers.

After about ten minutes of running over the plant, the ants return to the subterranean enclosure and vigorously stroke the caterpillar with their antennae, apparently coaxing it to move. The caterpillar, now emancipated, ascends the "clean" stem, shepherded by its carpenter ants and eventually settles on a tender leaf near the top of the plant to begin feeding within safety.

Feeding persists intermittently throughout the night, with the ants constantly in attendance by crawling over the caterpillar, pausing occasionally to imbibe droplets of honeydew, and running up and down the croton plant in search of marauders and potential enemies. The caterpillar, meanwhile, frequently emits its pheromone and vibrates its bladelike beaters, causing the ants to become more active and attentive. Between 4:30 and 4:45, just prior to dawn, the ants herd their charge downward and into the underground chamber. The ceiling is replaced, and before even the first streaks of light cross the tropical sky, both cow and herders are secure within their corral until the next twilight, when the wily tale is brought once again, full circle.

The daily cycle is rarely altered or interrupted during the summer and fall months. Even torrential rains present no observable deterrent. The underground pens are invariably positioned on sloping terrain of heavy red clay, which provides excellent drainage; as a result, the pens are rarely flooded. Besides, the larvae feed atop the croton plants during darkness when rains are most common.

CHAPTER 5: CASE OF THE KIDNAPPED CATERPILLARS

I found it odd that while my laboratory-reared specimens required up to two months of growth to complete their development, the in-situ insects did not require such. In fact, I judged that development in the field required merely half that time. My hypothesis to explain this discrepancy is that under natural conditions, the tactile stimulation of attending ants induces a speedier development.

Returning to the field experiments, I learned that metamorphosis of Ross's metalmark takes eleven days. The process begins with the *Anatole* chrysalis in its chamber, attached to the subterranean portion of the croton stem or to its root Although the structure does not produce honeydew, it does possess glandular openings corresponding in position to the pheromone-producing organs of the caterpillar, and so I conclude that a similar chemical is released into the air. At any rate, the ants remain in the pen for nine days. Eventually as the adult form (imago) nears perfection and all pupal structures have been transformed, the ants depart, leaving the pen open. The butterfly then emerges from the old pupal skin, climbs out of the previous darkness it has inhabited during the daylight hours for nearly two months, and enters the bright, sunny world of the pine ridges. After an hour of drying and exercising its newly formed wings, the butterfly departs for a free, aerial existence, which it enjoys for as long as a month, apparently oblivious to its past ant associates, i.e., "hijackers."

Many questions arose during my observations. Do the same ants remain with their charge throughout their development or do individuals return to their own nest site as replacements arrive? What would happen if the caterpillars were isolated from their ants? Is the association between the ants and caterpillars of benefit to only the ants, or do the caterpillars benefit as well?

I experimented. First, I carefully opened a pen, removing the ants one by one. I then dabbed each with a drop of quick-drying paint. I repeated this procedure with four nearby pens, using a different color for each. Three days later, I observed that all the painted ants had been either replaced by unpainted ones or else had moved to different, nearby chambers. Evidently, the ants practice a periodic changing of the guard. The ants' nest may be up to fifty feet away located in a rotting log or stump, its inhabitants exploiting a variety of resources—saps, flower nectars, and anything else sweet; the *Anatole* caterpillars seem to be just one source of food. Whether or not the ants' response—confining the unwieldy prize in a hole instead of attempting to carry it back to the nest—has evolved specifically to cope with the *Anatole* caterpillars is unresolved; similar behavior has been observed with several species of myrmecophilous ants. I am of the opinion that the herding behavior may be a specialized behavior of the *Camponotus* ants to the *Anatole* caterpillars in the isolated Popolucan habitat.

In another experiment I divested the ants from several croton pens and placed net cages around the plants to keep the ants from returning. Absent their associated ants, the caterpillars did not return to their subterranean cells each day after feeding through the night; instead, the caterpillars remained on the leaves throughout a twenty-four-hour period, feeding intermittently

throughout both day and night. My theory, not definitive, but substantively credible, is as follows: the nightly rituals of scaling the plants from subterranean enclosures are behaviors forced on the caterpillars by the carpenter ants.

Next, I removed several caterpillars and placed them on croton plants that were outside the butterfly-caterpillar colonies. Left unattended, the caterpillars were invariably ravaged: by workers of *Ectatoma tuberculatum*, large reddish ants festooned with numerous hairs and spines, and/or by domesticated chickens. The ant is a member of a taxon, the Ponerinae. Among entomologists (and humankind in general), the medium-size reddish ants are distributed worldwide and infamous for their aggressive ability to sting and their relentless, voracious predatory habits for any other creature. Indeed, the Popoluca's name for this species translates as "The Robbers," appropriate for six-legged malevolent creatures that pillage the pinelands not to seek sugary treats but to snare any manner of fresh protein-rich insects that are carried back to their tree-hole nests, which usually are at the base of trees.

I was personally well acquainted with the legendary *Ectatoma*. A few days prior to my relocation experiments, I had been stung on the thumb as I leaned against an oak tree. My finger was numb for nearly twenty-four hours and swollen for another day. The incident was so traumatic that I could not even imagine the damage such venom would inflict on a lowly caterpillar. I have since learned that when stung, a butterfly larva undergoes extensive tissue destruction within only a few minutes. "The Robbers" within the Popolucan pinelands are surely an indomitable force to be feared by "All Creatures Great and Small," to quote the poet/hymnologist Cecil Frances Alexander.

The relationship between the carpenter ants and the metalmark caterpillars thus appeared to be one in which the larvae furnish the ants with tasty sweets, and in return receive protection from a vicious armed predator, another ant species. To confirm this, I carefully investigated the crests and upper slopes of the pine ridges, exclusive habits for the metalmark colonies. The *Ectatoma* ants infested these open areas and spent the daylight hours solitarily staking potential prey. During darkness, they remained secluded in their nests. The *Anatole* caterpillars and their wood ant guardians constituted prime targets; they, however, were hidden beneath the ground during the day when the predators were on patrol. At night, with the plundering halted as the *Ectatoma* ants remained in their own nests, the caterpillars could feed in safety, exposed on their plants. Also, the caterpillars are secure from household chickens. Therefore, the relationship between the carpenter ants and metalmark caterpillars is mutually beneficial, a textbook example of symbiosis.

There is at least one other chapter to this story. During the cooler months of winter and early spring, the ant-caterpillar activities are somewhat altered. Between November and April, nighttime temperatures may drop to 50 degrees F. Adult butterflies are no longer on the wing, having died as the cooler, damp weather set in. The ants deepen the pens into five-to-six-inch vertical tunnels, probably to increase insulation from the cold air. The butterfly's larval stage is greatly lengthened as the caterpillars and their attending ants become sluggish. A caterpillar will frequently crawl up a plant during the early dark hours, take a few bites, and then be herded quickly back into the pen. At times, particularly during very cool spells, the caterpillars do not emerge at all for many consecutive nights, presumably able to subsist on stored nutrients due to reduced metabolism.

As spring, with its warmer temperatures, begins in the Sierra de Tuxtla, so does the dry season. Much of the undergrowth in the various ecological communities withers, drying rapidly. At this time, humans become an important factor in the perpetuation of the metalmark's life cycle. The

Popoluca men toss lighted matches alongside the numerous trails on the pine ridges adjacent to their villages. The pine needles and dried undergrowth make excellent tinder, and the flames spread rapidly along and down the ridges. Because the ground is only sparsely covered, there is no widespread inferno, only low ground fires that creep in irregular patterns. The goal of this annual activity is to clear clutter from the ground to encourage the growth of fresh grasses that depend on fire for regeneration and that will serve as nutritious fodder for mules, burros, and horses. This permits the work animals to be pastured only short distances from the Popoluca villages.

By mid-to-late April, selected sections of the pine ridges—and practically all butterfly-caterpillar colonies—have been burned over. Be that as it may, because the wood ants previously had deepened the pens during the cool months, the fires do not harm the secluded insects. They emerge the night after the fire. There, they are presented a new world, one devoid of food plants and littered with burned debris. Undoubtedly, a bad omen.

The absence of food for these winter-season caterpillars triggers the onset of their long-delayed pupal period. Approximately twelve days after fire passes through a colony, all the caterpillars metamorphose into chrysalises. In two more weeks—by late April or early May—a fresh generation of butterflies is flying about in venues that had been burned earlier. And because *Croton repens*, a fire-dependent species and the singular host plant for the metalmark butterfly, is rampant, the butterflies encounter hallowed ground.

Soon mating occurs, and the females begin to lay their eggs. They select only the small shoots of croton plants that have recently sprouted within the bare, scorched patches of ground near the original larval food plants. The nascent greenery appears much healthier than others growing in unburned localities; the fresh shoots are shorter, brighter green, and have relatively smooth leaves—presumably new sprouts from hardy root stocks untouched by fire. The butterflies instinctively avoid placing their eggs on larger, more spindly plants with hairy leaves due to age. While rearing caterpillar in my field laboratory, I observed that the young larvae could not penetrate the velvety surface of the larger plants; shortly thereafter, the larvae became emaciated and died, presumably from starvation and dehydration.

Scientifically, the distinctive growth form of the crotons in the metalmark colonies may be a response to the increased sunlight that pours into the burned-over areas. In unburned, grassy areas, even newly sprouted crotons produce hairier leaves. This difference, important to the young caterpillars, remains in effect throughout the year. Thus, both the spring burns initiated by the villagers along with the selectivity of the egg-laying butterflies ensure colony stability. The small Popolucan settlements create ideal breeding habitats for the metalmark. And because burns usually occur in the exact areas of previous butterfly colonies (near villages), the annual fires guarantee long term viability of the species in the region over time.

With the reproduction of the "spring crop," the metalmark's life cycle closes. Summarily: Ross' metalmark reproduces exclusively in an environment that is hostile to most other defenseless insects. The butterfly species lives in a restricted habitat—pine ridges close to Popoluca Indian villages, a habitat that is burned systematically by the Indigenous population and is the hunting territory of a potentially devastating ant predator, and within the feeding territory of family chickens. The butterfly thrives, where others cannot, because of its benevolent liaison a "pact," if you will, with a specific wood ant and an Indigenous culture. If for whatever reason this biological imperative were to fail, the butterfly species would probably face immediate extinction.

EPILOGUE: The future of Ross' metalmark appears to be secure. And that is because the Sierra Popoluca culture appears to be secure. Reason? The strong cross-cultural bonds that developed between the Lind family and other American/Mexican linguist/missionary associates has made the Popolucas healthier and more economically secure than ever before. And perhaps even more importantly, now emboldened by salient literacy and a new spirituality and morality, the modern Popoluca not only understand and appreciate their unique cultural and biological heritage in their specialized homeland, but also feel confident in their ability to affect their own future. Put simply, today's Popolucas enjoy a bulwark against extinction. Furthermore, the Mexican government has constructed an all-season road into the previously inaccessible pinelands of Volcán Santa Marta to assist with the Popolucas various concerns in our increasingly techno-savvy times.

This new globalization has exposed the formerly and provincial Popoluca to amenities of the twenty-first century. With the increased ability to market their agriculture products (principally coffee and corn), the Popoluca have increased income to purchase outside items that were unimaginable decades earlier. For example, computers, cellular phones, and substantial housing with clean water and plumbing are commonplace throughout many villages.

In response, the Popolucan population has increased—now approximately 30,000 speakers living in 58 different communities, up from the 1960 estimate of a few thousand scattered in 30 small settlements. This rapid expansion has necessitated an increase in the need for housing, grazing lands, coffee groves, and cornfields.

When I last visited the Popoluca area during the summer of 1978, I was able to locate at least 15 metalmark colonies—more than triple the number I had studied in the '60s. That made the metalmark the most common butterfly in the region. As new Popolucan home sites have created more disturbed lands, the croton plants along with the metalmark butterflies and their attending ants have followed. Furthermore, small butterfly colonies were stretched out along the new road—even into the relatively gnarly oak forest below the pine community. The road constructed for human access into and out of Ocotal Chico has ostensibly become a corridor for the dispersal of the metalmark from the pinelands. Because human traffic along the road is sporadic, and government does not have the means to maintain the road adequately, Popolucan men have taken upon themselves to burn the median grassy strip and bordering ditches during each spring/dry season. These annual scorched areas continually renew the supply of appropriate larval food plants—a non-pubescent variety that "fits the bill" for the metalmarks. And in all cases that I investigated, the attending carpenter ants were present, too. The unique ecological niche for the butterfly—arguably with the most complex natural history of any extant lepidopteran—seems to be responding positively to the human expansion, and therefore, for the moment at least, intact.

That said, I cannot foresee the future, of course. Given that human civilizations in most parts of the world are responsible for extensive damage to virtually every ecosystem on Planet Earth, it is comforting to proclaim that in the Popoluca homeland on Volcán Santa Marta, one small, rare species of metalmark butterfly and a common species of carpenter ant are thriving. For me this has a personal impact. And I am optimistic!

One final caveat: In 1981, the scientific taxon, *Anatole rossi*, was synonymized to *Lemonias caliginea*, a species described from a single damaged male specimen collected in 1867 and housed in the prestigious Natural History Museum in London. The vintage specimen was labeled simply "Mexico," and was illustrated with a drawing in an arcane scientific English journal. And enigmatically, the species (or possibly a separate cryptic species, or different subspecies) has been reported from a few isolated locales in Oaxaca and Tabasco, states that are adjacent to Veracruz. No information on the life history of those insects has been reported. Consequently, the definitive classification and distribution of the butterfly, which I collected and chronicled between 1962 and 1965, remain uncertain.

[Published originally as "The Case of the Vanishing Caterpillar. *Natural History*, November 1985 (Vol. 94:11), pages 48-55, 112. Reprinted with permission of the publisher, and with minor editing. The original essay constitutes my introduction into the genre of commercial, popular scientific writing.]

SELECTED REFERENCES

Andrle, R.F. 2014 (1964). *A biographical investigation of the Sierra de Tuxtla in Mexico*. Robert F. Andrle with CenterSpace Independent Publishing Platform. Virginia Beach, VA. 219 pages.
Butler, A.G. 1868. Mr. A.G. Butler on the species of *Lemonias*. *Journal of the Linnean Society*, 9:213-229.
Callaghan, C.J. 1981. Notas sobre un caso de sinonimia entre las riodinidae Mexicanas. *Revista de la Sociedad Mexicana Historia Natural* VI (2): 41-42.
Clench, H. K. 1964. A new species of Riodinidae from Mexico. *Journal of Research on the Lepidoptera* 3(2):73-80.
De la Maza Ramaríez, R. 1987. *Mariposas Mexicanas*. Fondo de Cultura Eonomica, S.A. de C.V. Mexico, D.F. 302 pages.
DeVries, P.J. 1989(1991). Detecting and recording the calls produced by butterfly caterpillars and ants. *Journal of Research on the Lepidoptera* 28(4):258-262.
DeVries, P.J. 1992. Singing caterpillars, ants, and symbiosis. *Scientific American* 267(4):76-82.
DeVries, P.J. 1997. *The Butterflies of Costa Rica and Their Natural History*. Volume II: Riodinidae. Princeton University Press, Princeton, NJ. 288 pages.
Editor, 1963. Animal husbandry in the animal kingdom. *Time* December 6: 98.

Gifford, N.A. and S.P. Campbell. 2019. Blue blazes: In pursuit of a butterfly effect. *Natural History*, September (Vol. 127:8), pages 30-31.

Glassberg, J. 2007. *A Swift Guide to the Butterflies of Mexico and Central America*. Sunstreak Books, Inc. Morristown, NJ. 265 pages.

Grove, D.C. 2014. *Discovering the Olmecs: An Unconventional History*. University of Texas Press. Austin, TX. 197 pages.

Haddad, N. 2019. *The Last Butterflies: A scientist's quest to save a rare and vanishing creature*. Princeton University Press, Princeton, NJ. 264 pages.

Ross, G.N. 1964. Life history studies on Mexican butterflies: II. Early stages of *Anatole rossi*, a new myrmecophilous metalmark. *Journal of Research on the Lepidoptera* 3(2):81-94.

Ross, G.N. 1966. Life-history studies on Mexican butterflies. IV. The ecology and ethology of *Anatole rossi*, a myrmecophilous metalmark (Lepidoptera: Riodinidae). *Annals of the Entomological Society of America* 59(5):985-1004.

Ross, G.N. 1994. Winged victory. *Wildlife Conservation* 97(4):60-67.

Ross, G.N. 1997. *Lemonias rossi*. IN: Soriano, Enrique, Rodolfo Dirzo, and Richard Vogt (editors). 1997. *Historia Natural de los Tuxtlas*. Pages 323-328. Mexico, DF: Universidad Nacional Autónoma de México, Instituto de Biología, Apartado Postal 70-143, Instituto de Ecología, Apartado Postal 70-275, 94510, 647 pages.

Ross, G.N. 1975-77. An ecological study of the butterflies of the Sierra de Tuxtla in Veracruz, Mexico. *Journal of Research on the Lepidoptera*, 14(2): 103-124; 14(3): 169-188; 14(4): 233-252; 15(1): 41-60; 15(2): 109-128; 15(3): 185-200; 15(4): 225-240; 16(1): 87-130.

Ross, G.N. 2010. Caterpillars, ants and Populuca (sic) Indians: An adventure in remote Mexico. *News of the Lepidopterists' Society*. 52(1), 34-41, 44.

Ross, G.N. 2010. Living with the Popoluca: Another adventure in remote Mexico. *News of the Lepidopterists' Society*. 52(4), pages 118-127.

Ross, G.N. 2024. Insects in Mythology and Religion. Chapter 5, pages 95-117. IN: *A Cultural History of Insects in the Modern Age*. Volume 6, 217 pages. Edited by Robert K.D. Peterson. IN: *A Cultural History of Insects*, Volumes 1-6. General Editor: Gene Kritsky. Bloomsbury Academic. London, UK.

CHAPTER 6: "A CLOCK-WORK ORANGE"
THE TRANS-GULF MIGRATION OF THE MONARCH BUTTERFLY

If there is one quintessential universal butterfly, that surely would be the monarch (*Danaus plexippus*). The storied narrative goes something like this:

(1) The vary name *monarch* denotes royalty, literally. In fact, the insect's original name, "King Billy," was penned by United Empire Loyalists who had migrated to Canada following the American Revolutionary War. The name "King Billy" refers to King William III (1650-1702), King of England, Prince of Orange, and Stadholder of Holland. The butterfly's emblazoned orange color is an endearing reference to William's heritage from the royal House of Orange of the Netherlands. Because King William championed the divergent Protestant religion, the leader was held dear in the hearts of Protestants, who often were routinely condemned for their beliefs. Through time, the charisma of the orange *Danaus plexippus* earned the species a place in the hearts of many Americans and Canadians.

(2) The monarch is the favored species in texts to illustrate a metamorphic life cycle, that is, an indirect form of development that encompasses four distinct stages: egg, larva (caterpillar), pupa (chrysalis), and adult (butterfly).

(3) Monarchs and milkweed plants (*Asclepias*) have an inextricable relationship that has evolved as a textbook example of co-evolution between the animal and plant kingdoms. The paradigm goes something like this: Milkweed plants

contain toxins that render their leaves, stems, and flowers unpalatable to most herbivores, especially vertebrates such as deer and cattle. Monarch larvae (caterpillars), though, have developed physiological strategies that not only detoxify these chemicals, but literally sequester the toxins in their blood and tissues. In turn, these plant-larval toxins are passed on to the pupa (chrysalis) and eventually to the adult during the different stages of metamorphosis. Thus, the monarch species is protected from most vertebrate predators such as birds, bats, and reptiles, for example.

(4) The monarch is recognized as the de facto national insect for the United States and the official butterfly for eight states. And throughout the United States and Canada, the monarch is considered as the poster child to champion biological conservation in general.

(5) Trumping all, is the monarch's annual migrations. Those, along with the annual migrations of the painted lady butterfly (*Vanessa cardui*) in Europe, Africa, and South America, constitute the longest annual migrations within the insect world, and the most populous periodic population movements in the entire animal kingdom. Both the monarch and painted lady butterflies are regarded as international travelers of storied fame.

Here are the specifics for the eastern United States and southeastern Canada: Each fall, hundreds of millions of monarchs begin winging their way southward from as far afield as Ontario (Canada) and New England, to central Mexico. This constitutes 95 percent of the entire North American population of monarchs. Target? The high montane forests within the Transverse Neovolcanic Belt—a mineral-rich mountain system composed of high, inactive volcanoes that stretch across the southern end of the central Mexican plateau within the neighboring states of México and Michoacán. There, the butterflies congregate into a dozen or more enclaves where they spend the winter months in a state of reduced activity: clutched together on limbs and branches of oyamel fir trees (*Abies religiosa*) and Montezuma pine ("ocote") (*Pinus motezumae*) during cool/cloudy weather, and taking brief flights to secure water from nearby seeps on warm/sunny days to rehydrate themselves. [NOTE: Maximum numbers occurred in the 1996-1997 winter when the total was estimated to be 383.8 million. In the winter of 2023-2024, the number was estimated to be between 10 and 40 million, second lowest in recorded history. In contrast, west of the Rocky Mountains, monarch butterflies overwinter along the Pacific coast between Ensenada, Baja California (Mexico) and Marin County, California, in 200-300 small colonies. Historically, numbers were estimated to be about five million. In 2020, the number plummeted to just under 2,000—a 95 percent decline. But in 2023 the population rebounded to 233,000, still far fewer than in the past.]

The following March, the butterflies become more active, including courtship and mating. Afterwards, the butterflies embark on a return flight northward. En route, females lay eggs on milkweed plants they encounter, but then, soon die (males die shortly after mating) because of physiological exhaustion. The new generation matures within three to four weeks; new generation adults fly farther northward, lay eggs, and within a week or two, die. With the approach of the

Autumnal Equinox (September 20-22), the butterflies, which now have completed three to five generations, respond to new genetic programming: reproductive urges cease, energy is channeled into building fat reserves, and the internal compass is reversed from north to south. Voila! The monarch's autumn migration is primed. By the end of October and early November most butterflies end up in central Mexico—a place they have never been, but a place familiar to their ancestors the previous year. This return to Mexico encapsulates the multi-generational species' annual cycle.

Historical dogma proffered that adult monarchs were restricted to daylight travel overland during their autumn and spring treks. The consensus was that the butterflies would *not* fly over large bodies of water or during the night. Then, in 1990, a Mississippi entomologist named Bryant Mather (1916-2002) published in the July/August issue of *News of the Lepidopterists' Society* the following:

> "On the 17th and 18th of October, every year for the past 18-19 years, monarch butterflies in immense numbers alight on and rest on an offshore oil production platform out in the Gulf of Mexico. Mrs. Hylma Gordon of Hattiesburg, Mississippi, told me about this on January 12, 1989, when I was speaking about Lepidoptera at a meeting of the Pine Woods Chapter of the National Audubon Society in Hattiesburg. She later gave me more details in a letter dated 31 Jan. 1989. In her words: The experience on the rig was certainly an unforgettable one to see the cloud coming from all around in a mass that settled on every available space from the top of the derrick to the floors. Everything was covered to the depth of several layers. There were butterflies on top of butterflies. The deck hands were busy with wash-down hoses and had to keep it up to be able to handle the gear while drilling. Some of the older hands said it was a yearly occurrence in the area. We were about 150 miles S. of Cameron, LA. One of the men who had worked in the area for 18-19 years said they came through on the 17th-18th of October. They thought the butterflies were using the rig to rest on and fly around in the daytime and come back each night to rest for three nights. The idea that they were different groups on the same flight route had not occurred to me until you mentioned it."

Suddenly, the traditional concept of monarch migration was in question. I thought: "Should I begin a new research project?" A daunting proposition. With the city of Lafayette, a convenient forty-five miles from my home in Baton Rouge, and because I had unlimited spare time because of my recent retirement, I was bolstered to try to verify the report.

Summer 1991. I visited the Cajun city in the heart of Louisiana's "Acadiana." Turns out, in 1989—the date quoted by the original observer—there were no permanent man-made structures as far as 150 miles into the Gulf of Mexico. (Louisiana currently registers over 3,400 man-made oil and gas producing structures—greater than any other state—that fan out nearly 170 miles into the northern Gulf.) I soon was directed to visit Petroleum Helicopters, Inc. (PHI)—the largest company that ferries men and supplies to points within the Gulf. There, I learned that two PHI pilots, Charles

CHAPTER 6: "A CLOCK-WORK ORANGE"

"Chuck" Williams and Thomas "Tom" Schaal, both of Lafayette, serviced drilling rigs and production platforms south of Cameron Parish—the most southwestern and second largest political unit within the state (Louisiana has 64 political divisions called parishes). As lagniappe, both gentlemen were interested in wildlife, particularly the rehabilitation of birds that become injured or stranded offshore.

The PHI pilots were quick to inform me that on at least a half-dozen occasions, they had observed monarch butterflies in masses so thick that they appeared to be a stream of smoke moving southwest from the coast. The butterflies were flying above normal altitudes for helicopters (150-1,000 feet). Furthermore, one pilot observed upwards of a thousand monarchs resting on the wire fence surrounding a heliport on an offshore structure. Many of the butterflies routinely flew to a gas production platform known as West Cameron Block 280 (WC-280) a day or two after the passage of a strong cold weather front from the north in mid-October. Constructed in 1982 and located 72 miles south of the Cameron coast, the platform was owned and operated by UNOCAL Corporation (Union Oil Company of California)—the company boasting the distinctive logo of an orange circle enclosing a blue/white number 76. Further questioning revealed that the butterflies were orange and black: MONARCHS!

Intrigued, I contacted UNOCAL and California's Moody Institute of Science (a well-established medium renowned for producing educational films for schools and the public). Both were interested in my proposal to document monarch butterflies using oil and gas drilling rigs and platforms as rest stops during their migrations across the Gulf. After all, the publicity could be very advantageous for Louisiana's much maligned petroleum industry, and Moody could document another one of Mother Nature's wonders. Upping the ante, UNOCAL was prepared to host me and a cinematographer free of charge—a great offer since neither I nor Moody had funding.

If the passage of a cold front foreshadowed a migration of monarchs, my timing to board the offshore structure would be crucial. Weather data over recent decades purported that cold fronts pass though Louisiana circa every seven-to-ten days in October, and that the dates of October 17-18 were probably approximations. I decided to target the first week in October (1991).

Thursday October 1. Donald Valentine (cinematographer for Moody) and I rendezvous with Tom Schaal, a PHI pilot, in Intracoastal City, LA—a small community south of Lafayette, and PHI's hub for operations in the Gulf of Mexico. The helicopter flight is my first. From an elevation of 700-1,000 feet, the interface between the endless blue-green water domed by an azure sky creates an optical illusion: The aircraft seems to hover in space rather than move. After about forty-five minutes, Tom points directly ahead: "There she is—WC-280," he quips. Within 10 minutes we touch down atop a seemingly impossible tiny landing site 92 feet above the water.

WC-280 is a gas production platform anchored in 90 feet of water above the continental shelf. The structure is painted a bright yellow—a trademark color for UNOCAL. For safety, the platform consists of two components separated by a long walkway: a large assemblage containing the actual pumping equipment and huge cranes, and a smaller multi-level unit that houses filtering and dehydrating equipment, the heliport, and living/dining quarters for a crew of 18. (Personnel quarters are small but adequate: bunk beds and a common bathroom, a kitchen and dining room for preparing and serving three meals a day, a recreational area, and a room packed with electronic and communication equipment.) Furthermore, there are two metal boats suspended from two sides of the platform for emergency evacuation. Railings and safety signs are ubiquitous.

Luck is with us. Just two nights later, a mild cold front from the north passes through. I can feel the entire structure sway a bit as I lay in my bed. With the blustery weather, I don't get much sleep. The next morning the Gulf waters remain turbulent: eight-to-ten-foot billows with whitecaps lash and rock the platform. Then at about six o'clock in the evening, a single monarch sails past headed in a westerly to southerly direction.

October 7. No butterflies during the morning hours, wind is slowing, and seas are balmy. Then, EUREKA! In the afternoon, several monarchs fly past the platform; by dusk, several butterflies land on the wire safety guard on the heliport. At this same time, personnel from WC-196, a UNOCAL platform slightly closer to shore, telephones to report approximately a dozen monarchs resting on their platform. As darkness descends, a dispatcher from WC-593, another UNOCAL platform farther from shore in about 250 feet of water, sends this message: *"Approximately 1,000-2,000 monarchs are circling equipment and lights."* Sadly, the darkness precludes a helicopter flight. By maintaining intermittent contact with WC-593 during subsequent hours, I learn that the butterflies were not persnickety about their perches—anything they could grasp with the small spines on their feet. At dawn, the butterflies departed in a south-southwesterly direction.

During my eighteen-day tenure on WC-280, cold fronts continued to move through every five to seven days (including one on October 15). Always, monarchs followed once the inclement weather cleared. The butterflies seemingly take advantage of the mild tail winds. Never was I personally privy to a melee of butterflies. Instead, small groups of 5-10 individuals sailed past the WC-280 platform every hour. And during this same period, small numbers of monarchs were reported from 25 different platforms near WC-280. No structure, however, hosted more than several dozen butterflies at any given time. With dusk, I was able to collect and tag nearly 100 monarchs during 1991 and 1992 on WC-280.

The tagged butterflies were released with the hope that at least one would eventually be recovered from the monarch overwintering sites in Mexico; regrettably, none was. The cinematographer, Don, was able to capture singular footage of much of the activity. [NOTE: Edited footage of the monarch spectacle is included in the MOODY INSTITUTE OF SCIENCE/QUESTAR VIDEO release titled "The Wonders of God's Creation." That same title is offered in a six-disk set of DVDs distributed by QUESTAR, INC; the monarch's migration is highlighted in Volume 5: "Animal Kingdom."]

Because the venture was disappointing, I petitioned to resume my association with UNOCAL and the WC-280 platform. That was granted. As a result, each October between 1992 and 1995 I returned to WC-280—usually for a period ranging from two to three weeks. The helicopter pilots, Tom and Chuck, always spread the word to their PHI colleagues (about 400-500 helicopters fly the Gulf on any given day) to report any butterfly sightings to us aboard WC-280. Additionally, PHI headquarters circulated a special bulletin describing my project. Result? (1) A cumulative total of 52 platforms and rigs ranging from eastern Louisiana to eastern Texas reported a cumulative total of hundreds of monarchs flying over Gulf waters each year. To my surprise, most sightings occurred on or near structures located south of the coastline of southwest Louisiana (Cameron, Lake Charles, and Lafayette are metropolitan areas to the north)—not south of New

Orleans and the Mississippi River Delta where the majority of platforms and drilling rigs occur; (2) the majority of sightings occurred in mid-October, actually, close to October 17-18, and always after the passage of a cold front; (3) the majority of sightings—seventy-two percent to be exact—occurred on or near platforms and rigs painted bright yellow or orange. No one, however, ever reported a "cloud" of butterflies as described by Mrs. Gordon in 1990. (Be mindful that the Gulf is a massive body of water, and most structures are unmanned. Therefore, most structures are not visited except for emergencies.)

And there were other details. For instance, butterfly sightings were not random; most migrants were observed during the heat of the day, that is, mid to late afternoon. Often the butterflies would be in tandem pairs or small groupings of 20-40. The butterflies always flew 30-150 feet above the warm waters of the Gulf, presumably taking advantage of warm thermal uplift (water temperature in October is usually 77-78 degrees F—warmer than ambient temperatures). If an individual set upon the water's surface, it was quickly nabbed by a fish. Another point: whenever a monarch would come within the vicinity of the UNOCAL platform—principally constructed of metal—the insect would slow and circle as if to "check it out." After a brief inspection, the insects carried on with their prescribed trajectory.

That is, until dusk. Then, the butterflies would usually settle onto various structures such as machinery, pipes, chains, wires, ropes, railings, and especially, the wire fencing that encircled the heliport. There, the monarchs would remain until the following dawn, when they would take off in their typical south-to-southwest direction. (Although night flights are very unusual for butterflies in general, the behavior was reported as far back as 1899.)

I remain confident that my observations disprove the theory that monarchs shun flights over water. To clarify: Based on my data, I posit the following: Many migrating monarch butterflies each autumn track a consistent over-water Gulf trajectory that is approximately 90-100 miles wide, and that extends southwesterly from the southwest coast of Louisiana and extreme southeastern Texas. By extrapolation, this path would take them to the northeast coast of Tamaulipas, Mexico, approximately 400 straight-line miles from the U.S. coastline. And again, by extrapolation, once onto the Mexican Gulf coast, the butterflies are able to access a series of geographic passes that dissect the eastern Sierra Madre, gaining a foothold onto the Central Plateau. Forthwith, the butterflies face an unencumbered pathway towards their ultimate target—the montane evergreen forests of the Transverse Neovolcanic Belt of central Mexico west of Mexico City.

That said, two salient questions remain. First, how monarchs navigate over the open waters of the Gulf and locate the offshore structures remains a mystery. Research suggests that magnetism and color both play key roles. In the past, studies have proven that body parts and sections of wings of monarchs contain quantities of magnetite, an oxide of iron that acts as a biosynthetic compass. For clarification, many birds, dolphins, rays, sharks, and the migratory locust possess magnetite. (Magnetite is a mineral (an oxide of iron) which in theory, is responsible for an animal's ability to orient to earth's natural geomagnetism.) Because the offshore facilities of the petroleum industry are constructed of massive amounts of iron, and house telecommunication and electrical generating equipment, these structures generate substantial electromagnetic fields. (I could easily demonstrate this by observing the deflection of a compass, or "Directional Gyro," aboard a helicopter as it approached an offshore facility. Beginning about two tenths of a mile out, the compass began deflecting between seven to ten per cent. On deck, the deflection was approximately twenty percent.)

Likely, migrating monarchs are fooled by false readings from their internal compasses. Furthermore, numerous reports by land-based researchers indicate that monarchs have a propensity for the colors yellow and orange, the usual palette of their fall nectar plants such as goldenrod (*Solidago*) and sunflowers, particularly swamp sunflower (*Helianthus angustifolius*) in Louisiana. Here again, the monarchs are lured to many offshore structures that are interpreted as "pit stops." With the potential for food and rest, the butterflies descend and alight. Because the enticement is bogus, though, the next day the butterflies resume flight. Beyond the range and influence of the offshore structures, the butterflies find themselves past a point of no return. After perhaps another ten to thirteen hours of non-stop flight that covers a remaining distance of approximately 300 miles, the insects at last are treated to rejuvenating food, water, and trees. Over the new landmass, the internal compasses probably are reset to a more westerly orientation. In the end, by playing "hopscotch" between the petroleum industry's offshore structures in Louisiana, migrating monarch butterflies can navigate a safe passage across the waters of the Gulf of Mexico to the eastern coast of Mexico.

Second, where are the launch site/sites for migratory autumn monarchs? Louisiana's coast is principally a treeless marshland. Only three major geographical venues support trees and beaches that abut the Gulf: the cheniers (ancient beach ridges) of Cameron Parish, Grand Isle in Jefferson parish, and Avery Island in Iberia Parish. The most strategic are cheniers. These lone topographic features consist of dry land with elevations just a few feet above the wet marshlands. From the air, cheniers resemble great ships afloat in a sea of grass. Historically, these bits of elevated land offered early settlers engaged in hunting, fishing, and trapping the only dry land in the region. As such, cheniers have been a continual source of natural resources for animals and people. For example, cheniers support natural woodlands dominated by live oak (*Quercus virginiana*), sugarberry/hackberry (*Celtis laevigata*), black/honey locust (*Gleditsia triacanthos*), and toothache tree (*Zanthoxylum clava-herculis*). In spring and fall, wildflowers are ablaze—a great benefit to pollinators.

Because of their east-west orientation, the Cameron cheniers present an ideal broad front for staging a launch site for monarchs flying southward out to sea in the fall—or a landing site for migrants moving northward over the waters of the Gulf in the spring. With that in mind, I opted to include a study of the cheniers in my monarch studies. A prime venue was the Baton Rouge Audubon Society's *Peveto Woods Sanctuary* near Johnson Bayou. There I learned that many monarchs from more northeastern locations congregate on Louisiana's chenier coast between mid-September and early October. At night, the insects take refuge in the boughs of the numerous moss-hung trees—all in full sight and sound of waves pounding the nearby Gulf beach.

During the day, the butterflies feed on the numerous nectar and pollen rich wildflowers. There is, however, one plant that stands out above all others: chloracantha/spiny aster (*Chloracantha spinosa*). This species, found in Louisiana exclusively on the southwest cheniers, attains a height of two feet and bears numerous fall-blooms that have white petals surrounding a yellow disk. The flowers are attractive to monarchs, but also to a small, diurnal wasp moth. Identified as the yellow-collared scape moth (*Cisseps fulvicollis*), the moth is black with a pronounced orange-red collar—a combination that suggests aposematic (warning) coloration. Intrigued, I question: "Could both the moth and the monarch butterfly be securing vital protective chemicals from the aster?"

The inordinate attraction of these two insects to a single plant species is highly suggestive of a strong symbiotic/mutualistic relationship. In an attempt to confirm my hypothesis, I contacted Ronald B. Kelley, a natural-product chemist at Moorhead State University in Minnesota. The scientist had conducted some of the original research on pyrrolizidine alkaloids (PAs), the toxins found in monarchs that are thought to confer distastefulness to the insects. As per his instructions, I shipped a considerable quantity of fresh flowers of the spiny aster to him for analysis. Regrettably, the analysis was inconclusive, thus the question remains open. With such strong empirical data, it doesn't take much of a leap of faith to imagine that the abundant aster plants on the cheniers do produce such powerful toxins, and that the bright colors of the scape moth and monarch indicate that they extract these during their feedings on nectar. Fundamentally, cheniers offer monarchs not only a Gulf-coast launching site, but also, a rich banquet for securing food and defense chemicals.

Come spring, monarchs backtrack from Mexico. Although I was not aboard offshore structures in March or April, I did make observations in 1991 and 1992 from Holly Beach and

Rutherford Beach in coastal Cameron Parish. During both years, I counted large numbers of monarchs sailing in from the Gulf and onto the beaches. All butterflies were flying within a hundred feet of the surface and directly from a south/southwest direction, frequently despite prevailing breezes and headwinds from the north. Numbers of butterflies ranged from 15-30 every fifteen minutes, with peak hours between 11:00 AM through 4:00 PM.

With an abundance of shade trees and spring wildflowers displaying on the cheniers behind the beaches, the butterflies are treated to a bonanza, particularly important because of the aged and emaciated state of the spring migrants. The trees serve as nocturnal roosts and for resting during copulation (mating usually commences after the noon hour and peaks near dusk). Besides, an abundance of nectar sources such as southern dewberry (*Rubus trivalis*) bull thistle (*Cirsium horidulum*), tickseed (*Coreopis lanceolata*), and Indian blanket (*Gaillardia pulchella*), provide high-octane food for renewing energy.

Meanwhile, there is another critical plant: green antelopehorn/spider milkweed (*Asclepias viridis*). This monarch host plant is a local but common component of chenier vegetation. Migratory female monarchs lay their first clutch of eggs, thus jump-starting the year's first generation. Adults from this generation quickly travel north, laying their eggs en route. By summer's end, adults from the final brood begin the same epic journey undertaken by their direct antecedents the previous year. The species' cycle of life is now complete.

The other two coastal highlands, Grand Isle and Avery Island—both slightly east of Cameron Parish—offer tree cover for migratory monarchs, but only Avery Island has a thriving population of *Asclepias viridis,* a suitable host that is utilized in the spring. The two venues, however, are used by monarchs during both spring and fall migrations as rest stops, but the cheniers of Cameron Parish seem to be the primary locations used by the migrants.

Here's my take: The over-water migration of the monarch probably was initiated in some long-forgotten time by a few wayward individuals flying along the United States Gulf Coast being blown offshore primarily from the cheniers of Louisiana's Cameron Parish following the passage of an autumn cold front from the north. Had the vagrants maintained a south-to-southwest trajectory, they would have had an above average chance of surviving. I postulate this because: (1) the Gulf offers a shortcut to the eastern coast of Mexico, (2) the cheniers offer monarchs a banquet of flowers for stockpiling fat reserves, and (3) the cheniers provide an unmatched opportunity to sequester potent chemicals for their defense system. During the subsequent spring, the offshore flyway again shortens mileage and offers a quick source of nectar-rich flowers and host plants. Furthermore, if per chance monarchs encounter a late spring cold front moving southward while they are traveling over the Gulf, offshore platforms and rigs provide temporary sanctuary during the severe weather; once on the cheniers, trees provide additional safety. Because the new route proved advantageous for the species, Darwinian natural selection, and its tenet, "survival of the fittest," postulate that what started as a minor aberrant pathway to Mexico, was reinforced over and over again. Today, the progeny of those deviants comprise a well-established annual Gulf flyway.

Whether or not the Gulf flyway originated as a byproduct of the petroleum industry's colonization of northern Gulf waters is contentious, of course. For the industry, however, the idea is a vaunt for public relations. [NOTE: For many decades, ornithologists (bird scientists) have documented that neotropical songbirds streaming southward in autumn and northward in spring also cross the Gulf to and from Mexico and Central America. These feathered creatures use offshore man-made structures and chenier trees as sanctuaries during storms in the same way as monarch butterflies.] Regardless, because the flyway now affects the safety and economics of the monarch as a species, the flyway is now most likely a mix of learned and programmed (instinctual) behavior. From an environmental/political viewpoint, the event is a poignant example of how an apparent unholy alliance between industry and nature is often only a question of personal aesthetics and spurious opinions. In the words of a UNOCAL spokesperson: "Oil, water—and wildlife—CAN mix!

Such ideas are compelling. But what of the future? In theory, at least, fall monarch migrants from eastern Canada and United States that arrive on the Gulf Coast (say Florida, Alabama, Mississippi, and Louisiana) should increasingly take advantage of a Gulf crossing. (Migrants that move through the central sector of the United States should, of course, continue to funnel through Texas.) Not unexpectedly, with no permanent offshore monitoring projects in place (and none projected), data is lacking. Furthermore, with the overall monarch population dwindling,

CHAPTER 6: "A CLOCK-WORK ORANGE"

comparisons of numbers of trans-Gulf migrants from year to year are rather meaningless. Bottom line: The final chapter in the ongoing saga of monarch migration remains an unknown.

When all was said and done, I formally—and brashly—christened the previously undocumented flyway " 'A Clockwork Orange': The Monarchs Trans-Gulf Express." My title pays homage to the butterfly's historic reference to a historic monarch: King William, III, of England, who was from the House of Orange (Netherlands). The title has a metaphoric component pursuant to a 1971 Stanley Kubrick film of the same name. The theme of the blockbuster cinematic giant centers on a young sociopath who terrorizes the countryside in a futuristic England. Kubrick uses the word "orange" as a metaphor for "rusty", hence, a broken clock. The inference is that a sociopath, like an "orange" clock, is useless. For me, the monarch's trans-Gulf flyway, like the protagonist in the Kubrick film, deviates from the norm—a bit "orange," if you will. But unlike in the film, the sullied behavior of the butterflies is not at all destructive. For monarch butterflies, "orange" individuals can be productive.

EPILOGUE: During the early twenty-first century, southwest Louisiana was pummeled with several strong hurricanes. As a result, most of the cheniers were inundated with salt water that remained for upwards of ten days. Surveys of the region over recent years indicate that *Asclepias viridis*, the monarch's host in the region, could not be located. Whether or not the plant will resume growth in the future is, of course, an unknown.]

[This is excerpted from chapters in "The Monarch Butterfly." *Louisiana Wildlife Federation* magazine, special issue "Monarch Magic" (Vol. 29:4), pages 4, 13-40, front cover (inside, outside), back cover (inside, outside) by G.N. Ross, 2001. The special issue was the dominant force behind my being recognized as "2001 CONSERVATION COMMUNICATOR OF THE YEAR" by The Louisiana Wildlife Federation and The National Wildlife Federation. The award was presented at The Louisiana Wildlife Federation's 63rd annual convention on March 2-3 at Paragon Casino and Resort in Marksville, Louisiana. Reprinted texts used with permission of the editor and with minor edits.]

SELECTED REFERENCES

Auld, L.B. and G. Hoff. 2022. Chasing the monarch migration. *Southern Lepidopterists' News*, June (Vol. 44:2), pages 161-166.

Brower, L. 2015. The remarkable monarch. *Natural History*, July/August (Vol. 123:6), pages 26-29.

Butler, C. 2015. The monarchs and I. *Natural History*, July/August (Vol. 123:6), 22-25.

Ross, G.N. 1993. The trans-Gulf express. *Louisiana Conservationist* (Vol. 102:9), pages 15-17.

Ross, G.N. 1994. Butterflies descend on offshore rigs. *Louisiana Environmentalist* (Vol. 2:5), pages 12-15, cover.

Ross, G.N. 1996. The trans-Gulf migration. *MMS Today* (Minerals Management Service, U.S. Dept. of the Interior (Vol. 6:1), pages 11-13, cover.

Ross, G.N. 1998. Monarchs offshore in the Gulf of Mexico. *Holarctic Lepidoptera* (Vol. 5:2), page 52.

Ross, G.N. 2010. The monarch's trans-Gulf express: "A clockwork orange." *Southern Lepidopterists' News* (Vol. 32:1), pages 11-24.

Ross, G.N. & D.A. Behler. 1993. The trans-Gulf express. *Wildlife Conservation* (Vol. 96:3), page 8.

Ross, G.N. 2020. Louisiana's Avery Island and its Enigmatic Butterflies. *Southern Lepidopterists' News*. Supplemental Issue, Vol. 42. 95 pages.

Ross, G.N. 2022. Monarch butterfly and native milkweed in coastal southwest Louisiana. *Southern Lepidopterists' News*, September (Vol. 44:3), pages 265-272.

Schappert, P. 2000. *A World for Butterflies: Their Lives, Behavior and Future*. Key Porter Books Limited. Toronto, Ontario, CA. 320 pages.

Schappert, P. 2000. *A World for Butterflies: Their Lives, Behavior and Future*. Firefly Books Inc. (U.S.), 320 pages, back jacket cover.

Stutz, B. 1993. Butterfly flyby. *Audubon* (Vol. 95:1), page 16.

Suchan. T., C.P. Bataille, M.S. Reich, E. Toro-Delgado, R. Vita, N.E. Pierce, and G. Talavera. 2024. A trans-oceanic flight of over 4,200 km by painted lady butterflies. *Nature Communications* 15, 5205 (2024). https://doi.org/10.1038/s41467-024-49079-2.

Talavera, G. & R. Vila. 2017. Discovery of mass migration and breeding of the painted lady butterfly *Vanessa cardui* in the Sub-Sahara: the Europe-Africa migration revisited. *Biological Journal of the Linnean Society* (Vol. 120, Issue 2) pages 274-285.

Walton, R. 1993. Tracking North American monarchs. Part 1. The East. *American Butterflies* (Vol: 1:3), pages 11-16.

Internet: https://journeynorth.org.

CHAPTER 7: BUTTERFLY WRANGLING IN LOUISIANA

Cajun cowboys and caterpillars share a Gulf Coast habitat

More than half of Cameron Parish, located in the southwestern corner of Louisiana, consists of open water, and most of the land is a marshy labyrinth. The parish's few patches of solid land are its cheniers; composed of sand, shell, and organic material, the formations rise one to twelve feet above the surrounding muck. Geologically, cheniers are ancient, dry beach ridges, originally built up near a delta and separated from other high ground by extensive intervening marshland. Long and narrow, cheniers parallel the coast and exist where a voluminous river has periodically changed its course. The Louisiana cheniers, which are anywhere from several hundred to 2,700 years old, result from the meanderings of the mighty Mississippi River. Such distinguished lands occur nowhere else in the United States, and in only four or five other places in the world.

Louisiana's cheniers were once all wooded, dominated by live oaks and other water- and salt-tolerant hardwoods such as hackberry (sugarberry) and locust. (Coined by early Cajuns, the word *chenier*, pronounced "shin-ear" or "shin-a-ree," means "Oak place.") They were biological islands, upland forests afloat in a grassy sea. Until roads were constructed through the marshlands linking the cheniers to higher ground farther north, local folk had but one form of transportation: boat. In today's world, practically all chenier lands are privately owned and are used for cattle ranching, which was introduced from eastern Texas decades ago. Over the years, the local people have cut down most of the forest for wood and to create pastures and farmland. Cattle roam mazelike trails through the pastures and the remaining patches of woodlands, and Cajun speaking cowboys float the cattle to market on oil-drum rafts.

Because sea level is rising and the coast of Louisiana is subsiding because of the weight of sediments deposited by the Mississippi River over eons, the southern faces of several cheniers are currently under assault by even normal waves of the Gulf of Mexico. Storms originating farther south also funnel through the area. Although erosion is proceeding at an alarming rate, this precarious world remains a haven for an odd collection of plants and animals. Where else can one find, growing within just a few feet of one another, water hyacinths, Louisiana irises, lantana, prickly pear cactus, gigantic live oak trees festooned with Spanish moss, and Spanish bayonet? And where else could a lepidopterist like me have a better adventure?

CHAPTER 7: BUTTERFLY WRANGLING IN LOUISIANA

My odyssey began on March 23, 1991, while I was tagging migrant monarch butterflies on a wooded chenier as they arrived from their wintering grounds in Mexico. My attention was diverted by a small, white butterfly flying lazily in the dappled light. I reflexively thought "falcate orangetip," but then my academic training quickly asserted itself: (1) *Anthocharis midea* (family Pieridae), normally appears only in early to mid-April and only in upland oak-hickory forests, such as those of central and northern Louisiana; (2) the species has but one generation each spring (univoltine). But when I netted the butterfly, I was able to confirm my first impression: it had a falcate, or hooked, tip on each forewing, as well as other identifying characteristics of the species as reported in popular butterfly field guides. (A slightly tattered female, my specimen lacked the distinctive orange wingtips, found in the male.) I concluded it was a rare stray that had traveled from the northern part of the state, or perhaps, even from eastern Texas.

The event was filed away in my mind until the following year. On March 19, 1992, I noticed another lone falcate orangetip in that same enclave of hardwoods. Because of the signature orange wingtips, I identified the butterfly as a fresh male. By day's end I had counted nine fresh butterflies, five males and four females. And even better, I was able to track a female as she began to lay her eggs. The host plant she chose, appropriate for this species of butterfly, was Pennsylvania bittercress (*Cardamine pensylvanica*), a plant with fine leaves and tiny white flowers. An annual, the plant grows only eight to twelve inches high in this hot locale, going to seed earlier than in most temperate areas.

The butterfly usually deposits a single conical, orange egg per plant, on a bud or open flower or at least near the flower head. I noticed that the water-loving bittercress flourished in patches on the northern slopes of the cheniers, in the soggy boundary between the light-colored soil of the chenier proper and the black muck of the marsh. The plants were growing near partly shaded patches of woodland, frequently bordering the branching cattle trails that were etched deeply in the shaded landscape. The most robust plants had sprouted in the actual hoof prints of cattle.

Concluding that I had discovered an unrecorded breeding site for the falcate orangetip, I spent the next two days combing the region for other colonies. By dusk on March 21, I had mapped four colonies on four different cheniers, a total population of fifty-six butterflies. But the next day was disappointing: I located only a handful of butterflies throughout the four colonies. And the following day, I found none. My fifty-six research subjects had disappeared, as if into thin air. And because of heavy thundershowers the previous evening, coupled with poor drainage, three of my four study plots were under nearly a foot of water. I wondered if I had just witnessed the demise of this nascent population.

I awoke early on March 24 and made my way from the motel where I was staying to the nearest plot for another search. Wearing rubber boots, I waded cautiously about, trying not to alarm any of the cattle and keeping an eye out for venomous cottonmouth snakes. I noticed that the bittercress plants were still evident, although for the most part, only their tips were above the waterline. Crouching to inspect one plant, I was gratified to see a tiny orange egg, unmistakably that of the falcate orangetip. I moved on. By day's end I had painstakingly counted sixty-three eggs, usually one per plant, distributed throughout my four study plots.

Apparently, in less than one week, the adults had mated, and the females had deposited their eggs. Their reproductive drives satisfied, the delicate butterflies probably had become too weak to fly and had been eaten by the fire ants that actively patrolled the ground within the sites. Although I was relieved to learn that the butterflies had safely laid their eggs in preparation for next year's generation, some questions persisted. How could the larvae (caterpillars) and, later the pupae (chrysalises)--the mummy-like forms that eventually open to reveal the adult butterflies—survive the next eleven months in a habitat prone to floods? How could they survive the cattle's constant browsing and trampling? All profound questions, but all absent answers.

Rather than hang about to watch the caterpillars hatch and develop, I collected a batch of twelve eggs and several host plants and brought them back to my home in Baton Rouge, 120 miles away. I planted the bittercress in a three-foot tall glass terrarium and set the eggs carefully on the plants' leaves. Within three to four days, all the eggs hatched. The small, yellow-green caterpillars quickly ate the eggshells and then crawled to the tips of the bittercress where they began feeding on the delicate flower petals, never descending to sample the leaves. This behavior was reported to be characteristic of falcate orangetip caterpillars. And the caterpillars' uncanny resemblance to the elongated seed pods that appear on the tips of the plants, probably protects them from potential predators. Striking camouflage, indeed.

Bittercress is a member of the mustard family, and the mustard oils the caterpillars consume while munching on the plants are believed to render them and the adult butterflies distasteful to predatory birds. Possibly the caterpillars avoid the leaves because the concentration of the oils in them is too high (cattle certainly avoid consuming bittercress)? In any case, by remaining on the top of their host plant, caterpillars that live on the cheniers significantly reduce their risk of drowning.

After three weeks, my twelve house-reared caterpillars changed from green to brown, an indication that they were nearing the end of their larval phase. It was time to see how the "wild" caterpillars were doing; I packed the terrarium, along with my other gear, into my truck and returned to the cheniers. There, I observed that the formerly inundated habitats were now dry, except for a few natural depressions and many of the cattle paths. Most of the bittercress plants had already gone to seed and were yellowish and withered. In damp depressions, some plants were quite healthy; on eight, I observed a few plump, mature caterpillars.

I had a problem to solve, however. Where did the caterpillars pupate, that is, transform into a chrysalis? They could not attach themselves to the bittercress plants, which were soon to wither away. They needed a place where they could remain secure until the following March, nearly a year away. Using ice cream sticks, I marked the eight plants hosting caterpillars. When I returned to inspect the plants the following morning, I learned that half the caterpillars were missing. The larvae apparently traveled at night. I would have to pull an all-nighter if I wanted to see where they went.

At dusk, I transferred four of my house-reared caterpillars onto the abandoned host plants. I then drenched myself with insect repellent, mindful of local folk wisdom: "If you can't complete any outdoor activity by sunset, forget it!" (Mosquitoes in the marshlands of Louisiana can be so numerous that one has the impression that the air is vibrating, alive. I refer to these pests as Louisiana's singular "plankton of the air.") With flashlight in tow, I located a more-or-less comfortable spot near the tagged plants, spread my poncho on the ground, sat, and began to mark time as the mosquitoes buzzed about relentlessly.

In the wee hours of the morning, when I had just about decided that I could not contend any longer with buzzing misery, a break came. One of the caterpillars began to crawl down its host plant. Keeping my distance to keep from directly illuminating the caterpillar with my flashlight, I maintained a watchful eye. The individual made its way to the ground before continuing onward. After traveling without pause about thirty feet onto slightly higher ground, the caterpillar encountered a small hackberry tree. The larva then crawled about ten feet up the trunk where it rested. I remained with the caterpillar for nearly a half-hour, although nothing further seemed to be happening. After marking the trunk with a strip of white cloth, I backtracked to check on the other three caterpillars. All three had disappeared from their host plants. Consequently, I began scanning the ground for them. In short order, the beam from my flashlight fell on something I did *not* want to see: a fat, two-foot-long cottonmouth. Fortunately, the serpent was slithering in the opposite direction. When I recovered from the shock, I spotted two of my caterpillars on the damp, bare ground, crawling to higher ground. When they encountered the bases of trees, they, too, ascended to a height of six to ten feet. By four in the morning, they had begun to weave silken threads to attach themselves to the trees.

Content that I had discovered where the caterpillars pupate, I made the rounds to check on all the other caterpillars. By this time, they, too, had departed from their host plants, presumably in search of trees to attach in preparation for their transformation into pupae. Finally, I returned to my truck to observe the eight caterpillars that remained in the terrarium. I found that they had crawled to the upper ends of some dead twigs I had provided for them and had attached themselves to begin their transformation. Exhausted but satisfied, I drove to my motel for a much-needed shower and a couple hours of sleep.

By mid-morning I was back at my research sites. The caterpillars were still attached to their trees. By late afternoon, each had shed its skin to reveal its pupa, which was anchored at its base and middle. Basic brown in color, with yellow, green, and tan mottling, the structure has a pointed front end that makes it look very much like a thorn or bark protrusion—another remarkable example of camouflage, echoing that of the previous larva. Moreover, the pupa's high perch is reasonably secure from flood waters and marauding cattle.

My curiosity was mostly satisfied, but I was intrigued by one detail: the manner in which the bittercress plants flourished best near, within the cattle tracks. I decided I should investigate conditions on a chenier free of cattle and people. I chose Little Pecan Island, which at 2,700 years is Louisiana's oldest extant chenier. As a result of extensive dredging to create navigational ditches and canals for petroleum exploration this chenier is surrounded by open water, not marsh. Although it was homesteaded by a few families in the late 1800s, Little Pecan is now uninhabited, managed by The Nature Conservancy as a preserve for research and nature-oriented recreation. Because the chenier is accessible only by boat, I had to hire a local fisherman.

In a two-day survey of the island I could find only two dozen bittercress plants, all growing in natural depressions under the parasol-like branches of ancient live oak trees. None showed any signs of having hosted falcate orangetip caterpillars. (I suspected there were too few plants to sustain a colony of the butterflies from one year to another.) If ever the butterfly had lived there, it probably had died out a long time ago.

I came away from Little Pecan Island convinced that the cattle on the other cheniers played a part in making Cameron Parish hospitable to falcate orangetips. The cattle tracks create countless small catch basins that retain water long after the surrounding terrain has dried out. These damp micro-habitats help the bittercress plants grow larger and taller. This may matter little in a spring with normal rainfall. During unusually dry years, which are not that infrequent, the mini pools are probably crucial to the plants and therefore to the caterpillars. In addition, the churning of the ground by the cattle creates and maintains relatively clear areas free of competing, congesting vegetation such as grasses. This promotes the dispersal of bittercress, a pioneer species known to do best in recently disturbed areas.

Cattle thus appear responsible, at least indirectly, for maintaining this small population of butterflies in southwest Louisiana. How long this relationship has prevailed is hard to say. Before many trees were cleared, the falcate orangetips were likely more widely distributed across the cheniers. The butterfly population may have been an eastern extension of the population in Texas. As the forest was cut, the butterflies' foothold in the cheniers probably became more precarious, and the cattle became a significant factor in the survival of this isolated population. Alternatively, the butterflies and the cattle may have been introduced into the region at the same time. The least probable scenario is that the chenier butterfly population was once connected to the more northerly Louisiana population; the distance seems too great. Perhaps in the future, genetic tests will reveal how these various butterfly populations (demes) are related.

In 1992, after I returned to my home in Baton Rouge, I placed the terrarium containing the eight remaining pupae near a window. A year later, on March 19, 1993, two of the pupal cases split open to free two perfectly formed female butterflies. The following day, one had eclosed (emerged) as an adult male. I drove to Cameron Parish to check my field site. All the plots were relatively dry because of the lack of heavy spring rains. On March 21, a single female appeared, and on the following day both a male and female were on the wing. By March 25, they had vanished. For the next four days I searched in vain for butterflies—this was probably the shortest flight period on record for a population of butterflies. But I did see a few of their orange eggs—on bittercress growing in cattle tracks.

Another year passed. The weather was warm, and although I was skeptical, I decided to place the terrarium with its five remaining pupae in an outdoor patio. On March 12, 1994, a shower during the night saturated the soil in the enclosure. To my surprise, between March 19 and 26, two females and one male emerged, a full two years after beginning their deep slumber. During this same period, I observed a relatively large number of adults throughout the four colonies in Cameron Parish. It was a bumper year for falcate orangetips. And in March 1995, the remaining two pupae in my terrarium (one male, one female) broke their hibernation, donning their fresh wings.

What at first seemed to be a life strategy teetering precariously close to oblivion has turned out to be one that is singularly fine-tuned for survival. Consider: In a dry spring, when the bittercress plants are unlikely to flourish, pupae may remain in their mummy like, protective state for another twelve months (perhaps even for several years). When the spring rains are adequate, the butterflies emerge in pristine condition, mate, and females lay eggs within only a few days, particularly in the micro-habitats created by cattle. The new caterpillars race through their brief life cycle and then, as pupae, lie low in a hostile environment until, once again, they are awakened by some yet unknown quantity of spring rainfall.

My research into this extraordinary butterfly life cycle of *Anthocharis midea* in the isolated Cajun wetlands of southwest Louisiana has been unceremonious. Nonetheless, it has been personally rewarding. And although not definitive, I am confident that the data are plausible, and therefore, of scientific value. Regrettably, the species faces an uncertain future.

[Published originally in *Natural History*, May 1995 (Volume 104, No. 5), pages 36-43. The illustrated article was the recipient of The John Burroughs Association's ANNUAL AWARD OF RECOGNITION for "Outstanding Published Natural History Essay in 1995." Award was presented on Monday April 1, 1996, at the annual meeting/awards luncheon of the association in the Audubon Gallery of the American Museum of Natural History, New York City. Text reprinted here with permission of the publisher and with minor editing.]

SELECTED REFERENCES

Glassberg, J. 1999. *Butterflies through Binoculars: The East*. A Field Guide to the Butterflies of Eastern North America. Oxford University Press. New York, NY. 242 pages.

Opler, P.A. and G.O. Krizek. 1984. *Butterflies East of the Great Plains.: An Illustrated Natural History*, The Johns Hopkins University Press, Baltimore, MD. 294 pages.

Krotzer, M.J. and S. 2023. Wanted alive in your garden: Falcate orangetip. *Butterfly Gardener*, Spring (Vol. 28:1), pages 12-13.

Marks, C. 2018. *Butterflies of Louisiana: A Guide to Identification and Location*. Louisiana State University Press, Baton Rouge, LA. 462 pages.

Ross, G.N. 1996. Orangetips die hard in Louisiana. *American Butterflies*, Winter (Vol. 4:4), pages 4-10.

Ross, G.N. 2009a. Louisiana's lost world. *Louisiana Wildlife Federation*, Fall (Vol. 17:1), pages 14-20.

Ross, G.N. 2009b. Orangetips and marsh cattle: An adventure in Louisiana's Cajunlands. *Southern Lepidopterists' News*, December 31. (Vol. 31:4), pages 151-160.

Ross, G.N. 2016. Return to "Louisiana's lost world." *Southern Lepidopterists' News*, September 30, (Vol. 38:3), pages 185-203.

Scott, J.A. 1986. *The Butterflies of North America: A Natural History and Field Guide*. Stanford University Press, Stanford, CA. 583 pages.

CHAPTER 8: BIRDWING BUTTERFLIES AND STONE AGE TRIBES

Walking in the shadow of a Victorian naturalist

I first became aware of Alfred Russel Wallace in the spring of 1961, as a biology major in my junior year at college. The professor of a course in "natural history," an enthusiastic young ornithologist with a propensity for biogeography, introduced us to Wallace's six zoogeographic regions and the "Wallace Line." Given that my passion was for butterflies, he shared with me his personal copy of Wallace's *The Malay Archipelago*, in which Wallace describes his first field interaction with a birdwing butterfly. This took place in 1859 on Batchian, today Bacan, in the Maluku Islands (formerly, the Spice Islands), an archipelago just west of the world's second-largest island, New Guinea—itself a celebrated venue as the home of many of the world's the most unusual animals and human languages.

"During my very first walk into the forest at Batchian, I had seen sitting on a leaf out of reach, an immense butterfly of a dark colour marked with white and yellow spots. I could not capture it as it flew away high up into the forest, but I at once saw that it was a female of a new species of *Ornithoptera* or "bird-winged butterfly," the pride of the Eastern tropics. I was very anxious to get it and to find the male, which in this genus is always of extreme beauty. During the two succeeding months, I only saw it once again, and shortly afterwards I saw the male flying high in the air at the mining village. I had begun to despair of ever getting a specimen, as it seemed so rare and wild; till one day, about the beginning of January, I found a beautiful shrub with large, white leafy bracts and yellow flowers, a species of *Mussaenda*, and saw one of these noble insects hovering over it, but it was too quick for me, and flew away. The next day I went again to the same shrub and succeeded in catching a female, and the day after a fine male. I found it to be as I had expected, a perfectly new and most magnificent species, and one of the most gorgeously coloured butterflies in the world. Fine specimens of the male are more than seven inches across the wings, which are velvety black and fiery orange, the latter colour replacing the green of the allied species. The beauty and brilliance of this insect are indescribable, and none but a naturalist can understand the intense excitement I experienced when I at length captured it. On taking it out of my net and opening the glorious wings, my heart began to beat violently, the blood rushed to my head, and I felt much more like fainting than I have done when in apprehension of immediate death. I had a headache the rest of the day, so great was this excitement produced by what will appear to most people a very inadequate cause." (*The Malay Archipelago*, pages 257-258).

The obsessive exuberance of the young Victorian naturalist-writer hooked me on tropical biology; I vowed to someday experience a live birdwing butterfly for myself. I pined: "Could I ever have such a first-hand experience?" For now, though, I needed to learn more about Wallace and his "pride of the Eastern tropics."

Fast forward twenty-nine years to 1990. Holbrook Travel, Inc., announced a nearly three-week-long collecting and photographic expedition to Irian Jaya. The easternmost territory of the nation of Indonesia, Irian Jaya, today, Papua or West Papua, occupies the western half of New Guinea, whose eastern half is the nation of Papua New Guinea. The expedition was to be led by Thomas C. Emmel of the University of Florida, who had previously led expeditions to Papua New Guinea. Emmel was both a fellow butterfly specialist and a longtime personal friend. According to the brochure from Holbrook, the trip offered "A wealth of spectacular *Ornthoptera* species and subspecies, occurring from the lowlands to above 6,000 feet." And to tantalize further: "…to see native settlements almost untouched from the Stone Age." I signed up immediately.

To prepare for the trip, I re-read *The Malay Archipelago* to reacquaint myself with Wallace's adventures. He spent eight years, from 1854 to 1862, traveling through the chain of more than 25,000 islands, including New Guinea and the Philippines, that separates the Indian and Pacific Oceans as well as mainland Southeast Asia from Australia. Wallace estimated that he traveled 14,000 miles on some sixty to seventy separate journeys, collecting 125,660 specimens, including 13,100 butterflies. Among the latter, the birdwing butterflies.

Birdwings are classified within the swallowtail family (Papilionidae). The common name "birdwing" is applied explicitly to thirty-six species clustered within three genera: *Ornithoptera*, *Trogonoptera*, and *Troides*. All species are sexually dimorphic, that is, males and females differ in coloration and size: males are brightly colored, often with large areas of iridescence set against black; females usually are relatively drab and larger. The moniker "birdwing" refers to the butterflies' exceptionally large size, their angular bird-like forewings, and because their flights resemble those of small birds. Birdwings are break-out extremes in evolution. They are island neighbors with an equally singular excess of natural selection: the seemingly impossible Birds of Paradise (family Paradisaeidae). All birdwings utilize plants within the family Aristolochiaceae (pipevines) as hosts. Because such plants are medicinal (aristolochic acid is the main toxin), the butterflies are considered toxic (at least unpalatable) to potential vertebrate predators. Birdwings are endemic to Wallace's Oriental and Australian Zoogeographic Regions, ranging from as far west and north as the Indian subcontinent to as far east and south as Papua New Guinea and northern Australia. Finally, regardless of species, all birdwings can best be described, in my opinion, by a single word: *elegant*.

Wallace was responsible for scientifically describing four new taxa of birdwings. The specimen encountered on Bacan Island he named *Ornithoptera croesus* (1859) honoring Croesus, the king in ancient Anatolia renowned for his wealth (gold). Present-day entomologists recognize five subspecies of *O. croesus*, each endemic to one or more islands within the Malukus. All are commonly

CHAPTER 8: BIRDWING BUTTERFLIES AND STONE AGE TRIBES

referred to as Wallace's golden birdwing, although whether Wallace ever set eyes on any besides the subspecies on Bacan, is debatable. Another species he named *O. brookiana*, for James Brooke, the first "White Rajah" of Sarawak (now a Malaysian state) on the island of Borneo. Since placed in the genus *Trogonoptera*, the butterfly is celebrated as Rajah Brook's Birdwing—the National Butterfly of Malaysia. What's more, Wallace's named two of the eight recognized subspecies of the oblong-spotted birdwing, *Troides oblongomaculatus*: *T. o. papuensis* from New Guinea and *T. o. bouruensis* from Buru Island and Sula Islands (Malukus). Of the birdwings named by Wallace, I could hope to collect only the latter since it was, as the name implies, native to Papua.

Wallace spent three months in Dorey, New Guinea, a small Papuan, and missionary settlement on the northwestern coast. There he was plagued by malnutrition, fevers, colds, dysentery, and insect bites, as well as by a foot infection that kept him housebound for nearly a month.

Had Wallace been able to travel farther inland, into what is currently considered the epicenter for *Ornithoptera* diversity, he likely would have encountered such alluringly named members of that genus as the Goliath birdwing, the chimaera birdwing, and the paradise birdwing. And had he trekked into the coastal rainforest of northern Papua and the nearby island of Bougainville, he could have encountered Queen Alexandra's birdwing. Females of the latter have a wingspan of nearly ten inches (7.3-9.4 average), making them the titans of the butterfly world, and listed in Appendix I of CITES (the Convention on International Trade in Endangered Species of Wild. Fauna and Flora), prohibiting its commercial international trade; other birdwings are listed in Appendix II, requiring permits for export.

October 17, 1990. Our group of 23, accompanied by Emmel and the president of the agency (Giovanna Holbrook), boarded a *Garuda Indonesia* overnight fight of 7,000 miles from Los Angeles via Hawaii to Biak, an island north of the Papua mainland. With free time, we organized a short collecting foray in the morning. Slightly later, we flew 250 miles southeast to the capital, Jayapura, on Papua's northern coast.

As it turned out, my first encounter with a birdwing came sooner than expected, as we rode by bus to a collecting site approximately a dozen miles west of the capital. Suddenly from my window seat I glimpsed a large, dark-colored butterfly moving among some hibiscus flowers, and because of the insect's enormous wings, I blurted out, "female birdwing!" Moments later, I spotted a brilliant green-and-black butterfly, again very large. Emmel commented: "Two species of birdwings are common throughout New Guinea: one is the common green birdwing—*Ornithoptera priamus*—in which the male is a brilliant green and black, whereas the female is black with grayish spotting and larger. The second is the oblong-spotted birdwing (*Troides oblongomaculatuus*) in which both sexes are black and bright yellow, although females are a bit larger. The two individuals we just viewed are unmistakably a pair of *O. priamus*." Everyone on the bus smiled as I mused: "Not bad for our first full day out and for a road sighting!"

My first close encounter with a storied birdwing occurred during an early trek in a national park in the foothills of the Cyclops Mountains. After disembarking from our minibus, I quickly assembled my collecting net: a lightweight, collapsible piece of equipment that featured a large diameter and deep see-through bag, and most important of all, a segmented aluminum handle that permitted the easy addition of eighteen-inch extensions. I optimistically added two one-foot segments to my net, bringing the total length to ten feet.

The forest was sumptuous, mysterious, but different from its counterparts in the Americas. the juggernauts of the American rainforest, for example, are usually anchored by flaring buttresses ("plank buttresses"). Instead, trees here in New Guinea were less statuesque and less buttressed. Common species included banyan (*Ficus*) as well as an abundance of pandanus, wild bananas, and a profusion of palms of varying sizes. Too, trees featured fewer epiphytes; these consisted not of bromeliad and cactus species but rather a great diversity of aroids, ferns–including the popular greenhouse bird's-nest ferns (*Asplenium nidus*) and staghorn or elkhorn ferns (*Platycerium*)—as well as *Dendrobium* spp. orchids. Understory vegetation, also, was heavy with species such as feathery ferns, young pandanus, large aroids (arums) such as, *Aglaonema* and *Alocasia*, and an unending number of unrecognizable woody species that bore heavy loads of epiphytic lichens and mosses.

CHAPTER 8: BIRDWING BUTTERFLIES AND STONE AGE TRIBES

Access to the forest was informal. A well-trodden trail was being maintained by locals who periodically raided the "protected" forest for wood to be used for cooking and building. Our group assumed train formation. This guaranteed personal space for each individual; I elected to bring up the rear. Within minutes we were soaked—not the result of strenuous walking but because of high temperature and humidity, our proximity to the equator and ocean, and stagnant air. I soon began to feel queasy and light-headed. Nonetheless, I was distracted by the abundance of butterflies: I could walk only a few feet before encountering an unfamiliar species.

And then: MY WALLACE MOMENT!

My physical condition caused by heat exhaustion and dehydration continued to deteriorate; and I was out of drinking water. As I passed over the crest of a knoll and began to descend into a small, forested ravine, I heard the welcoming sound of running water. As my spirits lifted, I noticed a large butterfly—a female common birdwing similar to the one I had spotted from the bus window—flying upwards along the trail toward me. The butterfly was about twenty-five or thirty feet above the trail, too high for my net, but due to the incline of the trail, the individual was getting ever closer to the ground. "Would it remain along the trail?" I quickly spread my legs for balance, positioned my net in front of me close to the ground, my hands as far back on the handle as possible, and remained motionless with bated breath. At once, like a winged apparition, another butterfly began tailing the first as if trying to engage it. The iridescent green was telltale: a male of the same species. My heart rate soared as I contemplated the nearly unfathomable: "Could I possibly net the pair with a single swing?"

Time seemed suspended. My eyes locked onto the butterflies. As the duo came within netting distance, I closed my eyes, uttered a short prayer, and swung my net with as much force as I could muster. As the net plunged to the ground, I closed my eyes hoping that my aim was on target. Before I could open my eyes, I realized that I had indeed netted *both* because the massive and powerful wings could be heard as they beat against the cloth—reminiscent of a captured bird or bat trying to escape a paper bag. I quickly realized luck had smiled on me. Regaining my composure, I carefully removed the two specimens. Upon examination, I could confirm that both were in mint condition, plus. I quickly dispatched the two. (With most butterflies, a strong pinch to the body is the quickest and most humane way of dispatching a butterfly, but with these heavy-bodied birdwings, I had to repeat and hold until the insects were lifeless.) Following, I placed each in a glassine envelope before depositing it in my satchel. I sat for a few minutes, savoring the fact that I now was living a lifelong dream!

Soon, my mind quickly was forced back to reality: my intensifying nausea and weakness—no doubt exacerbated by the excitement of netting the birdwings. Acquiring drinking water was still a primary directive, and thus, I kept along the trail in the direction of the gurgling sounds of water. Within just a few minutes I encountered a narrow, fast-running, rivulet of clear water cascading over boulders. Educated that moving water is usually free of most pathogens, I disrobed to my briefs, immersed myself by sitting on a submerged rock, and pumped water from my portable filtering device into my canteen. As I drank and my body cooled from the ambient heat, I began to feel better. I retrieved a "power bar" from my satchel to restore my energy, all the while keeping a watchful eye for lurking serpents, which according to rumor, were rife in this forest.

During this respite, I began to reflect on Wallace's impassioned comments upon netting his first golden birdwing. My mind seemed to meld with that of the Victorian naturalist. We both were enraptured by the glory of nature, a reverence that usually is reserved for religious artifacts. As with Wallace, who probably was also suffering from heat exhaustion and dehydration as well as various tropical illnesses, I, too, relied on abject grit. Our experiences were equally visceral and exhilarating. (I must admit, though, I didn't suffer a headache!) Wallace wrote that his capture of his first birdwing changed his life forever. My capture of my first birdwing changed me, too. Today, in my senior years, my experience in that steamy forest in the wilds of New Guinea gets banked as profound, even epiphanic.

During the next days, I had two additional gainful encounters with birdwings. First, our group was in the lowland rainforest on the island of Supiori off the northwest coast of Papua. Our group had split into several teams. After about an hour, my team of four happened upon a gap in the forest canopy where a large tree had fallen. Here the sunlight had encouraged the growth of an understory clump of *Clerodendrum speciosissimum* (family Lamiaceae) identified locally as "Java glorybower," a species often marketed in the United States horticulture trade. The large-leaf shrubbery was crowned with nearly head-high panicles of bright red flowers that seemed to be magnets for birdwings.

Within an hour or so, both *O. primus* and *T. oblongomaculatus* visited the *Clerodendrum* blossoms. The sunlight patch proved to be both an exceptional venue for collecting, as well as arena for observing the insects' behavior. For instance, the butterflies were "highflyers," preferring open space above the forest canopy. Wing beats were relatively slow—but not shallow—and often interspaced with short glides. (The flight has been described as "poetry in motion.") To me, the insects closely mimicked the aerial dynamics of swallows and swifts, two birds common in the region. I could easily understand why early explorers coined the name "birdwing butterflies." When a butterfly sighted the bright red flowers, the insect descended directly. The sizable panicles of the *Clerodendrum* inflorescence, as with the wide corollas of the hibiscus flowers, provided a substantial landing platform for the heavy-bodied butterflies, an example of co-evolution between the plant and animal kingdoms. Nevertheless, specimens continued to flutter their forewings in order to balance s in typical swallowtail behavior.

My final encounter with birdwings was in the vicinity of Wamena in the Baliem Valley. This is an interior insular region at about 5,300 feet in altitude and surrounded by high cloud-enshrouded mountains that peak at 8,000-10,000 feet. The village is served by a small airport that accommodates

CHAPTER 8: BIRDWING BUTTERFLIES AND STONE AGE TRIBES

tourists who are interested in viewing the Dani—an anachronistic Stone Age tribe discovered by the outside world only on June 23, 1938.

The Dani consists of about 90,000 speakers of Melanesian descent. The tribe represents one of many ethnic and linguistic groups in New Guinea lumped together as "Papuans." All individuals are black-skinned and frizzy-haired. They remained Stone Age farmers/warriors for thousands upon thousands of years—right up into the 1970s. Even today when steel implements are common because of outside influence, some individuals prefer ancient stone adzes, stone and boars' tusk scrapers, knives made from sharpened bamboo, wood spears, bows and arrows, and digging sticks. Regardless of tool, these highland peoples adhere to relic Stone Age principles of hunting, gardening, pig husbandry, fighting, and body decoration.

Women are bare-breasted but wear low-slung grass or fern-fiber skirts. String bags (*noken*) are an integral part of the female apparel. These bags are relatively large, loosely knit from bark fibers, and are used to carry sweet potatoes (a modern replacement for the more ancient crops of taro and yams), wood, a child, piglet, or anything else that needs to be transported. The bags are supported by the forehead much like a tumpline; when empty, they serve as a wrap to help ward off early morning chill.

Men, by contrast, are virtually naked. Their chief item of clothing is the penis sheath (*holim/kotkepa*), technically, a *phallocrypt*. These are constructed from gourds attentively cultivated in cottage gardens and then hollowed out and dried. Gourds of various shapes and sizes are retained for different occasions and to distinguish their status at social events. Sometimes the gourds are painted and enhanced with a long feather or two. For additional adornment, men often augment their sparse attire with caps, wrist bands, and "magical strips" suspended from the neck (all made in part from silken fibers of spider webs), bones, bore tusks, and shells--principally to accent noses and ears. Often, feathers from birds of paradise, fur from the marsupial cuscus or tree kangaroo (*Phalanger maculatus*), and body paint from clay are used to further adorn the body.

Children are usually naked. Older lads often wear tattered items of Western clothing —usually gifted from American and Dutch missionaries.

The Dani typically live in round, grass-roofed huts organized into small compounds consisting of two to five families to form small bucolic settlements near their arable land. Each house usually features small food gardens (primarily sweet potatoes of which seventy-plus varieties are cultivated) and adjacent land for pig husbandry. The house-garden compound is bordered by plank fences amidst a profusion of flowering plants, especially hibiscus, coleus, crotons, dracaenas, angel's trumpets (*Brugmansia*), and New Guinea impatiens or "balsam" (*Impatiens hawkeri*). Many of the fences are entwined with pipevine plants (*Aristolochia*)as mentioned previously, the exclusive hosts for birdwings. The residents grow the flowers and vines to encourage female birdwings to exit the forest to feed and to lay their eggs on the *Aristolochia*, a project sponsored by the government as "butterfly ranching." The eggs, the largest in the butterfly world—are placed in netted enclosures for protection. After the butterflies eclose (emerge), a major portion of the stock is harvested for the flourishing international collectors' trade while all remaining individuals are released into the free-ranging populations. Butterfly ranching has proven to be profitable for isolated villages in both Papua and Papua New Guinea (the latter is where the practice began). And there is more: the simple act of releasing a portion of the raised stock is an asset to local butterfly conservation—and an asset to conservation in general.

At scarcely a mile high, the Baliem Valley provided a respite from the almost incapacitating sultry lowlands. Understandably, our group caused local excitement. Because of this interest, we had no problem locating local men to escort us into the dense forest in nearby ravines. The tribe's men always insisted on carrying our gear. Young adolescent boys often proved helpful as well. They would trail behind, and whenever we paused to rest, they would ask to borrow our nets in order to partake in our "fun." Within a short time, the youngsters demonstrated their ingenuity. They searched nearby for forked twigs and spider webbing, which they then crafted into their personal nets to capture low-flying specimens. At first, the specimens were mutilated. Apparently, the boys initially thought that we needed the insects' bodies, not their wings. But after a little training, most lads quickly became adept at handling butterflies. For compensation, we paid about a quarter for each specimen in good condition. The payment triggered ear-to-ear grins, and as one might expect, touched off a run on the construction of ingenious spider-web nets.

At the end of our five-day stay in Wamena, our group was treated to a cultural bonanza: a demonstration of a Dani ritual. That included the enactment of a mock battle and a traditional feast featuring pit-roasted pig, sweet potatoes, and taro. By nightfall, during discussions of the preceding days, our collective sense was candid: The drama of the Dani would remain one of our more salient memories. On a personal note, I felt a tinge of hubris: the Baliem Valley exposed me to flora and fauna and an arcane Indigenous culture that was unknown even to the preeminent Alfred Russel Wallace. By trip's end, I had collected a total of 728 specimens of butterflies representing 122 species. Of these, nine specimens were *O. priamus poseidon*, and 12 were *Troides oblongomaculatus papuensis*.

Contemplating the distributions of the three genera of birdwing butterflies as we understand them today, it seems that the Wallace Line—that invisible frontier that Wallace erected to illustrate the separation of Australian and Asian animal life—applies, also, to birdwing butterflies. Specifically, *Ornithoptera*, with thirteen species and many subspecies and forms, are found exclusively east of the line, in Wallace's Australian Region. On the other hand, *Trogonoptera*, with two species—one on the Thai-Malay Peninsula and surrounding islands, the other exclusively on Palawan Island in the Philippines—occur west of the line, placing them in what Wallace called the Oriental, currently identified as the Asian, Region. And *Troides* with twenty-one species, is also found west of the line, as far as India. There is one exception, and it is a lone subspecies: Wallace's *Troides oblongomaculatus papuens*, named in honor of Alfred Russel Wallace himself.

[Published originally as "My Wallace Moment: On the Trail of Birdwing Butterflies" in *Natural History*, September 2015 (Vol.123:7), pages 34-39. Reprinted with permission of the publisher and with minor editing.]

SELECTED REFERENCES

Bates, H.W. 2002. *The Naturalist on the River Amazons*. The Narrative Press, Torrington, GB. 432 pages.
Berry, A. (editor). 2003. Infinite Tropics: An Alfred Russel Wallace Anthology. Verso, New York, NY. 430 pages.
Flannery, M.A. 2011. *Alfred Russel Wallace: A Rediscovered Life*. Discovery Institute Press, Seattle, WA. 165 pages.
Haugum, J. & A.M. Low. 1978-1980. *A Monograph of the Birdwing Butterflies*. Volume 1, Part 1: Introduction, Ornithoptera (Aetheoptera), Pages 11-84; Part 2: Ornithoptera (Ornithoptera), Pages 85-192; Part 3: Ornithoptera (Scoenbergia), Pages 193-308. Scandinavian Science Press Ltd., Klampenborg, DK.
Lamas, G. 2004. *Atlas of Neotropical Lepidoptera. Checklist: Part 4A: Hesperiodea-Papilionoidea*. Scientific Publishers, Gainesville, FL. 439 pages.
Muller, K. 1990. *Irian Jaya: West New Guinea*. Periplus Editions, Inc. Berkeley, CA. 167 pages.
NABA. 2001. *Checklist & English Names of North American Butterflies*. Second Edition. North American Butterfly Association, Inc., Morristown, NJ. 60 pages.
Parsons, M. 1991. *Butterflies of the Bulolo-Kau Valley*. Bishop Museum Press, Honolulu, HI. 280 pages.
Ross, G.N. 2016. On Alfred Russell (sic) Wallace, birdwing butterflies, and my experiences in New Guinea. *News of The Lepidopterists' Society*, Spring (Vol. 58:1), pages 9-15.
Wallace, A.R. 2007. *The Malay Archipelago*. Tenth Edition. Cosimo Classics, New York, NY. 515 pages.

CHAPTER 9: DIANA IN AMERICA

A glamorous, legendary, and revered butterfly haunts woodlands in Arkansas and Appalachia

July 4, 1992, 7:30 pm CDST. The sun has barely dipped below the western horizon. I am seated behind the steering wheel of my pickup/camper that is parked on a narrow, lonely forest service road that loops around the rim of the plateau atop Mt. Magazine in northwest Arkansas. I have a panoramic view of a long valley 2,000 feet below. To my immediate right and left are patches of scraggy oak/hickory forest. In front, is a precipitous sandstone escarpment with an east-west orientation. Here and there, a singular gnarly cedar tree shaped by wind adds a touch of drama. Between me and the escarpment is a small meadow filled with vibrant yellow wildflowers. The valley below is pastoral, a checkerboard of verdant pastures and woodlots. At this instant, the vista is particularly breathtaking because the sky is its most sublime: a bright azure halo on the western horizon is being captured by deeper indigo tones advancing from the east. Like an extravaganza of fireworks honoring the nation's birthday, fireflies are beginning to punctuate the air with flickering neon light.

Yet, it is not these serene surroundings that have prompted my 550-mile journey from Baton Rouge. No, my quest is the Diana fritillary butterfly (*Speyeria diana*), or simply, "Diana" –a medium size, elusive lepidopteran that has been reported to fly in mountainous regions of northwest Arkansas.

Having arrived on Mt. Magazine on July 3, I discovered, by happenstance, this deserted road with a patch of native eastern purple coneflowers (*Echinacea purpurea*) growing within the understory shade of the surrounding forest. Word has it that female Dianas are especially fond of purple coneflowers. About a dozen of the plants, approximately two feet in height, were capped with elegant daisy-like flowers, each consisting of a droopy whorl of pink petals surrounding a yellow-orange pincushion-like center. I've been holding vigil here since midday, hoping to spot a Diana fritillary. So far, I've counted nine species of butterflies, but no Diana.

It is now 5:30 PM. My eyes are tired, and my attention is waning. Before exiting the vehicle for a short break, I suddenly notice a sizable butterfly with black and blue wings open atop one of the coneflowers. Yes, it is my "Diva," a female Diana! I grab my binoculars for a close encounter. The butterfly is impressive, not only for its large size and exceptionally long, spindly legs and equally disproportionate proboscis, but also because of its resolute behavior. Unlike many butterflies that are skittish when feeding, the Diana walks slowly on the flower's spiky center, probing into each crevice to access the tiny reservoirs of high-octane nectar. She often tilts forward in a headstand to tap deep recesses. On occasion, she flies upward three or four feet, circles the patch of flowers a few times, but then re-settles on an adjacent flower to resume feeding. She is unfettered by my presence, or anything else.

As the glowing disk continues to sink, a few rays of sunlight intersect with the patch of flowers. In response, the Diana closes her wings as if to shield herself. The dark color of her under surface reminds me of a dead leaf. But once the beams fade, the butterfly re-opens her wings, revealing the striking blue and black coloration; after another twenty-five minutes on the flower head, she flutters up to move to an adjacent flower spike. At no time does she depart into the brighter meadow as did all other species I had observed earlier. Caught up in the moment, the chic "flower-strider" seems insatiable, and oblivious to the sun's impending disappearance.

Although exhausted, I stick to my voyeurism. Experience has taught me that temperate zone butterflies depend upon warmth from the sun for flight energy and usually cease feeding long before the sun sets. This allows the butterflies sufficient energy and time to locate safe nighttime roosts. I questioned: "How was this Diana up so late?"

At 8:50 PM the butterfly finally closes her wings and launches straight up. She alights upside down on the underside of an old leaf of a hickory tree, about eight feet above the ground. After a few seconds she partially tucks her two forewings into her hind wings. The overall effect is uncannily similar to that of a frayed leaf—an excellent example of camouflage. I keep watch for another ten minutes for assurance that the butterfly has truly settled in. When satisfied, I retire into my camper, quickly downing two cans of ENSURE®--my usual haute cuisine when in the field. Shortly, I fall into my own nocturnal slumber.

Speyeria diana is the largest of some fourteen species in a genus of butterflies commonly referred to as The Greater Fritillaries, family Nymphalidae (see Chapter 10). Members of the genus typically sport a checkerboard foundation of black spots on their wings against an orangish background (the name "fritillary" is from the Latin word for "dice box"); the undersides of their wings are brown with shiny, silver spots. Entomologists hypothesize that the reflective nature of the ventral surfaces of the wings assists in heat regulation since most fritillaries are addicted to sunny venues.

CHAPTER 9: DIANA IN AMERICA

In most species within the taxon, males and females look alike, although females are slightly larger. All live in regions with cold winters and significant snowfall. Whereas most butterflies have a straightforward life cycle (egg, larva, pupa, adult in a sequential, reasonable short period of time), the Greater Fritillaries are exceptions. Their paradigm goes something like this: Males emerge (eclose) from their pupal stage (chrysalis) in late spring or early summer, usually three to four weeks before females. Subsequent to mating, males become tattered and die shortly after mating. By contrast, females live for three or four months after mating, but do not begin depositing eggs until late autumn (October/November). Each female deposits between 1,000 and 2,000 eggs during a three-to-four week during the cool days of autumn. Eggs are deposited singly on ground litter, not on host plants (violets) that are desiccated at the time. Although larvae (caterpillars) hatch in late autumn and partly consume their egg casings, they cannot feed on dried hosts. Instead, the minuscule larvae hibernate in ground litter and snow throughout the entire ensuing old season. Come spring when the violet plants renew growth, the caterpillars re-energize and start munching on the tender foliage. After several molts to accommodate growth, they pupate as chrysalis near ground level, and then emerge as adult butterflies on the time scale as described earlier.

Many of these life strategies of *Speyeria* are extreme for butterflies. Even among these atypical fritillaries, though, the Diana is quirky, a maverick. To clarify: Whereas in most species, the sexes are identical or very similar, male and female Dianas are markedly different (termed sexual dimorphism).

The upper surfaces of a female Diana's wings are black with pale blue splashes and dots; the undersurfaces are a rich mottled mahogany color. By contrast, male wings are dark brown with extensive orange outer margins, while beneath they are a cinnamon color. And whereas most fritillaries are at home in sunlit flower-filled meadows, Dianas are partial to shadowy forested habitats. (In Roman mythology, *Diana* was the "Goddess of woodland, childbirth, and fertility." Her Greek equivalent, *Artemis*, commonly portrayed with a cocked bow, was "Goddess of the hunt.")

Named in 1775 from specimens in Jamestown, Virginia, the species was historically common throughout the temperate deciduous forests of the southern Appalachian Mountains and westward to the Ozark-Ouachita Mountains of the Midwest. Presumably, it once had a continuous range, but *Butterflies East of the Great Plains,* published in 1984, recorded merely four separate populations, two of which had recently disappeared:

> *"The largest population occurs in the southern Appalachians from central Virginia and West Virginia southwestward in the mountains to northern Georgia and Alabama. A fourth population persists in the Ozark mountains of Arkansas and Missouri."*

To that, I add that investigations by others had concluded that the population in Missouri had been extirpated as well. In response, in 1990 I made it my business to learn how and why the extant populations of Diana survive, and, paradoxically, in two regions separated by some 600 miles.

CHAPTER 9: DIANA IN AMERICA

I began with several exploratory late-summer road trips from Baton Rouge to northern Georgia and southwestern North Carolina. During my visits I observed but a few of the butterflies, all females, but enough to conclude that the ideal domain for the Diana is forested land between 2,100 and 2,500 feet in elevation where summers are uncommonly cool, and mornings often cloaked in pea-soup fog. I discovered the Dianas along shadowy forest roadsides in patches of wildflowers such as butterfly milkweed (*Asclepias tuberosa*), joe pye weed (*Eupotorium fistulosum*), and fall blooming thistles (*Cirsium* spp.) The butterflies were docile and approachable. The forests, consisting of hardwoods and hemlocks, were tall and moist, and violets—presumably, ideal hosts for hungry larvae—were common. Following that initiation, I launched research in early July 1992 (as described earlier) in Arkansas' Mount Magazine. For the next several summers, I traveled to Mount Magazine for a week. I funded the work personally, although in 1996, I was bolstered for twelve months by a modest grant from the *National Geographic Society* (see Preface).

Mount Magazine is in Logan County near the small community of Paris (about 100 miles northwest of the City of Little Rock). The mountain is essentially a 2,500-foot plateau—albeit a 2,753-foot knob (Signal Hill) logs it in as the highest point in the state. The monolith rises from the Petit Jean River Valley. In the 1850s the top of the plateau became a seasonal respite of town-size proportion. During the Great Depression (1930s), homesites were abandoned and the land was purchased by the federal government to become the Magazine Division of the Ozark National Forest. A summer resort consisting of a two-story lodge, 18 rustic cabins, and a primitive campground followed. Unexpectedly, in 1971, the then unoccupied lodge burned to the ground and the cabins abandoned shortly thereafter. Except for occasional nature and recreational enthusiasts (primarily hang gliders) and forest service personnel, the area remained relatively undisturbed—a natural Eden.

As my truck began ascending state highway 309 up the mountain, I was surprised to find a very different forest cover from that of the southern Appalachians. Specifically, Mount Magazine is drought-prone and dominated by oaks and hickories of medium stature at best. I did note that violet plants were common, often growing in seemingly hostile places such as cracks in old asphalt roadbeds where moisture can accumulate. Apart from the violets, the Arkansas site seemed an unpromising haunt for the shade-loving *Diana* of classical Roman antiquity.

That said, to quote an adage: "Things are seldom as they seem." After two weeks of searching in vain for Dianas on the mountain's lower slopes, I eventually headed up to the plateau proper. There I found sunny swaths of wildflowers, including butterfly milkweed, banking the untended roadsides. And before I knew it, I viewed perched on one of the flowers, a butterfly that I instantly recognized to be a male Diana. During the remainder of the day, I logged in six Dianas, all male, some even helping themselves to minerals and salts from the scat of a coyote or fox. It took but another day or two to unearth the "secret garden" where I was finally able to observe my female

Diana. Having returned to Mount Magazine periodically for fifteen years, I am now privy to the fundamentals of the species' atypical life cycle.

A classical maxim in biology is that the morphology, anatomy, physiology, and behavior of an organism represent ancient adaptations to specific environmental parameters. Furthermore, the extraordinary high number of eggs deposited by females was a hint that the life cycle was extremely problematic. Thus armed, I assumed that the peculiar attributes of both sexes of *S. diana* could be explained if I could observe the details of the insect's lifestyle. First, I concentrated on the obvious: sexual dimorphism. Once adults elcose (emerge), males are relatively short-lived, surviving just long enough to mate. The marked contrast between the bright orange and dark tones on the upper wings may make them more vulnerable to predation by birds, but may also serve to attract females, which reside for the most part, within the shade of forest cover. Consider: the bright orange is a close match to the petals of the male's favorite nectar source, butterfly milkweed, so that in addition, the color may serve as camouflage.

Females, by comparison, face more Herculean challenges. A female, for example, doesn't eclose until June or early July. She mates immediately with males that are at the end of their flight season. Each female usually lives through the summer's heat, that is, until September and October when she then begins to deposit her eggs. I was perplexed by a nagging question: How does a female Diana manage to secure nutrients and evade predators for such an extended period?

I became a "Sherlock Homes" to sleuth on female Dianas. I soon learned that on warm, sunny days, females spend most of their time perched quietly atop leaves of understory vegetation within the deep shade. Although they station themselves in close proximity to favored sources of nectar—eastern purple coneflower (*Echinacea purpurea*—they usually exit the forest during the cool morning hours (arising as early as 8:00 AM) and again during late afternoon and early evening (retiring as late as 8:50 PM). Other times are spent resting in the shade of the forest, where if an individual over cools, she will fly into a sunlit patch, spread her wings, and slowly fan to adjust body temperature. After a few minutes, she returns respite—inconspicuous to all, including lepidopterists. Only on warm cloudy days are females likely to feed in the open regardless of the hour. And if daytime temperatures are cool, females remain secluded all day—a prowess befitting the "Goddess of Woodlands."

The female's habits change in autumn. When temperatures are cooler, and when she is laying eggs, the butterfly will not begin feeding until about 10:30 in the morning. An individual will spend as much as two to three hours on a single thistle flower head (the favored nectar plant during autumn). By one o'clock in the afternoon, the female will take flight into the canopy of the nearby forest. There she descends and alights on the shaded ground. Walking about and probing dried detritus with the tip of her abdomen, she finds a site that suits her, and curling her abdomen under dead plant material, deposits a single egg. Within four or five seconds, she moves a few inches and repeats the probing.

After depositing up to a dozen eggs in the perpetual shade, she apparently needs warmth and therefore will fly to a sun-drenched spot to bask with her wings outstretched. She continues laying eggs and basking until about 3:00 in the afternoon, by which time she will have laid a total of between thirty and forty-five eggs. She then abandons the forest to resume feeding, usually on the same thistle visited earlier in the day. Near 4:45 she seeks shelter for the night. A female will follow this routine each sunny day until she deposits her full load of eggs (several thousand), or until she becomes so tattered that disease or predators easily overtake her.

My conclusion? The dark coloration of a female Diana is a direct adaptation to energy conservation—of evolutionary significance. During summer, for example, restricting feeding to only morning and afternoon hours helps conserve energy during the most exhausting hot parts of the day. During autumn, dark coloration facilitates the maximum absorption of heat from less direct sunlight. Such behavior, patently, is important for laying a prodigious number of eggs late in the growing season. (But there may be another factor at play, too. Over the years, several evolutionary biologists have hypothesized that the black-and-blue coloration mimics/imitates that of the pipevine swallowtail (*Battus philenor*), a common butterfly species reputed to be unpalatable to vertebrate predators, and a species common throughout the entire historic range of the Diana. Hypothetically, the guise between the model (pipevine swallowtail) and the mimic (Diana fritillary) is so similar that neither is attacked. The question, of course, remains open-ended.)

Source of nectar is crucial, too. Although adult Dianas feed on the flowers of a variety of plants, the butterflies are fussy. Example: Male Dianas decidedly favor *Asclepias tuberosa*—peak bloom in June. Females, by contrast, exploit specific summer/fall flowering species: eastern purple coneflower, wild bergamot (*Monarda fistulosa*), mountain mint (*Pycnanthemum tenuifolium*), gayfeather (*Liatris aspera*), pasture thistle (*Cirsium altissimum*) and tall thistle (*C. discolor*). These plants share relevant characteristics. First, all are locally common in disturbed, sunny to partially shaded habitats in the vicinity of forest cover. These habitats enable high levels of photosynthesis and therefore high nectar production. Second, all are "composites," that is, they possess a flower head (inflorescence) that consists of multiple individual flowers, each with a nectar reservoir that encourages a pollinator to spend extended time aboard, thus conserving energy. Third, all have spiky flower heads that cater to pollinators endowed with long legs and mouth parts for deep penetration, such as *Speyeria*. Finally, all contain phytochemicals, those torrents of plant-derived compounds that are known to be pharmacologically active in human beings. (Popular examples: nicotine, caffeine, gingko, St. John's wort, lycopene, echinacea, peppermint, menthol, saw palmetto, beta carotene, vitamin C, herbs in general; and the list goes on and on.) Such complex chemicals exhibit vital *in situ* functions on the cellular level of virtually all organisms. Functions might include: attract pollinators and dispersers of seeds, repel herbivores, and impart resistance to inflammation, mutations, viruses, bacteria, and fungi. Tellingly, an analysis of the major nectar sources of female Dianas confirms that all possess strong anti-bacterial and anti-inflammatory properties. Besides, feeding on specific nectars, aged females lessen the impact of dehydration by imbibing moisture directly. (On four separate occasions I observed a female siphoning water directly from dew coating roadside detritus.)

In 2003 and 2009, I published articles (see "Selected References) on the relationship between butterflies' sources of food and longevity. I proposed that the dictum "we are what we eat" must apply not solely to humans, but to the entire animal kingdom. Specifically, I suggested that female Dianas sequester phytochemicals from nectars in their diet. If so, the insects are primed with an arsenal of health promoting pharmaceuticals. This, coupled with coloration and behavior that make the insects super-efficient with energy conservation, and I can easily understand how female Dianas are able to endure months of environmental abuses. As corollary, I proposed that these same medicinal agents are transferred via adult to egg, and later to young larvae. There, these compounds

are stored (perhaps in body fluids or even in the bulbs of the long protruding hairs) to assist delicate larval stages outwit for nearly six months, the dangers of forest floor debris rife with fungi and small predators. Additionally, the accumulation of dead leaves in autumn and winter snowfall(made up mostly of trapped air) help conceal/insulate the fasting (diapausing) larvae from colder ambient temperatures, thus further enhancing survival. While such hypotheses lack scientific experimentation, I find my empirical data compelling. Succinctly, the *Speyeria diana* complies with its genetic legacy by developing a life strategy that enables success in a problematic environment.

Extending this train of thinking, I proffer that the present (and probably past) geographical range of *S. Diana* is governed not by the extirpation of violet host plants in the East as has been promulgated by hard-core

ecologists (factually, *Viola* remains common throughout most of the butterfly's former range). Instead, the females may have been deprived by urban sprawl of critical drug-rich nectar plants that bloom in sequence throughout her lengthy life. With its unique history of human settlement and abandonment, Mt. Magazine seems to have been primed to fulfill the Diana's stringent requirements.

That no longer is the case. Mt. Magazine has been rediscovered by the American public. The mountain top has become a popular state park and tourist destination. Inspired by my extended research and widespread media publicity, in 1997, the Paris Chamber of Commerce launched the annual "*Mt. Magazine International Butterfly Festival*" (July 31-August 2). The event brought nearly 10,000 visitors to the mountain and Paris community. The event continues. Since the early 2010s, however, it has been scaled down to lessen human impact on the sensitive nature of the park. More recently, the Diana fritillary has been designated the poster species for Mt. Magazine State Park, and on February 28, 2007, the Arkansas General Assembly passed legislature enacting the butterfly as the official butterfly of the State of Arkansas (the honeybee is the official state insect). Finally, I and others have further championed Mt. Magazine's Diana in published articles, posters, television productions, and presentations at meetings and butterfly events across the country.

Today, "Mt. Magazine" and "Diana" resonate in concert among butterfly aficionados and conservationists. Residents in nearby communities (Paris, Magazine, Havana, Booneville, and Subiaco) champion Arkansas' iconic mountain and butterfly.

In fact, Dianas occasionally visit the gardens of residents who cultivate pollinator-friendly plants such as phlox, onions, and especially zinnias. Yet, fame can be a cautionary tale, a double-edged sword. Because Mt. Magazine is public-friendly, the insular and fragile ecosystem is under increased pressure, making the Diana's extended presence tenuous. How this celebrity butterfly with its fitting mythological name and reputation will fare in the future is anyone's guess, of course. Meanwhile, I wish what I have daubed my "winged muse," well.

[This is an integration of two of my previously published illustrated essays: "Diana's Mountain Retreat," IN: Naturalist at large. *Natural History,* March 2008 (Vol. 117:2), pages 24-26, 28, 72; and "Diana still reigns in Arkansas: A natural history essay," in *News of the Lepidopterists' Society*, Winter 2011 (Vol. 53:4), pages 116-123, cover. Portions of texts are used with permission of the publisher/editor and with minor editing.]

CHAPTER 9: DIANA IN AMERICA

SELECTED REFERENCES

Adams, J.A., and I.L. Finkelstein. 2006. Late season observations on female Diana fritillary (*Speyeria diana*) aggregating behavior. *News of the Lepidopterists' Society* 48(4):106-107.

Allen, T.J. 1997. *The Butterflies of West Virginia and Their Caterpillars*. University of Pittsburgh Press. Pittsburgh, PA. 388 pages.

Brock J.P. & K. Kaufman. 2003. *Kaufman Field Guide to Butterflies of North America*. Houghton Mifflin Co. NY. 392 pages.

Carlton, C.D., and L.S. Nobles. 1996. Distribution of *Speyeria diana* (Lepidoptera: Nymphalidae) in the highlands of Arkansas, Missouri, and Oklahoma, with comments on conservation. *Entomological News* 107(4):213-219.

Editors. 1997. IN: Field notes: Searching high and low: Butterflies are free.. *National Geographic* January (191:1), page 107. (In addition, the single photograph was used in two different "Renew Subscription" brochures and as example for "Research" on the web site of the *National Geographic* home page for six months.)

Editors. 2001. Butterflies losing habitat. IN: Geographica: NGS Research Grant. *National Geographic* November (200:5).

Evans, W.H. 1959. The saga of an orphan *Speyeria diana* larva. *Journal of the Lepidopterists' Society* 13(2):93-94.

Fessenmyer, K. August 2006 species spotlight: Diana fritillary butterfly. Wild South Society. Website: www.wildsouth.org/index.php/species-spotlight/37-diana-fritillary-butterfly.

Flaschka, H. 1989. Disinfection during rearing. *Southern Lepidopterists' Society News* 2(4):36-37.

Glassberg, J. 1999. *Butterflies Through Binoculars: The East*. Oxford University Press. New York, NY. 242 pages.

Glassberg, J. 2010. *Butterflies of North America*. Fall River Press. New York, NY. 202 pages.

Hammond, P.C., and D.V. McCorkle (1983(84). The decline and extinction of *Speyeria* populations resulting from human environmental disturbances (Nymphalidae: Argynninae). *Journal of Research on the Lepidoptera* 22(4):217-224.

Heitzman, J.R. and J.E. Heitzman. 1996. *Butterflies and Moths of Missouri*. Missouri Department of Conservation. Jefferson City, MO. 385 pages.

Hovanitz, W. 1963. Geographical distribution and variation of the genus *Argynnis*. III. *Argynnis diana*. *Journal of Research on the Lepidoptera* 1(3):201-208.

Howe, W.H. 1975. *The Butterflies of North America*. Double Day & Co. Garden City, NY. 633 pp.

Iftner, D.C., J.A. Shuey, and J.V. Calhoun. 1992. *Butterflies and Skippers of Ohio*. Ohio Biological Survey Bulletin, New Series, Vol. 9(1):1-212. Hillard, OH.

James, D.G. and J. P. Pelham. 2011. Observations on the seasonal biology and apparent migration of *Argynnis* (*Speyeria*) *coronis* (Nymphalidae) in Central Washington. *Journal of the Lepidoperists' Society* 65(4):249-255.

Louisiana Public Broadcasting. 1997. An Enchantment of Butterflies. Video and CD. Donna Lafleur producer. Louisiana Public Broadcasting. Baton Rouge, Louisiana. www.lpb.org.

Marks, C.W. 2008. Dianas in southwest Arkansas at Rick Evans/Grandview Prairie WMA. *Southern Lepidopterists' Society News* 30(4):136-140.

Mattoon, S.O., R.D. Davis and O.D. Spencer. 1971. Rearing techniques for species of *Speyeria* (Nymphalidae). *Journal of the Lepidopterists' Society* 24(4):247-256.

Moran, M.D., and C.D. Baldridge. 2002. Distribution of the Diana Fritillary, *Speyeria diana* (Nymphalidae) in Arkansas, with notes on nectar plant and habitat preference. *Journal of the Lepidopterists' Society* 56(3):162-165.

NABA Butterfly Counts. *Reports* from 1992-2010. Region 10 (Southeast), Region 11 (Central Midwest), Region 14 (Great Lakes) and Region 16 (South Atlantic). North American Butterfly Association. Morristown, NJ.

National Geographic Society. 1997. Butterflies are free. IN: Field Notes: Committee for Research and Exploration (Gary Noel Ross). *National Geographic*, 191(1):107.

National Geographic Society. 2001. Butterflies losing habitat. IN: Geographica (Gary Noel Ross). NGS Research Grant. *National Geographic*, 200(5): Geographic Section.

Opler, P.A. & G.O. Krizek. 1984. Butterflies East of the Great Plains. The John Hopkins University Press, Baltimore, MD. 294 pages.

Opler, P.A. & V. Malikul. 1992. *A Field Guide to Eastern Butterflies*. The Peterson Field Guide Series. Houghton Mifflin Co. New York, NY. 486 pages.

Paulissen, L.J. 1975. *Arkansas butterflies and skippers*. Proceedings of the Arkansas Academy of Science 29:57-61.

Price, L. 2011. Notes on the Diana fritillary. *Southern Lepidopterists' Society News* 33(3):99.

Pyle, R.M. 1981. *The Audubon Society Field Guide to North American Butterflies*. Alfred A. Knopf, New York, NF. 915 pages.

Reese, M. 2003. Hot seens: Summer/Fall 2003. *American Butterflies* 11(4):38-39.

Ross, G.N. 1995. *Everything You Ever Wanted To Know About Butterflies: 100 Questions and Answers by Gary Noel Ross, Ph.D.* Gary Noel Ross. Baton Rouge, LA. 52 pages.

Ross, G.N. 1997. Preliminary inventory of the butterflies of Coweeta Hydrologic Laboratory, Nantahala National Forest, North Carolina. *News of the Lepidopterists' Society* 39(4):70-71, 88, front cover.

Ross, G.N. 1998. Butterfly festivals: Fun and education for all! *American Butterflies* 6(2):16-23, front cover.

Ross, G.N. 1998. Definitive destination: Mount Magazine State Park. *American Butterflies* 6(2):24-33.

Ross, G.N. 2002. Social butterflies. IN: The Lives of Butterflies: Tails & Tales. *News of the Lepidopterists' Society* 44(2):55, 63.

Ross, G.N. 2003. What's for dinner? A new look at the role of phytochemicals in butterfly diets. *News of the Lepidopterists' Society* 45(3):83-89, 100, outside back cover.

Ross, G.N. 2005. A time to drink. *News of the Lepidopterists' Society* 47(4):107, 111.

Ross, G.N. 2005. Rain, rain, go away! *Butterfly Gardener* 10 (full year issue):4-5.

Ross, G.N. 2009. Herbs and spices for man and butterflies. *News of the Lepidopterists' Society* 51(3):95-100.

Ross, G.N. 2011. The accidental visitor. *Butterfly Gardener* 16(1):4-5, 14.

Ross, G.N. and M.C. Henk. 2004. Notes on eggs and first instar larvae of three species of *Speyeria* (Nymphalidae). *News of the Lepidopterists' Society* 46(2):53-57, 62-63.

Rudolph, D.C., C.A. Ely, R.R. Schaefer, J.H. Williamson, and R.E. Thill. 2006. The Diana fritillary (*Speyeria diana*) and great spangled fritillary (*S. cybele*): Dependence on fire in the Ouachita Mountains of Arkansas. *Journal of the Lepidopterists' Society* 60(4):218-226.

Scholtens, B.G. 2004. Survey of *Speyeria diana* in Sumter National Forest (Oconee Co., SC). *Report to National Forest Service*. 3 pp.

Scott, J.A. 1986. *The Butterflies of North America: A Natural History and Field Guide*. Stanford University Press. Stanford, CA. 583 pages.

Showalter, A.H. 1980. Bilateral gynandromorphic *Speyeria diana* (Nymnphalidae). *Journal of the Lepidopterists' Society* 34(4):340-344.

Shuey, J.A., J.V. Calhoun, and D.C. Iftner. 1987. Butterflies that are endangered, threatened, and of special concern in Ohio. *Ohio Journal of Science* 87(4):98-106.

Skillman, F.W. Jr., and J.B. Heppner. 1992. Gynandromorph *Speyeria diana* from Georgia (Lepidoptera: Nymphalidae). *Tropical Lepidoptera* 3(1):35-36.

Spencer, L.A. 2006. *Arkansas: Butterflies and Moths*. Ozark Society Foundation. Little Rock, AR. 314 pages.

The Encyclopedia of Arkansas History & Culture. 2011. www.encyclopediaofarkansas.net/encyclopedia/entry-detail.aspx?entryID5236.

Wagner, D.L. 2006. *Caterpillars of Eastern North America*. Princeton University Press. Princeton, NJ. 512 pages.

Wells, C.N., L. Spencer, and D. Simons. 2011. Reproductive behavior of *Speyeria diana* (Nymphalidae) in Arkansas. *Journal of the Lepidopterists' Society* 65(1):51-53.

Wells, C.N., L. Spencer, and D. Simons. 2011. Reproductive behavior of *Speyeria diana* (Nymphalidae) in Arkansas. (Literature Cited). *Journal of the Lepidopterists' Society* 65(2):136.

Winter, W.D. Jr. 2000. *Basic Techniques for Observing and Studying Moths & Butterflies*. The Lepidopterists' Society. Memoir Number 5. Natural History Museum. Los Angeles, CA. 444 pages.

Author observing social feeding of regal fritillary (*Speyeria idalia*) butterflies on butterfly milkweed (*Asclepias tuberosa*): Wah'Kon-Tah Prairie Preserve, El Dorado Springs, MO. June 15, 1998. A controlled burn by the Missouri Department of Conservation the previous summer encouraged a rich growth of subsequent spring wildflowers, especially butterfly milkweed and pale purple coneflower (*Echinacea pallida*); both are favorite nectar sources for regal fritillaries. Photograph by author using self-timer on camera mounted on a tripod.

CHAPTER 10: A PRAIRIE ROYAL

The regal fritillary butterfly holds on to its tenuous reign in the nation's heartland

For numberless by-gone years, grass held sway across 42 percent of Earth's terra firma. Commonly referred to as grassland, prairie, steppe, veldt, pampas, or plains, all were lumped by ecologists into the Grassland Biome, the largest terrestrial ecosystem on Planet Earth. Within these spacious worlds, long blade-like leaves and stalks of feathery tassels undulated across a rolling earth beneath a domed heaven. The horizon was always in view but never within reach. In the past, explorers coined metaphors such as "great green seas" and "seas of grass." One anecdote describes the grass as taller than a "horse and rider." And although the landscape was dominated by expanses of grasses, the blade-like greenery was often punctuated with wildflowers that carpeted the deep, rich black soil with kaleidoscopic colors. The landscape was unique, its pedigree derived from a timeless interplay between moderate rainfall, four distinct seasons, diversified deep-rooted and warm-season grasses, large herbivorous mammals, and fires generated periodically by both lightning and native peoples. Together, the tableau presented a pastoral scene of subtle beauty.

In North America grasslands originally dominated the center of the continent—the nation's heartland. There, the greenery was distributed into three distinct longitudinal belts that began in south central Canada, then southward into the Midwest, and finally deep into western Texas and New Mexico. Each realm was codified according to maximum overall height of the grass: Tallgrass Prairie, Mixed Grass Prairie, and Short Grass Prairie (also known as Great Plains). The three growth patterns were determined by a gradient of rainfall, which is the highest in the east, lowest in the west. Grasslands were punctuated with extensive displays of colorful wildflowers, particularly in the spring.

These habitats birthed an array of the nation's most endearing animals: American bison (buffalo), antelope (pronghorn), deer (mule), elk, bear (grizzly), wolf (gray), mountain lion (puma, cougar), grouse (prairie chicken), ground squirrel (black-footed prairie dog), and black-footed ferret. But lesser critters made their home there, also. One of these, the Rocky Mountain locust, often swarmed in numbers comparable to a Biblical plague. All had integrated lives.

With western expansion by Euro-Americans, beginning in the 1800s, virtually all sod within the central grasslands had been plowed or mowed by the 1930s. Native grasses were replaced by corn, milo (sorghum), wheat, and fescue—agricultural grasses. Seeds from tree species common in the East were planted for shade, construction materials, firewood, and nostalgia. Most wildlife was devastated. And the natural grasslands—in reality only a transient ecosystem artificially maintained anyway—were easily transformed into what the nation needed: "The Breadbasket of the World."

Despite this extensive exploitation—especially of the Tallgrass Prairie—some remnants of native prairie still exist. And it is on those precious parcels that one of America's endemic and most celebrated butterflies, continues its reign, albeit tenuous.

The regal fritillary butterfly, *Speyeria idalia* (family Nymphalidae), is endemic to the prairies of North America. The species is a strong flier but is non-migratory. It is endearingly hailed simply as "regal," and compared to a "monarch butterfly dipped in chocolate." And in some places at the right time, the butterflies can be common, gliding above the greenery and quietly feeding atop a prairie purple coneflower or butterfly weed. In some years, regals number in the low thousands—not a sign that the species is thriving, but rather that it is coping. According to the US Department of Agriculture, the species is listed as Endangered in five states, Threatened in one state, and of Special Concern in four states. It is not yet on the IUCN Red List, CITES, or the US Endangered Species list. It recent times, the species has been designated the "poster child" for prairie conservation.

I was introduced to this distinguished lepidopteran back during the summer of 1959 when I was visiting an aunt/uncle in their home in Vienna, Virginia, a suburb of Washington, D.C. As a nascent entomologist, I had my net with me. On several occasions I took to a nearby sizable meadow to catch butterflies. One of the specimens I captured was a female regal fritillary. At the time, I was thrilled with the specimen's beauty and that I had not seen one before. But at the time, of course, I had no inkling that the eastern populations of the species were on the verge of collapse.

Another thirty-plus years had to pass before I encountered *S. idalia* again. During 1996 and again in 1997, I conducted brief butterfly surveys on prairies in southwestern Missouri as part of the North American Butterfly Association's "Fourth of July Butterfly Count." Regals were present in good numbers during both years. Finally, in May 1998, I accepted a contract from The Nature Conservancy of Missouri to become their "Lepidopterist in Residence." For six months (May-October) my "home" was a former livestock ranch of 872 acres in St. Claire and Cedar counties near the community of El Dorado Springs. The homestead had been recently purchased for prairie restoration and incorporation into the adjacent larger Wah'Kon-Tah Prairie. My mission was to inventory the butterflies—with special attention given to the regal fritillary. At the time, little did I realize that the regal fritillary butterfly would become one of my lifelong metaphoric muses. This is that story.

The life cycle of the regal fritillary is typified by a barrage of strategies that depart radically from rank and file nymphalid butterflies but is in line with related species termed "Greater Fritillaries" (see Chapter 9). Consider: there is significant behavioral disparity between males and females. The species reproduces but once per year (univoltine). And the only host for its larvae (caterpillars) are violets (*Viola* spp). Violets are ephemeral, however; their delicate leaves and flowers cannot tolerate the parching Sun of late summer and the dire cold of winter. To compensate, the plant in midsummer dries out (literally becoming a "shrinking violet") and remains dormant until the return of spring's warmth. Female regals respond to the blooming of the violets and produce a prodigious number of eggs—over 2,000—the most of any species of lepidoptera. Egg laying is delayed until autumn. Because host plants are "dead," eggs are deposited singly as females walk about ground thatch that is ubiquitous throughout the prairie. Volatile chemicals released by desiccated violets in the vicinity are theorized to trigger the egg-laying response. Eggs hatch after 3-4 weeks. Minuscule caterpillars first nibble their spent shells. They then enter a state of suspended animation (hibernation) for five to six months, protected from winter cold by thatch and periodic snow cover.

Torpor is broken when the warmth of early spring triggers violet plants to re-green. Caterpillars grow through five molts within the next four to six weeks feeding on violets. After, they pupate (metamorphose into a chrysalis) near the ground for about another three weeks. Finally, they emerge as adult butterflies—males primarily in early June, females another two weeks or so later. Mating occurs after females take to the air. Males may select multiple partners but females mate with only one. Wings of males tatter quickly, but individuals continue to fly through midsummer, or until prey such as birds, spiders, and mantids take their toll. Females, in contrast, remain quiescent throughout summer months, restricting their foraging to one-to-two hours during the heat of the day; consequently, their wings remain relatively intact. Both males and females are addicted to specific flowers for feeding even though the prairie supports many varieties of wildflowers.

Flowering is sequential: in early summer pale coneflowers (*Echinacea pallida*) and butterfly milkweed (*Asclepias tuberosa*) top the list. Later, wild bergamot (*Monarda fistulosa*), blazing star (*Liatris pycnostachya/L. aspera*), ironweed (*Vernonia* spp.), and finally field thistles (*Cirsium altissimum/C. discolor*) round out the pre-frost season of nutrients for remaining female regals. Soon thereafter, both thistles and butterflies die, their circle of life completed.

With so many critical environmental requirements, *S. idalia* could easily fall victim to the limitations created by expanding land development. The historical range of the butterfly, indeed, has already declined drastically. Early pioneer entomologists investigating pristine grasslands recorded that the insect was common in moist grassy areas from the Maritime provinces of Canada, through the northeastern United States, westward throughout the Midwest, and farther westward to the foothills of the Rocky Mountains—a cumulative total of 33 states and 5 Canadian provinces. There is today but a single extant colony west of Indiana: a military base in Pennsylvania; all other sightings occur primarily in isolated venues located on tallgrass prairie and mixed grass preserves west of the Mississippi River. Altogether, the species is flirting with extinction.

But this unorthodox life strategy in a hostile environment has been evolving for a long time. Because *S. idalia* is linked to present-day grasslands—what I view as the "grassland-regal paradigm"—it is reasonable to assume that the two co-evolved, perhaps during the last Glacial Period, aka "Ice Age" (Pleistocene Epoch, 115,000-11,700 years ago) when the interior of the continent remained ice-free and dominated by grasses.

What environmental factors could have spurred the idiosyncratic behavior of the grassland's hallmark butterfly? The first clue is the exceptional fecundity of females. Whereas most butterflies lay between 100-300 eggs during their annual life cycle, a female regal deposits between 2,000-3,000 eggs—and only during late summer and early autumn. Such a discrepancy cannot be downplayed. A blitz of eggs for any particular animal bespeaks of an adaptation to a poor rate of survival. Furthermore, female regals deposit their eggs not directly on viable host plants as with 99% of all butterflies but scatter them seemingly at random on the ground when hosts are dormant, and hence, unable to nourish offspring.

The second clue is that regals, especially females, are attracted to specific flowers for their nourishment, and these flowers are sequential. The nexus between the two indicates a correlation, logically. Turns out the favored plants are known to engage in pharmacology, that is, the production of phytochemicals, phytonutrients, or secondary plant substances—all complex compounds that have little or nothing to do with the plant's inherent metabolism, acting instead as cross-species repellents and attractants. Over 100,000 of such substances have been exploited for numerous purposes—herbs and spices for cooking; pigments to color our cosmetics and dyes to color our textiles, antioxidants to combat cancer, diabetes, and circulatory problems, drugs to combat memory loss and fortify our immune systems, narcotics to relieve pain—and so on. Specifically, many of the phytochemicals synthesized by the regal's "haute cuisine" have been shown to function in humans as anti-inflammatory and anti-microbial drugs. The compounds act first on the cellular level, but soon affect tissues, organs, and even organ systems so that general health is affected. Is it reasonable to assume that these same substances, which could be harvested and then sequestered from flower nectar, might contribute to female longevity, and later be passed on through eggs and larvae to assist with their difficult life stages?

With a colleague in the department of microbiology at Louisiana State University, I was able to coax a female regal to lay eggs in a paper bag. We secured several hatchlings covered with long translucent hair-like setae. Using a scanning electron microscope, we learned that the setae are not simply sword-like but are tipped with tiny swellings. Because several of these "bulbs" had collapsed, we assumed that they had been filled with liquid. I hypothesized: Perhaps, the setae serve a double function. First, they physically protect larvae. Second, they convey antifreeze and/or antibiotic substances –both important to protect nascent caterpillars during their lengthy hibernation on the ground. Could the adage 'We are what we eat' apply to butterflies as well?

Finally, I homed in on a problem that has haunted entomologists since the species was documented in 1773 in what is today, New York City: "Why have researchers not been able to locate eggs or larvae of regals in the wild? And how can a single violet plant—by nature, always diminutive in size—provide adequate forage for a caterpillar through its six larval stages?" These inconsistencies defied logic. (Fact is, virtually everything that is known about the immature stages of the species is derived from laboratory reared specimens.)

During a field trip onto the prairie in late summer I was able to observe, on more than one occasion, a female regal fly to a clump of sumac, drop to the ground, walk on the surrounding thatch, and every few minutes pause for a few seconds to deposit a single, tiny egg. The behavior was repeated until approximately four to eight eggs were laid. In each instance, the female took to the air to seek thistle flowers for feeding.

The following spring, I searched diligently these same areas for caterpillars. Freshly sprouted violet plants were common, but nary a caterpillar. Repeated attempts produced similar results, even though some of the violet plants showed evidence of heavy herbivory. Bolstered by the discovery of violets sporting partially eaten leaves, I decided to search at night. On a clear, warm night in late May—packing a Coleman lantern and a four-inch face flashlight covered with a makeshift red filter constructed from cellophane (subscribing to the tenet that most insects cannot perceive the color red)—I embarked on my first nocturnal foray. (Fortunately, unlike in my home state of Louisiana where nocturnal ventures can prove dangerous due to an abundance of venomous snakes—seven species—the prairies in the region were free of treacherous reptiles.) I selected the same areas in which I had observed egg laying the previous autumn, and that I had searched a month or so earlier. While probing through the thatch on my hands and knees I was surprised to uncover a shallow tunnel through what I had considered homogeneous debris. With a little teasing of the thatch, I located well defined passageways that I presumed were engineered by meadow mice or voles—small, common rodents documented to construct runways for easy, secretive travel.

And then I found life—no caterpillar, no chrysalis, only a slow parade of assorted Lilliputian-sized invertebrates. Within less than an hour I logged in several spiders, ants, pill bugs, centipedes, millipedes, and crickets (none of which seemed to be startled by the red light). The data were substantive, leading me to conclude that modern-day prairie thatch is not necessarily a ground cover that impedes small terrestrial residents. Rather, the seeming tangle of debris can be exploited by small rodents, and serendipitously, by both vertebrates and invertebrates. Understandably, the high traffic of "guests," likely assists mice with their housekeeping. My vigilance had paid off. And although I had extracted nothing definitive, I was able to postulate a workable theory.

Now empowered with new observations, my mind flooded with questions: "Might regal larvae also take advantage of these runways to move about the prairie safely in search of fresh violets when they exhaust any particular plant? Might these subsurface runs provide temporary sanctuaries during the heat of the day or cool of the night for regal larvae between feeding periods? And might secluded mouse runs be the reason why few regal larvae and pupae have ever been discovered in the field?" I think so.

Having spent much of one night on the prairie, searching with my improvised bug light, I opted to spend this new morning observing thatch mouse runs in daylight. As I returned to my parked vehicle for a field lunch, an El Dorado Springs police vehicle pulled up. The officer, a young amicable local, informed me that his headquarters had received a telephone call describing "suspicious white and red lights moving about on a section of prairie the previous night." I easily explained my project but was informed by the officer that there was heavy drug trafficking in the region, and for my own safety, I should cease my nocturnal research. I took his advice. Thus ended my investigations into mouse runs—ironically, not due to hazardous wildlife, but instead, curious humankind.

Current conservation theory posits that it is better to manage the entire landscape in which a rare species lives rather than manage the individual species. Termed the "ecosystem approach," the idea is to replicate or simulate an original habitat—as best as possible. For the tallgrass and mixed grass prairies of North America, methods have included grazing and browsing by cattle and/or goats to simulate the effects of original large foragers; haying/mowing with mechanical equipment to simulate browsing by the original, prodigious herbivores; removal of invading woody species either manually or by application of herbicides to maintain openness; periodic controlled burns to duplicate fires set by indigenous peoples to stimulate germination of grass seeds; and applications of synthetic commercial fertilizers to mitigate nutrient losses from animal organics (excrement and carcasses) as a result of traffic of terrestrial herbivores and carnivores, huge flocks of passerine birds, and periodic population explosions of the Rocky Mountain locust. In addition, the fertilizers supposedly helped compensate for the lack of natural "ecosystem engineering" (soil aeration) induced by bison and the black-tailed prairie dog. Bison behavior includes daily wallowing in dust and movement during grazing, as well as annual migrations. And prairie dogs (social ground squirrels) excavate elaborate underground colonies. These "towns" could be massive—the largest ever recorded occupied 25,000 square miles in the Texas Panhandle with an estimated population of 400 million individuals.

So far, each method has proven only marginally effective, that is, both unreliable for all species, and costly. And for regals, which have a life cycle spanning the full twelve months of every year—each stage having adapted through natural selection—the success rate has been very low. To date, no protocol has been standardized.

There is no one solution. Captive breeding programs, in which eggs, larvae, and adults have been reintroduced into the field, have had mixed rates of success (some with as much as 90-100% failure)—another indication that the current prairie environment no longer is ideal for the regal fritillary. To further complicate matters, prairies in contemporary settings *must* be managed on a timely scale. Otherwise, ecological succession will generate a forest of deciduous hardwoods, and both host plants and nectar plants of the regal fritillary are pioneer species, that is, plants that invade and thrive best on soils that are periodically disturbed. This has been dramatically proven for the single viable eastern population of regals on the Fort Indiantown Gap Military Reservation and National Guard Training Center near Annville, Pennsylvania, referenced earlier. Nearly 300 acres of training areas and ranges have been set aside as regal habitat. Since monitoring began in 1998 the population of butterflies has remained stable at approximately 1,000 individuals. The unusual success was not deliberate. The environmental manipulations were to accommodate military training—specifically, maintaining the integrity of an open grassland ecosystem by means of small-scale mowing, burning, and even maneuvers using live ammunition with heavy machinery. Furthermore, the alterations took place on a rotational schedule; no single area was permanently impacted. The system proved beneficial to regals, too. In effect, the butterflies were never deprived of some sanctuary—a "mini refugium." The arrangement has been so successful that since 2006 military personnel have been taking advantage of the butterfly's public persona by scheduling free summer tours of the butterfly's breeding venue. The events are actively advertised and have become increasingly popular. Visitors are educated about the rare butterfly in all of its life stages, the species' stringent environmental requirements, and how the military presence on the installation is vital to the butterfly's persistence.

If *S. idalia* is to be sustained, either entire preserves, or at least, designated sections of particular preserves will have to be managed in accordance with the specific requirements of the butterfly—in all its life stages. History has documented that simply fencing in land will fail. Likewise, ecosystem management such as mowing and burning on a scale that does not consider the feeding and reproductive requirements of this particular butterfly will fail, also. Simply put, there is too little critical habitat.

Patently, *S. idalia* walks the proverbial tight rope, teetering between survival and extinction in a micro-environment currently managed by humans. But the condition need not remain static. Human managers, actively involved in correcting the conditions, can determine a positive outcome. Not too long ago, another American prairie idol almost met its demise: American bison, aka American buffalo (*Bison bison*) North America's largest mammal. Weighing between 700 and 2,600 pounds, the shaggy herbivores were considered wild and ungovernable. Numbers were estimated at 60 million strong. Yet, by the late 1800s, that number plummeted to 541 individuals (300 in the United States), having been decimated for commercial and political purposes (to eliminate a critical resource for Indigenous people and force them into smaller confines). The American bison was on a fast track for becoming the first terrestrial mammal on the continent to become extinct. What happened?

Because American buffalo were so abundant, no one could conceive the notion that such a dominant animal could ever be over harvested. Therefore, bison were slaughtered wantonly.

In addition, the introduction of domesticated livestock spread exotic diseases to which the buffalo had no resistance. But this litany does not have a sad ending. Zoos began breeding programs, the New York Zoological Park being the first in 1905. President Theodore Roosevelt offered government protection. Concurrently, non-governmental agencies were established, and private ranchers began manipulating their practices to include breeding bison alongside their cattle to satisfy a burgeoning butcher market. Soon, the public began to embrace the "buffalo" as the symbol of the "Wild West." Today, the American Bison Association estimates there are 400,000 American bison in North America (4,000 graze within Wyoming's Yellowstone National Park, alone), and projects 1 million in the next few years. General consensus is that *Bison bison* is now firmly acknowledged as a living treasure—a legacy entrenched in America's cultural heritage.

So, why not a similar scenario for *Speyeria idalia*? Granted, the butterfly's life cycle is complicated and vulnerable at all levels. Thus, a conservation paradigm that is successful must address these dynamics. But with our current understanding, we should be able to design a construct in which the charismatic invertebrate will once again become an integral component of the prairie ecosystem, to be heralded as America's "Winged Prairie Royal."

EPILOGUE: My original work in southwest Missouri (1996 and 1997) inspired the premier of "*Festival of Butterflies*" at Powell Gardens. Located in Kingsville (Johnson County) the facility is 30 miles southeast of Kansas City, the largest metropolis in the state, and accessed by US Highway 50. The facility is exquisite, consisting of 907 acres of manicured gardens, educational buildings, and chapel, designed by renowned architect, E. Fay Jones. Co-sponsored by The Nature Conservancy of Missouri, the two-day event (August 16-17, 1997) was highly publicized in Kansas City and surrounding communities. I was interviewed extensively: radio, television, and newspapers. Consequently, the festival attracted approximately 14,000 visitors. (The official two-day count was logged as 12,000 because at least 500 vehicles were waved through the gates without a ticket purchase to accommodate the Missouri State Troopers, who complained that long backups at entrance gates were causing highways to become too congested.) That 1997 premier proved to be the top-ranking butterfly festival anywhere, surpassing even the "*Mt Magazine International Butterfly Festival*" in Paris, Arkansas on the weekend of July 31-August 2, 1997, two weeks prior to the Missouri extravaganza (see Chapter 9).

The Powell Gardens festival resumes each August; in some years, the event encompasses two weekends. Between 1997 and 2002, I was a featured guest, providing lectures, walks, and several different multi-media presentations, the highlight of which was my forty-five minute "*Born of Fire: A Prairie Saga*." The glitzy production centered on a PowerPoint presentation featuring my images associated with the Wah'Kon-Tah Prairie Preserve—all choreographed to music by Philip Glass and Katrina and the Waves. Besides the annual festival, since 2002 Powell employees and volunteers have conducted "Fourth of July Butterfly Counts" sponsored by NABA (North American Butterfly Association) within the gardens and surrounding neighborhoods. On several of these counts, one or two regal fritillary butterflies have been recorded, although no breeding colonies were revealed. All

CHAPTER 10: A PRAIRIE ROYAL

activities offer the public an opportunity to learn about butterfly biology, and especially, the plight of the regal fritillary. My fervent wish is that one of the new devotees to butterfly conservation will craft a comprehensive prairie management plan in which the regal fritillary will be able to maintain its aerial sovereignty over the historically important Tallgrass Prairie ecosystem. I remain positive.

[Published originally in *Natural History*, February 2023 (Volume 131, No. 2), pages 16-23, cover. The article was the recipient of The John Burroughs Association's "2024 John Burroughs Nature Essay Award for Outstanding Natural History Writing Published in Essay Form." The award was presented on Monday April 1, 2024, at the annual meeting/awards luncheon of the association in a banquet hall of the Yale Club of New York City. Text (with slight editing) reprinted here with permission of the publisher.]

SELECTED REFERENCES

Glassberg, J. 1998a. Army tries to crush butterflies: NABA fights back! *American Butterflies*, Summer (Vol. 6:2), inside front cover.

Glassberg, J. 1998b. Late breaking regal fritillary news. *American Butterflies*, Summer (Vol. 6:2), page 23.

Glassberg, J. 1998c. Regal fritillary update. *American Butterflies*, Winter (Vol. 6:4), inside front cover.

Hammond, P.C. and D.V. McCorkle, 1984. The decline and extinction of *Speyeria* populations resulting from human environmental disturbances (Nymphalidae: Argynninae). *Journal of Research on the Lepidoptera*, Vol. 222:4, pages 217-224.

Kopper, B.J., D.C. Margolies, and R.E. Charlton. 2000. Oviposition site selection by regal fritillary, *Speyeria idalia*, as affected by proximity of violet host plants. *Journal of Insect Behavior*, September (Vol. 13), pages 651-655.

Ladd, D. 1995. *Tallgrass Prairie Wildflowers*. A Falcon Field Guide. The Nature Conservancy, Falcon Press Publishing Company, Helena MT. 263 pages.

Ross, G.N. 1998. Butterfly festivals: fun and education for all! *American Butterflies* 6(2): 16-23, front cover.

Ross, G.N. 2001. Butterflies of the Wah'Kon-Tah Prairie. *Holarctic Lepidoptera*. Volume 8, Number 1-2, pages 1-30, four covers.

Ross, G.N. 2023. Review of regal fritillary (*Speyeria idalia*) on the Wah'Kon-Tah Prairie Preserve of Missouri. *Southern Lepidopterists' News*, March (Vol. 45:1), pages 15-51.

Shepherd, S. and D.M. Debinski. 2005. Reintroduction of regal fritillary (*Speyeria idalia*) to a restored prairie. *Ecological Restoration* (Vol. 223:4), pages 244-250.

Wagner, D.L 2005. *Caterpillars of Eastern North America: A Guide to Identification and Natural History*. Princeton University Press. Princeton, NJ. 512 pages.

Williams, B. 1999. Regal fritillaries in a tailspin: a story of East and West, DNA, and the urgent need for the conservation of a flagship species. *American Butterflies*, Winter (Vol. 7:4), pages16-25.

CHAPTER 11: AN AMERICAN BUTTERFLY WIZ

The zebra longwing butterfly can remember its home place

I garden for butterflies and other pollinators at my home in south Louisiana. My personal utopia sprawls in wild profusion across my entire front yard—all the way to the sidewalk. This provides an ever-changing tableau of color and activity throughout the four seasons. The semi-natural landscape is a neighborhood conversation piece.

In the late 1990s, the garden became a staging area for me to observe the zebra longwing/zebra heliconian (*Heliconius charithonia*), a medium-size butterfly common throughout the frost-free areas of Florida and southern Texas, although, occasionally encountered in Louisiana. The "zebra" gets its name from its dark, elongated wings, accented with vibrant yellowish stripes. But the insect is also recognized for several specialized traits, including a proclivity to ingest protein-rich pollen, exceptional longevity—upwards from 8-10 months—and most intriguing of all, the ability to learn visual cues for navigating.

After purchasing some eggs of the butterfly, and nurturing them to adulthood on their host, *Passiflora incarnata*, referred to as passionflower or "maypop" (a native vine I routinely cultivate in my home garden), I marked each butterfly by writing a number on the underside of its left hind wing with a felt-tipped pen. I then released the insects into my garden. They circled for a few minutes but then settled to feed on the flowers of their choice (zinnias and Mexican flamevine (*Pseudogynoxys chenopodioides*). Following their "breakfast," the butterflies flew off in various directions, but a few hours later they returned to the garden to feed once again. The next day I observed two female zebras laying eggs on my native passionflower plant. And so, the activities continued. The butterflies laid their eggs or fed as I watched with binoculars, taking note of the numbers marked on the butterflies' hind wings. My observations proved that the *same* butterflies were showing up day after day.

As the long days of summer progressed, the zebras spent less and less time in my garden, showing up at about mid-morning and again at about four o'clock in the afternoon. I was impressed by the fact that they habitually departed towards the southeast, flying about ten to fifteen feet above the street in front of my house, but always returned tailing each other along the side street that formed the northwest border of my corner lot. Even more uncannily, on their return the butterflies would execute a ninety-degree right turn at the stop sign on the corner, before flying the short distance to my emblazoned front garden.

It happened that at this same time, I had hired a construction crew to remodel a part of my house that bordered my side street. One morning, I was talking with them about the advantages of my unconventional, butterfly-oriented landscaping. They were skeptical, to say the least. To them,

CHAPTER 11: AN AMERICAN BUTTERFLY WIZ

my grounds were weedy, unkempt. I hoped to impress them by describing the extraordinary behavior of my zebra longwings. So, at the telltale hour that afternoon, I mentioned that we would soon be seeing some butterflies approaching the stop sign at the corner, turn right, and then fly to my vibrant garden.

Within minutes the procession was in sight. With their signature slow, fluttery flight about eight to ten feet above the ground, and striped wings, they could not go unnoticed. "You mean the butterflies can read and are going to stop at the corner" quipped one of the men. I simply smiled. Sure enough, as we stood there watching, the butterflies approached the intersection of streets, veer to the right, and fly direction toward my colorful garden. The workers' eyes popped as if they had a mystical vision. Immediately, they began hurling questions: How did you train them? What did you put on that sign? Do you have some kind of butterfly whistle? I simply smiled, and suggested they try to figure out the mystery. For the remaining several days they worked, each man put down his tools at 3:45 PM and positioned himself near the stop sign to try to figure out what was assumed as my "hocus-pocus." And on one day, a worker's wife and two young children showed up at the appropriate hour to witness the wizardry of my homespun and spellbinding magic show. Never was anyone disappointed.

There is, of course, a scientific explanation: The longwing butterflies had learned to travel through the streets, past various markers to locate the food and plants they require for feeding and reproducing. With large eyes and big brains, the butterflies remember these markings—clues, if you will—for securing their vital plants. Such "imprinting," as it is categorized, has been recorded to be typical within longwing (*Heliconius*) butterflies, a taxon that is common within and restricted to American tropical forests. And so, each day these butterflies endowed with a high IQ would make their "rounds" in much the same way as a human hunter or fisherman checks his trapline. Furthermore, the butterflies' Methuselah-like lives provide additional time for learning, and their high-octane, non-typical pollen-rich cuisines can supply the necessary brain food. In a sense, longwing butterflies are the "wise guys" of the world of lepidopterans.

In the end, I *think* I managed to educate my work crew about this academic quirk in butterfly biology—at least, I hope so. Regardless, the zebra longwing butterflies entertained me and a lot of other folks that summer and fall. Come winter, sub-freezing temperatures ended the lives of the butterflies along with their food and host plants. And that was that!

[Published originally as "Wise Guys." IN: Endpaper column, *Natural History*, July 2005, Vol.115(8), page 72. Used with permission of the publisher and with slight edits.]

SELECTED REFERENCES

Ajilvsgi, G. 1990. *Butterfly Gardening for the South*. Taylor Publishing Company. Dallas, TX. 348 pages.

DeVries, P. J. 1987. *The Butterflies of Costa Rica and Their Natural History: Papilionidae, Pieridae, Nymphalidae.* Princeton University Press, Princeton, NJ. 327 pages.

Ross, G.N. 1994. *Gardening for Butterflies in Louisiana: A Guide for Gardeners, Educators, and Enthusiasts*. Louisiana Department of Wildlife and Fisheries Natural Heritage Program. Wildlife Division. Baton Rouge, LA. 41 pages.

Ross, G.N. 1995. *Everything You Ever Wanted To Know About Butterflies: 100 Questions and Answers by Gary Noel Ross, Ph.D*. Gary Noel Ross. Baton Rouge, LA. 52 pages.

Ross, G.N. 2001. Brainy butterflies. *News of the Lepidopterists' Society*, Summer 2001, Vol. 43(2):43, 47.

Ross, G.N. 2010. A tale of homing in zebra heliconians. *Notes (Association for Tropical Lepidoptera)*, June 2010:1-2.

Ross, G.N. 2014. Planting memories: forget the opium, savor the poppy flowers. IN: Naturalist at Home. *Natural History*, April (Vol. 122:2), pages 10-13, front cover.

Ross, G.N. 2021. Notes on the correlation between the sightings of *Heliconius charithonia* in the east and passage of tropical cyclones in 2020. *News of the Lepidopterists' Society*, Winter (Vol. 62:4), pages 195-200.

Ross, G.N. 2022. Update to sightings of *Heliconius charithonia* and new sightings of *Anartia jatrophae* on the Gulf Coast in 2020, 2021, and early 2022. *News of the Lepidopterists' Society*, Summer (Vol. 64:2), pages 96-99.

CHAPTER 12: BUTTERFLIES AND THE ZUNI TRIBE OF NEW MEXICO

Messengers of a benevolent spirit

My introduction to the world of the Native American Zuni Tribe dates back to 2003. Robert Sherman, a Baton Rouge friend who had recently returned from an environmental work project in northern New Mexico, shared with me photographs he had taken of several medium-size paintings featuring "butterfly maidens"—humans with butterfly wings. The images were so uncannily realistic and dramatic that I could only conclude that the painter—Edward Lewis—had to be a master artist. Robert had also collected several attractive stone carvings of stylized butterflies that he called "fetishes." All were created in Zuni, a community in the heart of the Zuni Tribe and the prescribed Zuni Reservation. (Being a lepidopterist with a second love for ethnobiology, I have learned that diverse peoples throughout the world share an inordinate interest in butterflies, often incorporating their imagery into artistic expressions and rituals.)

In response, in 2006, I embarked upon an extended road trip through the Southwest, primarily to visit Zuni (July 14-20). In 2014, I returned to the reservation (October 15-November 10). What follows is a summary of those two adventures.

The community of Zuni, or officially, the Pueblo of Zuni (historically, *Halona Idiwan'a*) is located within the dedicated Zuni Indian Reservation—primarily within McKinley County in northwestern New Mexico. The Pueblo and its satellite community of Black Rock are about 37 miles south of Gallup and 11 miles east of the Arizona border. (The reservation is independent, encircled by the sprawling Navajo Nation, and supports no casino.) The venue is a part of the United States where the landscape vibrates with colors and textures. At an elevation of 6,309 feet, the reservation is relatively small, spreading across about 400,000 semi-arid acres, ecologically classified as a piñon pine-juniper (cedar) woodland; average annual rainfall is approximately 12 inches, the majority falling between July and September. Most of the pueblo lies in a flat valley punctuated with table-topped monolithic outcrops, aka, mesas. The closest and most significant of these is *Dowa Yalanne* ("Corn Mountain").

Geologically, *Dowa Yalanne* is a thousand-foot-high mesa of sandstone rocks dating back to the Triassic and Jurassic periods (the Age of the Dinosaurs). The formation is oriented in a more or less northwest to southeast direction. At sunset when the western façade is bathed in a red glow, *Dowa Yalanne* bears a decided resemblance to *Uluru* ("Ayers Rock") the iconic red monolith in the Northern Territory of Australia. For the Zuni people, *Dowa Yalanne* is considered sacred and historically important. It, for instance, has served in mythological history as a refuge from destructive floods, and in more recent history from invasions by the Spanish and neighboring

Apache. Today, *Dowa Yalanne* has become the emblem to identify the Zuni Tribe. Because the mesa is holy ground, it is off limits to non-Zunis.

The Pueblo is an artist colony. A whopping 80-90 percent of families are active in creating distinctive arts and crafts. Genres include pottery, silverwork (frequently with inlays of lapidary stones), Kachina dolls (small wooden carvings representing ancestral spirits), paintings on canvas, wood or drum surfaces, beadwork, and cotton weavings such as belts, sashes, and mantas (shawls). Of all handiwork, Zunis are most celebrated for their fetishes. These are small carvings in a medley of media: decorative stones, deer/moose antlers and bones, cedar wood, and recently, bowlerite (the outer layer of discarded bowling balls). Fetishes function as a spiritual charm or talisman, with no relationship to erotic objects often addressed by outsiders with the same name. Because all wild animals are believed to be endowed with a spiritual nature, subject matter for fetishes is virtually boundless. The carvings are believed to convey luck, power, protection, and good health to their owners. Put simply, fetishes are viable "spirits in stone"—unparalleled assets to humankind.

Zunis recognize two types of fetishes: "ceremonial" or "true" fetishes, and "commercial carvings." The ceremonial fetish has flourished for numberless years. According to oral tradition, this type of fetish has always been blessed by a spiritual leader of the tribe. Because the Zuni practice Animism (a belief system that acknowledges all objects, places, and creatures possess a distinct spiritual essence) everything in nature must be respected with dignity. As such, representations of these objects are tribal assets, which, except under unusual circumstances, should not be given or sold to outsiders. Consecrated fetishes may be either of a personal or communal nature. If, for instance, the fetish is personal, it is worn or carried in its own pouch at all times. Too,

it can be kept in a container that is placed on a mantle, in a curio cabinet, and even in the glove compartment of a vehicle.

On the other hand, if a fetish has communal significance, it is reserved for a sacred tribal ceremony and is frequently shared with other tribesmen during a time of celebration. Such sacred fetishes are housed when not in use in a special "fetish pot" (a storage jar or open bowl). Ceremonial fetishes are periodically "fed" traditional home-prepared blue corn meal. Gifts such as crushed turquoise and coral can be presented as well.

By contrast, if a fetish has not been blessed, it is more properly termed a "commercial carving." It is regarded as an *objet d'art*, that is, a collectible that can be given or sold to an outsider. However, the term "fetish" is frequently generalized to include any type of small animal carving. And while the Zuni produce other forms of art and crafts, commercial carvings, i.e., public fetishes, have recently surged in popularity, becoming the paramount object of desire by tourists and other outsiders.

It so happens that Edward Lewis, the artist whose paintings my friend Robert had originally introduced me to, was not merely a noted painter, but also a respected spiritual leader—a revered role model in a culture that is grounded in age-old traditions of spirituality and mythology. As Zunis tell it: "The landscape is a church, cathedral." Under Edward's tutelage, I learned that artists take great pleasure in caving representations of life. Power animals such as bear, bison, mountain lion, wolf, turkey, elk, raven, owl, and eagle are extremely common. "Ah," remarked Lewis brandishing a broad smile, "but butterflies are particularly adored." Lewis continued: "Butterflies are one of several insects that are significant to our beliefs and culture. We Zunis believe that butterflies are earthly representations of Butterfly Maiden (*Bu: lak'kya E:lash'dok'ee*). It is Butterfly Maiden who brings the rain—the life blood—to our village. The butterfly's metamorphosis is relevant to our beliefs in how we came into this world." Continuing his narrative: "The idea of painting butterfly maidens came to me when one day in middle school, I was outside eating lunch where I saw two butterflies chasing each other around a flower. My favorite species are the tiger swallowtail and monarch although I sometimes use the queen and mourning cloak as well. These are fairly common here on the reservation. I use a butterfly picture book as a guide for painting details of the butterflies." I learned that the butterfly is a "power animal," too. Butterflies, for example,

represent beauty, balance, change, transformation (including healing), movement, and air. Butterflies are endearingly referred to as "dancing flowers" and "air dancers." According to Zuni tradition, anyone who embraces the butterfly as a personal spirit usually exhibits a heightened sensitivity (including the wisdom to recognize when others are in a process of transformation). "Butterfly People" are acknowledged to be charming, successful in business and love, and sensitive to air quality. The butterfly in Zuni tradition represents both a literal and symbolic transcendental figure, patently.

Exotic animals are not off-limits, either. Moose, dolphins, elephants, dragons, dinosaurs, and monkeys are frequently depicted. Such figures are copied from images in magazines and books. An individual carving is an expression of personal imagination and interests. Given that each is handcrafted, no two cravings are ever exactly alike.

Raw stones are purchased from a trading post in the Pueblo, from distributors in Gallup, Albuquerque, and Santa Fe. Common varieties include serpentine, alabaster, South Dakota pipestone, jet, turquoise, malachite, lapis lazuli, Picasso marble, black marble, Mexican onyx, dolomite, travertine (especially a local variety called "Zuni stone" that exhibits many distinctive hues and that is hand-dug from several nearby mountain mesas, including *Dowa Yalanne*, known only to a few families). Other materials include amber, exotic shells (especially abalone), wood, and antler from deer, moose, and elk. Exotic shells, corals, fossilized walrus ivory, and unusual stones from distant parts of the globe are sometimes purchased from traveling traders. Turquoise, a stone that mirrors the sky in these semi-arid lands, is usually the most revered and expensive stone medium; it defines both Zuni and Navajo culture. (The color of turquoise is so revered by the Zunis and their Navajo neighbors that the county's emergency vehicles—fire and EMS trucks—are painted blue and white rather than the traditional red and white of vehicles throughout other areas of the United States.) Often bits of turquoise and other stones/shells (occasionally even diamond chips) are inserted as inlays in a base medium to enhance a carving.

Both ceremonial and unconsecrated fetishes are frequently augmented with gift bundles affixed to their backs. Such offerings are to the animal spirit and are believed to empower the fetish to provide extra aid to its guardian. The bundles usually consist of beads and arrowheads. Many carvings, particularly those of larger power animals such as bears and bison, have long lines on their sides. These so-called "heart lines" or "breath lines" represent the path of breath and energy used by the animal to charm its prey, and therefore, valuable to its human partner. The lines are created by filling grooves with thin inlays of stone or of stone dust (often turquoise) mixed with clear cement glue. Butterfly fetishes lack bundles and heart lines, in part as a matter of design aesthetics but also because butterflies are not prey animals whose spirits need to be appeased, nor predators whose hunting power needs to be cultivated. Instead, these fetishes feature elaborate inlays of semi-precious or precious jewels to accentuate the insect's exquisite wings. Except for Butterfly Maiden, most feature legs and antennae fashioned from thin gold and silver wires.

During my initial visit to the Pueblo of Zuni, I concentrated on gathering information and collecting samples of artwork. I took no photographs to minimize my intrusiveness. On my return in 2014, I hoped to photograph carvers in action. My lodging with Edward, who resided in Black Rock with a new wife and two young children, proved fortuitous. Edward was a font of knowledge. He was familiar with the most experienced and talented artisans, many of whom were residing in Edward's immediate neighborhood. His introductions afforded me the exceptional opportunity to watch and photograph the carving process from beginning to end. (As a token of my appreciation, I usually purchased the pieces that I had chronicled.)

Fetish carving relies on creativity and dedication. Because carvings are shaped by the cutting of dense materials, contemporary Zuni artists today have no hesitation about employing power tools. Work areas are usually small and ventilated: a table near a house window or in an outdoor shed, or even a simple bench beneath a tree or carport. The basic instrument is a small portable grinding wheel, and for detail, a small handheld *Dremel* rotary tool. The final product is never painted or lacquered but instead polished with a mild abrasive marketed as a stone polish. Some carvings are embellished with small inlays of precious and semi-precious stones. These are also used for eyes, mouths, horns, and hoofs. And as stated previously, some carvings are adorned with gift bundles and heart lines. When it comes to butterflies and other insects, thin wire of sterling silver and even gold are used to simulate legs and antennae. All contribute to the aesthetics of the final carving. To my surprise, working the stone moves along at a decided clip; many fetishes are completed in a single day. When content, the artist engraves his name or initials on an inconspicuous surface (men are the primary carvers of fetishes, but a few women have also taken up the art). If space permits, the word "Zuni" is engraved.

I learned that the raw stone may convey to the carver a specific vision of its potential. According to Travis Nieto a distinguished carver: "Sometimes the spirit of the stone speaks to me. All I have to do is release the spirit through my carving." When I asked Nieto about some not-so-inspiring-looking stones, he replied: "If an image does not jump out at me, I wet the stone to see its true color and rely on my imagination to create something I will enjoy. Often my first thought is not always my final; sometimes I change direction as I proceed with the carving." Over the years, several carvers and even entire families of carvers have become renowned for their specialized style. They may develop their own ways to illustrate intrinsic characteristics of an animal, such as stealth, power, cunning or ability to camouflage itself. Members of the Freddie Leekyla family, for instance, usually imbue their carvings with what I interpret as a "whimsical chubbiness." Such stylized fetishes are highly prized by collectors.

Working with stone generates a lot of dust. Finer particles are blown to the outside air by the fan attached to the grinding motor, but larger particles settle and accumulate underneath the saw blades and grinding wheels. This waste is periodically cleaned out but not discarded. Instead, it is eventually returned to the stone's excavation site, where it is devoutly returned to the earth. This ritual serves two purposes. First, the act honors the spirits of the mountain and the stone. Second, the act is a petition to the spirits to reconstitute the dust into new—and perhaps even more beautiful—stone for future carvers. In this way, both spirits and humans are graced throughout time.

The carving of fetishes can be traced to prehistory; occasionally old fetishes are unearthed in fields in the region. Ancient objects were simple, small, and not made of any particularly valuable stones. But the public's interest in Zuni fetishes began to burgeon in the early 1970s, when the

CHAPTER 12: BUTTERFLIES AND THE ZUNI TRIBE OF NEW MEXICO

exhibition *Two Hundred Years of North American Indian Art* was mounted at the Whitney Museum of American Art in New York City, accompanied by a book by the curator, Norman Feder. This coincided with an increasing influence of Japanese culture, which also venerates the collecting of small precious carvings.

In 1984, the Pueblo of Zuni organized to market Zuni arts. In 1987 the governing body that controls tribal commerce and business received one of its largest single orders. The request, from the Museum of Fine Arts, Houston, was for 300 fetishes, which were to be presented as gifts at the annual meeting of a Houston bank. Hollywood had an influence, too. Several movies appeared in which actors wore fetishes, and a few stars bragged that they collected these unique carvings. (Not surprisingly, today California is the largest market for fetish carvings.) From that point on, fetishes became prime *objects d'art*, sought by worldwide collectors as well as by individuals whose spiritual philosophy embraces nature.

Notwithstanding this popularity, Zuni artisans tend to avoid the avant-garde, preferring to be true to traditional standards of beauty, craftsmanship, propriety, and ethics. Several exceptionally creative artists have been producing carvings that seem to break out of the typical fetish mold. These pieces may be several inches in breadth/height and made up of different types of stone. Such sculpture-like pieces are not meant to be carried about, but instead to be decorative items displayed in the home. They probably take inspiration from the long-standing practice of carving "directionals," which symbolize the six directions in Zuni mythology: north, south, east, west, up, and down. Six different animals, usually shown in profile, form a composition standing for the different directions. These pieces, too, are above the average size for fetishes.

And then there is Esteban Najera, whom I met in the summer of 2006, when he was just thirty years old. Of mixed Zuni-Mexican heritage he has developed a singular flair for parodying human figures as skeletons—work reminiscent of the small, handcrafted skeleton caricatures associated with *Dia de los Muertos* ("Day of the Dead") celebrations in Mexico. Najera's pieces are carved from a single antler (usually deer or elk) primarily using the *Dremel*. To my delight, some of Najera's carvings were of skeletons holding butterflies, or skeletons adorned with butterfly wings (a popular metaphor for human transfiguration at death). Others were conceived as sets, such as musicians in a mariachi band, or an entourage of circus performers. The carvings in such groups are not attached to a base, allowing them to be repositioned at will.

During my 2014 visit I was impressed with the work of Enrike Leekya, a twenty-eight-year-old from a renowned family of fetish carvers. I asked him if he would be interested in creating a garden scene with several butterflies in fine turquoise. A broad smile said it all. Six days later the piece was complete. It consisted of an assemblage of five butterflies of different sizes, each resting atop a rose-shaped flower. All components were mounted on a flat stone that simulated the ground. Materials included Kingman turquoise, tijilite, leopard marble, Zuni stone, red coral, pink clam shell, black pen shell, and sterling silver wire. The overall carving measured nearly eight inches in diameter and weighed three and a quarter pounds. I wondered if such an elaborate and sizable assemblage could still be considered a fetish, but Enrike had no such reservations, calling the piece a fetish sculpture." Still, the work was out of the ordinary, becoming the talk of the neighborhood. If Enrike Leekya and other young artists decide to pursue such a direction in the future, the carving of fetishes might be propelled into the domain of modern fine art.

Having researched both Mesoamerican and Zuni cultural traditions on butterflies, I see differences. The ancient civilizations of Mexico and Central America seem to have been preoccupied with mythology concerning the relationship between gods and humans. The Butterfly Goddess for example, was a deity that could capture the human spirit upon death and transport it to the spirit world. The stylized butterfly image was incorporated into weavings, ceramics, clay stamps, painted murals, codices (painted picture books on leather or bark), large stone sculptures, and temple buildings. But to my knowledge, no artifacts exist to indicate that these cultures ever carved small objects that might be interpreted as stone charms, that is, fetishes. My experiences with nearly two dozen contemporary Indigenous cultures in Mesoamerica have confirmed that these cultures continue to honor past traditions, albeit in much-reduced practice. Regardless, I have failed to uncover the use of spirit charms, or any history of such use. [NOTE: In ancient Greek culture, there was but a single word to denote a butterfly and the human spirit or soul: "psyche." If you were Greek, the butterfly was your literal "soul mate." Patently, the nexus between butterflies and *Homo sapiens* dates far back—even into pre-history. To this day, English speakers use the word psyche to reference the "inner self," as well as a suffix for words that relate to the human spirit/soul (for example, psychology, psychiatry, psychoanalysis, psychopath, and so on and so on). Could it be that "butterfly worship" is part of our DNA, and not simply a social construct? I think so.]

The repository of Zuni oral history indicates, instead, that the butterfly did not have so great a mythological connotation. Instead, the insect embodied an intimate human-nature association that was—and remains—rooted in the ancient spirit world. The butterfly, whether a biological entity in real life or as an aesthetic and symbolic representation in a consecrated fetish, has the inherent power to affect one's everyday life experiences. For the Zuni, butterflies interact with humans at

CHAPTER 12: BUTTERFLIES AND THE ZUNI TRIBE OF NEW MEXICO

their moment of need. The interactions are personal and positive. Succinctly, Zunis believe that butterflies make us feel better and make us better people.

The source of such blessings is personified as "Butterfly Maiden." She is systemic throughout the culture—in the form of kachinas, consecrated fetishes and carvings, paintings, and even costumed dancers in ceremonial rituals. Butterfly Maiden straddles the spirit worlds of both humans and animals. Zuni carvings are collected and cherished by outsiders for their singular beauty, and, by some, as mystical symbols. These carvings, even if not consecrated, may offer a measure of hope. I usually carry my favorite butterfly carving in my pants left pocket. I consider this "butterfly therapy."

And what about actual butterflies?

The insects were scarce. In general, Zunis do not cultivate flower gardens around their residences, and commercial crops are not grown in the region, either. Therefore, there is little to attract pollinators into neighborhoods that can be dusty. The summer of 2006 was a particularly dry year. In fact, the Zuni River that runs through the pueblo, was completely dry. Edward suggested we drive to the base of the sacred *Dowa Yalanne* where native greenery was usually dependable. But there again, the drought was obvious: the earth was dry, minimal new growth; practically no plants were in bloom. Nonetheless, at *Dowa Yalanne* we did spot three stalwart butterfly species: one mourning cloak (*Nymphalis antiopa*), two western pygmy blues (*Brephidium exile*), and a single western tiger swallowtail (*Papilio rutulus*).

My visit in late 2014 was more productive even though most natural vegetation had ceased flowering. Nonetheless, because the summer rains had been adequate and the Zuni River had a remnant flow, some greenery and a few flowers persisted: Indian blanket (*Gaillardia pulchella*) and several small-flowering asters. Below are the ten species of butterflies that I observed. All sightings involved only a few individuals at most. Because of the Zuni belief in the sanctity of all life forms, I collected no specimens. My observations:

- dainty sulphur (*Nathalis iole*)
- checkered white (*Pontia protodice*)
- clouded sulphur (*Colias philodice*)
- Mexican sulphur (*Eurema mexicana*)
- western tailed blue (*Everes amyntula*)
- acmon blue (*Plebejus acmon*)
- sagebrush checkerspot (*Chlosyne acastus*)
- field crescent (*Phyciodes pratensis*)
- painted lady (*Vanessa cardui*)
- red admiral (*Vanessa atalanta*)

In addition to the lateness of the season, another factor contributed to the low number of species that I observed. Shortly after my arrival at the INN AT HALONA (a historic Bed & Breakfast in the heart of the community of Zuni), I had a serious debilitating accident. On the very day I arrived in Zuni (October 15), I slipped and fell in the parking lot of the B&B where I had reservations. During the fall, my head slammed into a wooden fence. The result was a significant gash across the bridge of my nose. The local EMS folks were summoned, and I was transported three miles to the ZUNI COMPREHENSIVE COMMUNITY HEALTH CENTER in Black Rock. Five stitches closed the gash. I then returned to the B&B.

But all was not well. Within a few hours my body began to shut down: slurred speech, difficulty in walking, sleepiness. The next morning (October 16) I could barely get out of bed. Upon trying to walk outside I fell twice, but fortunately, I did not hit my head. I returned to my bed, and EMS was called again. A CT scan at the health center revealed that I had a massive brain bleed. This prompted the physician in charge to initiate a call to GALLUP MED FLIGHT for a medical evacuation. Within an hour, I was transported via helicopter to the NEUROSCIENCE CLINIC OF THE UNIVERSITY OF NEW MEXICO HOSPITAL in Albuquerque, a distance of 124 air miles. There I underwent a craniotomy to remove what was diagnosed as a large and "acute subdural hematoma." The incision was closed with 17 staples, leaving a temporary drain in place.

My body responded almost miraculously. By the following day I could speak and coherently walk with only minor assistance. Having experienced no seizures, I was released on day seven. (The doctors at UNM hospital consider my rapid and full recovery a rare statistic—in essence, a medical mystery.) A registered/traveling nurse, Vicki Barker, who was part of the medical team caring for me, graciously volunteered to drive me in her vehicle 153 miles back to the Pueblo of Zuni. We departed UNM on the morning of October 23, absent a surgical drain tube but still brandishing staples, likely interpreted by onlookers as my pre-Halloween mask of "Frankenstein."

Upon my release, I was determined to complete my work. Unfortunately, the B&B where I had resided no longer had an available room. Therefore, Vicki and I returned to Gallup where I bedded down in a motel on HISTORIC ROUTE 66 for the next 5 days. On day six, my artist friend Edward Lewis who graciously offered to rent me a room in his home, retrieved me. Because I had lost a considerable amount of weight, I spent the next few days in and about my host's home speaking with neighboring artists that were accessible by foot. Also, I visited the local tribal health center for follow-up procedures to my surgery (removal of staples) and an assessment of mobility and cognitive skills. Each time I was given a "clean bill of health." Soon, I was able to renew my documentation of fetish carving and observations of local butterflies—the latter, albeit, with limited mobility. On November 10, I began the 1,400-mile drive back to Baton Rouge, arriving four days later on November 13. Upon exiting my vehicle, I acknowledged that *Bu:lak'kya E:lash'dok'ee* had assuredly watched over me. In my Cajun French, I reverentially murmured: *Joie de vivre*! ("Joy of Life!").

CHAPTER 12: BUTTERFLIES AND THE ZUNI TRIBE OF NEW MEXICO

[This is an integration of two of my previously published illustrated essays: "Air Dancers in Stone" in *Natural History*, April 2015 (Vol. 123:3), pages 12-17, front cover; and "My Experiences with Butterfly Imagery in Contemporary Indigenous Cultures. Part 2: Zuni Tribe of New Mexico," *Southern Lepidopterists' News*, June 30, 2015 (Vol. 37:2), pages 67-79. Texts used with permission of the publishers and with minor editing.]

SELECTED REFERENCES

Bahti, M. 1999. *Spirit in the Stone: A Handbook of Southwest Indian Animal Carvings and Beliefs*. Rio Nuevo Publishers. Tucson, AZ. 152 pages.

Dutton, D. 2009. *The Art Instinct: Beauty, Pleasure, and Human Evolution*. Bloomsbury Pres, New York, NY. 278 pages.

Ferguson, T.J., and E.R. Hart. 1985. *A Zuni Atlas*. University of Oklahoma Press. Norman, OK. 154 pages.

Gauding, M. 2006. *Personal Power Animals for Guidance, Protection and Healing*. Godshield Press, London, UK. 144 pages.

Glassberg, J. 2001. *Butterflies Through Binoculars: The West*. Oxford University Press. New York, NY. 374 pages.

Manos-Jones, M., 2000. *The Spirit of Butterflies: Myth, Magic, and Art*. Harry N. Abrams. New York, NY. 144 pages. McManis.

K. 1998. *A Guide to Zuni Fetishes & Carvings. Volume 1: The Animals & the Carvers*. Treasure Chest Books. Tucson, AZ. 56 pages.

McManis, K. 1998. *A Guide to Zuni Fetishes & Carvings. Volume 2: The Materials & the Carvers*. Treasure Chest Books. Tucson, AZ. 64 pages.

Opler, P.A. and A.B. Wright. 1999. *A Field Guide to Western Butterflies*. The Peterson Field Guide Series. Second edition. Houghton Mifflin Company. Boston, MA. 540 pages.

Rodee, M. and J. Ostler. 1995. *The Fetish Carvers of Zuni*. Revised Edition. The Maxwell Museum of Anthropology. The University of New Mexico. Albuquerque, NM. 112 pages.

Ross, G.N. 1986. The bug in the rug. *Natural History*, March (Vol. 95:3), pages 66-73.

Ross, G.N. 1997. Goddesses fly again: Butterfly images in Mexican myth and textiles. *American Butterflies*, Winter (Vol. 5:4), pages 14-18.

Ross, G.N. 2009. Butterfly designs featured in Zuni art exhibit at McGuire Center. *Southern Lepidopterists' News*, March 31 (Vol. 31:1), page 22.

Ross, G.N. 2009. Exhibit of Zuni butterfly art at McGuire Center extended through 2009.Notes. *Association for Tropical Lepidoptera*. June 2009, pages 1-2.

Ross, G.N. 2012. Zapotec Tapestries: A legacy of pre-Columbian Mythology. *Southern Lepidopterists' News*, Winter (Vol. 34:4), pages 197-215.

Ross, G.N. 2015. My experiences with butterfly imagery in contemporary indigenous cultures. Part 1: Mesoamerica. *Southern Lepidopterists' News*, March 31 (Vol. 37:1), pages 5-15.

Ross, G.N. 2018. Four new butterfly fetishes from the Zuni Tribe of New Mexico. *Southern Lepidopterists' News*, March 31 (Vol. 40:1), pages 11-12.

Ross, G.N. 2019. New Zuni carving in new medium added to collection. *Southern Lepidopterists' News*, September (Vol. 41:3), page 205.

Ross, G.N. 2019. Stone butterflies of New Mexico. *American Butterflies*, Winter (Vol, 27:4), pages 38-40, 48.

Ross, G.N. 2024. Insects in Mythology and Religion, Chapter 5, pages 95-117. IN: *A Cultural History of Insects in the Modern Age*. Volume 6, 217 pages. Edited by Robert K.D. Peterson. IN: *A Cultural History of Insects*, Volumes 1-6. 2024, General Editor: Gene Kritsky. Bloomsbury Academic. London, UK.

Rothschild, M. 1991. *Butterfly Cooing Like a Dove*. Doubleday. New York, NY. 315 pages.

CHAPTER 13: A LOUISIANA BUTTERFLY "HAPPY HOUR"

A rare butterfly survives by adopting an exotic habitat and becoming an alcoholic

Avery Island, a 2,200-acre ancient salt dome that rises 165 feet above the wetlands of coastal Louisiana, is home to the southern pearly eye butterfly (*Enodia portlandia*). Medium sized with eyespots and zigzag lines against a mousy background, the butterfly is cryptic when at rest—typically on ground litter or tree trunks. Distributed sparingly throughout the southeastern United States, pearly eyes prefer shadowy, dank hardwood forests bordered by native switch cane (*Arundinaria*), a type of caning grass, (i.e., bamboo), documented to be the proprietary host for egg-laying. Unlike rank-and-file butterflies, pearly eyes shun flower nectar, feeding instead on plant exudates such as sap.

Hardwood forests are plentiful on Avery Island; pearly eyes and switch cane are not. The butterflies are usually at home in a dense grove of giant timber bamboo near the island's high point. Known as moso bamboo (*Phyllostachys edulis*), the titanic grass is native to China and considered the most robust of grasses; canes (culms) can reach a diameter of five to six inches and a height of eighty to ninety feet. The species was introduced to Avery Island in the early 1900s for potential use in the construction industry by the legendary resident/conservationist Edward Avery McIlhenny. The island's moso grove soon became the largest outside China. Pearly eyes on Avery Island seem to prefer the related but more prevalent exotic bamboo over native switch cane, which occurs in restricted areas on the island.

Each February since 1998, the Louisiana-Gulf Coast Chapter of the American Bamboo Society convenes on the island to manicure the historic stand of moso—removing dead growth and thinning viable canes. The practice has proven effective in promoting the growth of larger canes. On February 23, 2019, I attended the annual event. For nearly an entire day, the air resonated with the sounds of chainsaws, machetes, lopping shears, and a huge diesel-powered woodchipper. Each cane was cut at its first node above the ground—about two to five inches. At day's end, the grove was at least 50 percent lighter.

I panicked! How could precarious pearly eyes, which according to published literature pass winter in their larval (caterpillar) stage, withstand such onslaught? Contemplating the situation, I realized that the species surely has been assaulted similarly over the previous two decades, and yet, the butterflies have endured. What was going on? I returned home, daunted and confounded.

In mid-March, I returned to Avery Island to observe the recently groomed moso grove. At once, I detected the distinctive odor of stale beer—a tell-tale sign of yeast fermentation. Scanning the ground, I located the source. Several of the amputated canes had become catch basins, filled with a clear cocktail, presumably of rainwater, sugary sap, and bits of organic debris. A white froth was accumulating along the round edges—evidence that the amputated canes were serving as microbreweries.

CHAPTER 13: A LOUISIANA BUTTERFLY "HAPPY HOUR"

A small number of fruit flies, gnats, and wasps were bellying up. Within a few minutes, two pearly eye butterflies arrived. Each circled for a few seconds before alighting on ground litter two feet away. Within minutes, each butterfly fluttered to the edge of the basin, extending its proboscis to imbibe. After ten to twenty minutes, the butterflies departed, only to return fifteen minutes later with a third companion. Flight was uncharacteristically labored; my proximity seemed of no concern. Indeed, on one occasion I coddled a butterfly for a more photogenic pose, triggering not even a wing flicker. Such camaraderie was a compelling clue to explain the behavior: Simply put, the butterflies were inebriated, intoxicated—drunk.

Mystery resolved! As a self-ordained "butterfly whisperer," I conclude that the annual thinning of the moso bamboo probably destroys a few developing *Enodia portandia*. Nonetheless, the loss is more than compensated for by the creation of windfall opportunities for those butterflies that complete their life cycle by securing an abundance of vital nutrients and water. As lagniappe, the practice creates a de facto bar that offers butterflies and their neighbors a "Happy Hour"—a local "*Cheers*!" [Published originally as "Barflies: Cheers!" IN: Endpaper column, *Natural History*, October 2019, Vol. 127:9, page 40. Used with permission of the publisher and with minor editing.]

SELECTED REFERENCES

DeVries, P.J. 1987. *The Butterflies of Costa Rica and their Natural History: Papilionidae Pieridae, Nymphalidae*. Princeton University Press, Princeton, NJ. 327 pages.

Dherraj, H., A. Krishna, U. Kodandaramaiah and F. Molleman. 2019. Lizards as predators of butterflies: shape of wing damage and effects of eyespots. *Journal of the Lepidopterists' Society*, Spring (Vol. 73(2), pages 78-86.

Glassberg, J. 1999. *Butterflies through Binoculars: The East*. Oxford University Press, Oxford, NY. 242 pages.

Marks, C. 2018. *Butterflies of Louisiana: A Guide to Identification and Location*. Louisiana State University Press. Baton Rouge, LA. 462 pages.

Ross, G.N. 1995. A butterfly roundtable: Ithomiines. on fruit (Lepidoptera: Nymphalidae). *Tropical Lepidoptera* 6(2), page 94.

Ross, G.N. 2019a. Report (13) on butterflies observed on Avery Island, Iberia Parish, Louisiana. IN: Reports of State Coordinators: *Louisiana. Southern Lepidopterists' News*, June (Vol. 41:2), pages 175-178.

Ross, G.N. 2019b. Humans provide southern pearly eye (*Enodia portlandia*) with a "Happy Hour" at an exotic Louisiana venue. *News of the Lepidopterists' Society*, Winter (Vol. 61:4), pages 186-190.

Ross, G.N. 2020a. Avery Island: An ark amidst a sea of grass. *Natural History*, March (Vol. 128:3), pages 14-21.

Ross, G.N. 2020b. Louisiana's Avery Island and its enigmatic butterflies. *Southern Lepidopterists' News,* June (Vol. 42: Supplement), 95 pages.

Scott, J.A. 1986. *The Butterflies of North America: A Natural History and Field Guide*. Stanford University Press, Stanford, CA. 583 pages.

CHAPTER 14: AN ADVENTURE IN THE AMAZON AND A MOTHER'S FINAL WISH

The rainforest offers both physical and metaphysical treasures

Westerners tend to regard science and spirituality as odd bedfellows. For me, though, the interplay between the physical and metaphysical constitutes an integrated fabric of life. Take my 1990-1991 expedition to Rondônia, a state located in the western Amazon Basin of Brazil. Professional butterfly surveys initiated in 1987 have documented that in just a few square kilometers of rainforest near Caucalândia ("Place of Cacao") almost 2,000 species were observable—a record (high numbers of many other groups have been documented, too.) Many biologists consider Rondônia to be a hot spot of biological diversity—the proverbial "Garden of Eden."

I was introduced to Rondônia in 1990 as a participant in an *Expedition Travel* tour led by Dr. Thomas C. Emmel (Florida Museum of Natural History, University of Florida). Our group of twelve resided for the first two weeks in December at Fazenda Rancho Grande, a 750-hectare (1,853 acres) agriculture/cattle ranch/field station owned and operated by the Harald and Barbara Schmitz family, repatriated German immigrants. Traveling to this insular real estate was an adventure in itself. First, we flew from Miami into the international airport of Manaus, Brazil (Manaus is the capital of the state of Amazonas and on the Amazon River), arriving after midnight. After a few hours of sleep at a hotel, we awoke early to board a small aircraft for the hour-long jaunt to Porto Velho (capital, state of Rondônia and on the Rio Madeira). After arriving, we boarded a large Greyhound-type bus for the 120-mile, three-hour trip to Ariquemas—usually the last name to show up on maps of Brazil. Finally, we boarded several vans for the 37-mile, one-hour drive to Caucalândia, a provincial village of 5,000 people. There we were greeted by Tomas Schmitz (charismatic son of Harald and Barbara) in an open-back truck outfitted with plank seats for our final seven-miles of dirt road.

My commitment to the Amazonian expedition was not without trepidation. You see, I had just returned from western New Guinea (then, Irian Jaya, now West Papua or Papua) with Emmel during early November. Ergo, the two ventures, were essentially back-to-back. My parents lived about 70 miles east of my home in Baton Rouge, and so I visited them for the Thanksgiving weekend. My mother was experiencing a nagging health problem: shortness of breath. Her physician had diagnosed this as chronic bronchitis, but not of grave concern. She, nevertheless, was apprehensive about my traveling to another exotic country especially during the impending Christmas season. But Thanksgiving went well. My family was fascinated with my exuberant recounting of chasing enormous birdwing butterflies along jungle trails and participating in a tribal dance and feast with the Stone Age Dani tribe (see Chapter 8). Consequently, when it was time for me to return to my home, my mother embraced me and whispered: "I know butterflies are your life. Go with my blessing."

Fazenda Rancho Grande was an outpost on the Amazonian frontier. Despite the isolation, the fazenda (ranch) featured running water pumped from a well, flush toilets, and diesel generated electricity 12 hours each day for TV, circulating fans, and freshly prepared meals by the affable

CHAPTER 14: AN ADVENTURE IN THE AMAZON AND A MOTHER'S FINAL WISH

Schmitzes. After breakfast, we maniacally vacated the breakfast table to begin a foray into the nearby primary rainforest as well as the peripheral banana/cacao plantations and pastures. Because of the rolling terrain at only 540 feet in altitude, walking was easy. Furthermore, our hosts had cut and maintained paths throughout the verdant landscape. At night, some participants set up black-light gear for collecting moths. The diversity of lepidopterans was so extraordinary that every day each of us collected dozens of different species, including many that had not been logged into the master roster being maintained for the site.

At departure time, all participants, that is, all except yours truly, exited. Because I was on sabbatical from my university, I had arranged to remain behind until late February 1991—another 10 weeks. But before I lost my companions, I arranged with one to carry a letter I had written to my family for posting from his home in Georgia. In the parcel I provided my contacts, but cautioned that all services were located miles away, making communications slow; any logistics for any emergency departure from the ranch could take a week or more. Lastly, I noted that I was in a two-hour advanced time zone.

Thus began my extraordinary and otherworldly odyssey. I took to the field each clear morning with an adventuresome perkiness. I carried a collecting net and backpack stuffed with a water-repellent poncho, camera equipment, lots of film (this was the pre-digital age), insect repellent, and a simple lunch consisting of a couple of dried salami sandwiches, a ripe orange or banana, and a canteen full of filtered water.

The Amazonian rainforest was a botanical cornucopia, a realm of majestic greenery. Within the boundaries of the ranch, two basic types of forest dominated: closed canopy and open canopy. In the former, a high proportion of heavily buttressed trees towered at least 125 feet. One of the tallest, identified by such monikers as "kapok" and "silk-cotton" (*Ceiba pentandra*), often emerged 40-50 feet higher than the emerald sea. Valuable trees such as mahogany (*Swietenia macrophylla*) and the Brazil nut (*Bertholletia excelsa*) were well represented. The fluted trunks and limbs of these titans acted as de facto aerial, miniature gardens composed of bromeliads (especially massive *Aechmea* and *Guzmania*), orchids, aroids, cacti, and a tangle of vines (lianas). Because of the heavy upper-story greenery, the ground was heavily shaded, creating an openness that facilitated walking. Open canopy sites, in contrast, were dominated by somewhat lower trees, including the acclaimed "chicle" (*Manikara chicle*), responsible for chewing gum. Here, light could penetrate, which in turn fostered an assortment of feathery palms, bamboos, gingers, and heliconias. Ground-cover vegetation was a potpourri of domestic shade-loving "hothouse" plants such as *Anthurium*, *Calathea*, *Caladium*, *Dieffenbachia*, *Peperomia*, *Philodendron*, and *Spathiphyllum*, to name but a few. The terrestrial, robust, and pineapple-like bromeliad, *Ananas*, often formed large impenetrable colonies. Walking here was often impeded, and so I usually confined myself to the established trails—also, with less likely hood of serpents.

The forest was an expo of butterflies, too. Consider: There were the charismatic and iridescent morphos (9 species) and super-sized owl-eyed caligos (4 species) (family Nymphalidae, subfamily Morphinae), as well as hundreds of pint-sized, zany metalmarks (family Riodinidae) that flaunted their dazzling colors and designs. I was especially impressed with the longwings/heliconians (family Nymphalidae, subfamily Heliconiinae)—25 species, and clearwings/glasswings/ithomiines (family Nymphalidae, subfamily Ithomiinae)—46 species; both groups are signature taxa for the American Tropics, and both are reputed to be distasteful to vertebrate predators. Rank and file longwings, usually with bright color schemes, were particularly common along sun-bathed corridors. There they patrolled in search of their favorite orange/yellow flowering vines (*Gurania* and *Psiguria*) from which they would extract both nectar and pollen. On the other hand, the ithomiines' guise of transparency epitomized the essence of the commonly used term for butterflies, "gossamer winged." With slow fluttery flights

CHAPTER 14: AN ADVENTURE IN THE AMAZON AND A MOTHER'S FINAL WISH

usually within the darkest recesses of the forest, the butterflies seemed illusionary—ghostly apparitions.

On two occasions I stumbled upon a lek, i.e., an arena where males of some birds, mammals, fish, frogs, and insects, assemble to display in order to attract females for courting. Two-dozen or so clearwing butterflies were gathered within an area of no more than 500 square feet. Most males perched on leaves 4-6 feet above the ground. Their abdomens elevated; they displayed their peculiar wing hairpencils (specialized scales located along the anterior margins of the hindwings whose function is to release volatile sex pheromones to attract females). On occasion, the ithomiine leks attracted a cameo pierid (sulphur) or riodinid (metalmark) that resembled the clearwings in appearance. (Such beguiling resemblances between unrelated species led in the nineteenth century to classical model-mimic theories currently celebrated as Batesian and Müllerian Mimicry.)

One morning, while resting and enraptured on a log beside a trail in a closed canopy forest, my solitude was interrupted by crackly sounds in the forest's ground litter. Within minutes I could view a mishmash of arthropods fleeing a raid of army ants (*Eciton*) known locally as "*marabunta*," and feared because of their powerful stings and carnivorous feeding habits. Because the "brigade" was barely 10-15 feet across, I was able to remain on the outskirts of the pillage to observe and remain unharmed.

And the ants had comrades. First, dozens of flies buzzed above—apparently waiting for an opportunity to parasitize the marauding ants. Second, two different species of small, dull-colored birds dubbed "antbirds" (passerine family Thamnophilidae) flitted within the low vegetation, systematically nabbing ants for food. Even several butterflies were part of the motley troupe. One was a large "tiger-striped" ithomiine that flew lazily three to four feet above the ants, searching out the conspicuous white bird excrement that the birds continually dropped. Finally, there were a half-dozen species of skippers (family Hesperiidae) flashing about, occasionally pausing to check out anything white. (Prevailing theory has it that several species of ithomiines and skippers exploit antbirds and indirectly, army ants to extract the nitrogen in the birds' excrement, which in turn aids the female butterflies with egg production.). Although this symbiotic behavior between army ants, ant birds, and butterflies was well known, this was my first encounter with the exclusively tropical phenomenon. Flying solo and lacking a schedule, I could immerse myself with observations, collecting, and photography, all supported by a seemingly endless tableau. All in all, the forest was a monumental place of wonder—my "happy place."

On Friday December 28 that all changed.

To clarify: The Schmitz family and I had just completed the evening meal. Outside was dark and rainy. Suddenly there was a knock on the kitchen door. A man, who had ridden in on a horse, stood in his drenched poncho holding up a plastic wrap. "Fax for the Americano," is all he uttered. With hands shaking, I accepted the damp paper.

"MOTHER VERY ILL…PLEASE CALL GRANT ROSS…
HIGHLAND PARK HOSPITAL…ICU WAITING ROOM… (phone no.)"

Time froze. Harald then broke the tension: "If the road is not washed out in the morning, we can drive to Caucalândia to try to place the call."

Mercifully, the following morning was rainless and the road passable, although we did pack a chainsaw in case we encountered a fallen tree. The telephone call went through so that I was able to speak to my younger brother, Grant. Apparently, the original diagnosis of bronchitis by my mother's doctor was not entirely correct. The major problem was a leaky heart valve, and that needed to be replaced. Surgery was scheduled for January 2 and would take about eight hours; there was an eighty percent chance of success. My mother understood that I would not be able to be present at the surgery. My brother promised to send a fax as soon as the surgery was completed.

January 2, 1991. Since my telephone call, I had tried my best to resume "lepping." But for this day I decided that I needed a more concentrated task to keep my mind off family matters. I decided to devote the day to photography. I packed my camera gear, bulky tripod, and set off for the pristine forest.

CHAPTER 14: AN ADVENTURE IN THE AMAZON AND A MOTHER'S FINAL WISH

After about two hours along a narrow, machete-hewn path within a tract of closed-canopy forest, I encountered what I first interpreted as a lek. Soon, though, I realized that most of the individuals were small, transparent-winged ithomiines, which were not displaying courtship behavior, but were instead seeking out tiny blobs of white organic matter lodged on the leaves of lower vegetation. There, they assembled in groups of from one to three individuals, each with its proboscis (tongue) extended as if imbibing a fluid. By tasting, I determined that the white "stuff" constituted bits of fruit, most likely fallen from the canopy and that now was fermenting. And the source? My attention was garnered by the raucous sounds from a small troop of howler monkeys (*Alouatta*) and a small flock of green parrots noisily feeding atop an enormous fig (*Ficus*) tree—a primary fruit-bearer in tropical forests. The tree with its vertebrate dinner guests was located about fifty feet off the trail. The monkeys and parrots were not only vocal, but messy eaters as well. Scraps of fruit were raining down like the proverbial "manna from heaven." And so, instead of a lek, I had stumbled onto an ithomiine feeding station—a "butterfly banquet" or "butterfly round table" in the jungle featuring non-typical cuisine.

With my curiosity piqued. I hastened to photograph. I had no difficulty in positioning my tripod as close to a feeding assemblage [My equipment consisted of a Cannon AE-1 camera equipped with a 50 mm macro lens and handheld electronic flash; film was Kodachrome 64.] The butterflies were totally indifferent to my presence. Pressing my luck, I dropped to my knees and inched the tripod closer. I learned that I could approach within two to three inches—a distance so short that even my deliberate slow exhalation of breath caused the wings of the butterflies to flutter ever so slightly as they prolonged their "snacks." For a quick fix, I resorted to leaning back, exhaling cautiously with my face turned away; I then inhaled a new breath and held it as I returned to the camera to focus, set the aperture, position the flash with my left hand, and finally trip the shutter with my right hand. With my mission accomplished, I once again leaned backward to exhale. This simple routine allowed me to shoot frame after frame with impunity, each time holding the flash at a different angle because I had no way of knowing what the film was recording. The limiting factor was my threshold for enduring the cramping of my legs and feet caused by my unorthodox/extended posturing. To stave off cramping, I sometimes backed up, retreating from my equipment to the path where I then stretched to recover. After a few moments to recuperate, I returned to my former venue for another round of filming.

Come lunchtime, I took a break from the surreal drama for my own nourishment. As soon as I removed my sandwich from its plastic wrap, a striking blue/black nymphalid butterfly (*Panacea divalis*), alighted on the bread and began probing with its proboscis. Another species (*Nessaea obrinus*) with soft-green underwings quickly muscled in. Both species normally are canopy dwellers. They are sometimes coaxed to the ground by the odors of minerals, salts, fermenting sugars, and nitrogen compounds found in a variety of substances such as feces, blood, sweat, tears, decaying flesh, damp soil, yeasty fruits, and other plant exudates—and yes, even sandwich meats. (Collectors in the tropics are known to employ "exotic foods" to bait trails and trap nets.) Although the behavior was entertaining, I soon became an impolite host by waving away my "lunch buddies" due to overkill.

But not easily intimidated, the intoxicated insects relocated to my sweaty hat I had placed on the ground to cool my head.

By mid-afternoon, my euphoria enticed me to venture into the forest to search for additional photo opportunities. But after an hour or so of battling vegetation while at the same time maintaining a watchful eye for a sleeping serpent, I detect nothing. Meanwhile, illumination began to dwindle—seriously dwindle because of the thick canopy of the forest and thickening clouds gathering above that. Heeding the clues, I begin backtracking.

The forest, although staggering, was also nebulous. Unwise, I had failed to note landmarks or mark my path. Not wishing to give in to panic, I thought: "Just how far could I have wandered from the trail?" So, I placed my tripod upon a fallen tree trunk so that the shiny metal would be visible above much of the ground vegetation. I then began making short sallies in various directions as my mind tried to recall my past movements. Nothing. The forest had me turned around and tapped out of energy, I returned to the tripod to face the hard truth: I WAS LOST!

Now I panicked! The hour was nearly five o'clock. I could spare only another 30 minutes before beginning my trek back to the ranch if I were to arrive before dark. (Remember, "twilight" varies according to latitude: lengthy at the poles, brief at the equator.) Otherwise, I would be facing a night within the forest—an onerous, spooky world ruled by jaguars, pumas, vipers, and a bevy of smaller but nonetheless potentially lethal creepy crawlers. (Indeed, my mind's eye conjured them all.) And what about tomorrow? Since the Schmitz didn't know just which trail I had taken, would I have any chance for rescue? My life was now at stake, undeniably!

Deflated and daunted by this specter of doom, I sat on the tree trunk to process my inattentive movements over the past hour. But all I could do was to gaze mindlessly as feelings of claustrophobia and helplessness intensified. Almost reflexively, I moved my lips in a silent prayer for guidance.

But just when I thought all hope was lost, my eyes paused on a pile of debris composed of small fallen limbs perhaps no more than twenty feet before me. A peephole in the canopy directly above—no doubt the result of the dislocated limbs resting before me—was pinpointing a faint ray of light highlighting the ground. My mind recalled: "I know I passed this same brush only minutes after I had veered off the path towards the fig tree." Electrified, I stood, raised my right hand, and while pointing at a forty-five-degree angle beyond the illuminated limbs. I exclaimed: "THE TRAIL IS THERE!"

With my internal battery recharged with adrenaline, and with certainty, I unleashed all my energy into a straightforward dash. (In hindsight, this was reckless: I could have tread on a venomous serpent or brushed against a poisonous insect or plant.) And there it was: the missing trail. Turns out, I hadn't deviated much from a straight-line, and I hadn't ventured far afield. But

CHAPTER 14: AN ADVENTURE IN THE AMAZON AND A MOTHER'S FINAL WISH

because of my eye-level view of the dense "jungle," I was unable to see the corridor, and I had miscalculated distance.

As I paused for my second wind, my body was racked by a commanding chill and racing heart. My mind flashed: *"Mother dead or dying.* Instinctively, I sank to my knees, and in piousness, reflexively whispered: *"Thank you, Mother."*

The once verdant forest suddenly grew black and ominous. A clap of thunder boomed overhead, and raindrops began to filter down. I rose, slipped on my poncho, and made a reality check of the hour: 5:30. Aware of the gravity of the hour, I set off at the best pace I could sustain, leaving my cumbersome tripod behind.

I arrived at the ranch house at 6:50—dusk. Rain persisted, and lights blazed in the welcoming Schmitz home. My hosts quizzed me about my unusual tardiness, but all I could relay is that I had been lost for several hours. None of us uttered a word about my mother; graciously,

Barbara had prepared an especially delicious meal in empathy for what she perceived had been a trying day for me.

The following day dawned cloudless. I decided to revisit the fig tree and employ my second Canon AE-1 camera—just in case there had been an undetected problem with the first. Sure enough, the butterflies (and tripod) were still present. This second day's performance was a repeat of the first—with one exception: I did not let myself lose sight of the trail. Satisfied that between the two cameras, I believed that I had an adequate number of "Kodak Moments." Once again, I returned to the ranch near dusk.

Although the day had been dry, rain was now falling. Once again during the dinner hour, there came a knock on the door. And once again, an intrepid messenger on horseback iterating that he carried a fax for the "Americano." Barbara Schmitz accepted and gestured to me. But I said: "I know what it says. You read it, please."

*"MOTHER PASSED AWAY AT 3:30 PM. JANUARY 2, 1991.
PLEASE CALL."*

My mind quickly converted the hour to 5:30 Rondônia time, the precise time of my revelation.

In the morning Harald and I drove to Cacaulândia to make the dreaded call. I learned that the surgery had gone well, but the final stitching didn't hold. And before the bleeding could be controlled, the heart failed. Doctors had no good explanation. The family was proceeding with the funeral for January 5 without my presence. Upon my scheduled return in February, they would organize a memorial service.

I decided to remain at the Schmitz ranch, observing and collecting until my originally scheduled departure in late February. The research continued to be productive although the number

CHAPTER 14: AN ADVENTURE IN THE AMAZON AND A MOTHER'S FINAL WISH

of rainy days steadily escalated, causing me to spend more and more time indoors preparing my collected specimens. On no other occasion did I encounter another treasure trove of butterfly activity. In fact, on January 5, the day scheduled for my mother's funeral, I returned to "my" fig tree. No longer were tidbits of fruit falling, and, understandably, no butterflies were gathering. The forest had returned to its status quo.

Finally, February 23 arrived. Since my truck ride to Caucalândia wasn't until noonish, I decided to take one final walk around the buildings. No net, no camera, just a perfunctory, dilly-dallied stroll to secure my memory. I spotted three species of butterflies that I had never encountered before—vivid testimony to the diversity of butterflies in the region, and a fitting "goodbye" to my adventure. [During my residency I logged a total of 1,571 specimens representing 400 species, more or less.]

Over these intervening years, my mind has frequently replayed my time at Fazenda Rancho Grande, especially those early days in January. Based solely on current cognitive science, I conclude the following: (1) the surprising tranquility of the butterflies was due to their alcohol intoxication from feeding on fruit that was rapidly fermenting because of high ambient temperature and humidity (see Chapter 13); (2) my sudden awareness of the location of the trail was prompted by the remembrance of a recent encounter resurfacing prompted by my respite on the log; (3) my electrifying emotions were triggered by apprehension, or perhaps, our poorly understood "sixth sense; and (4) the correlation between the time of my mother's death in Louisiana with my dramatic sensations in Brazil was an example of pure coincidence.

On the other hand, from a quasi-spiritual or metaphysical reference, I can believe that my encapsulated experiences and uncanny acumen in the forest were the result of providence or divinity, that is, some power greater than myself.

So, which is it?

Your call. But because I trust *both* science and spirituality, January 2, 1991, marks a cornerstone, albeit bittersweet, in my life. Clearly, the date immortalizes the loss of my family's matriarch, and so I mourn. However, the date is also a celebration of my mother's transcendence of time and space, an action that empowered her son in distress with her most precious and singular gift: LIFE.

> *"There are more things in heaven and earth, Horatio, Than are dreamt of in your philosophy."*

William Shakespeare: From HAMLET, Act 1, Scene 5.

EPILOGUE: Although the Amazonian rainforest is the world's bastion of biodiversity, it is not invincible, not immortal. The state of Rondônia has been experiencing widespread deforestation since the mid-1990s. And the over-exploitation continues. In fact, Rondônia is at the forefront of the burnings posted by international news organizations in 2019. Fazenda Rancho Grande remains the home place of the Harald Schmitz family. Because their property is technically guarded from encroachment, their section of rainforest endures. Fortunately, a Florida based organization (Association for Tropical Lepidoptera) raised sufficient funds to acquire in the late 1990s another 6,000 acres (about the size of JFK airport in New York City) of rainforest to preserve and to construct facilities for researchers. (The site is administered by a foundation within the Brazilian government.) So bolstered, Fazenda Rancho Grande has become an island of primeval and sublime splendor immersed within a mosaic of denuded landscapes. Moreover, the ranch serves as a template for safeguarding other sections of tropical forests. The percentage of the butterfly fauna I encountered that continues to thrive is unknown, of course. Additionally, just how much intact land is critical to sustain a viable rainforest ecosystem is equally dubious. Personally, I feel extremely privileged to have been able to experience this example of life—a paragon of the natural world.

[Published originally as "An Adventure in the Amazon and a Mother's Final Blessing" in *News of the Lepidopterists' Society*, Winter 2009 (Vol. 51:4), pages 140-145, outside back cover. In addition, published in part as "A Butterfly Banquet in the Tropics" in Natural History, February 2025 (Vol. 133:2), pages 16-21.] Reprinted with permission of the editors and with minor editing.]

SELECTED REFERENCES

Austin G.F. 1996. Hesperiidae of central Rondônia, Brazil: three new species of *Narcosisus* Steinhauser. *Journal of the Lepidopterists' Society*, Spring (Vol. 50:1), pages 54-59.

Austin, G.F. and T.C. Emmel 1996. Nymphalidae of central Rondônia, Brazil: Melitaeinae, with descriptions of two new species. *Tropical Lepidoptera*, 7(2), pages133-142.

DeVries, P.J. 1987. *The Butterflies of Costa Rica and their Natural History: Papilionidae Pieridae, Nymphalidae.* Princeton University Press, Princeton, NJ. 327 pages.

Emmel, T.C. and G.T. Austin. 1990. The tropical rain forest butterfly fauna of Rondônia, Brazil: species diversity and conservation. *Tropical Lepidoptera*, 1(1), pages 1-12.

Ross, G.N. 1995. One butterfly's poison is another's feast: ithomiines on droppings (Lepidoptera: Nymphalidae). IN: Note. *Tropical Lepidoptera*, 6:1), page 10.

Ross, G.N. 1995. A butterfly roundtable; Ithomiines on fruit (Lepidoptera: Nymphalidae). IN: Note. *Tropical Lepidoptera*, 6:2, pages 94-95.

Ross, G.N. 1998. Butterfly social clubs. IN: Note. *Holarctic Lepidoptera*, 5:1, page 22.

Ross, G.N. 2025. A butterfly banquet in the tropics. *Natural History*, February (Vol. 133:2), pages 16-21, cover.

CHAPTER 15: FLYING HIGH

Colorado's alpine butterflies offer a touch of whimsy

It was the first week of July 1990. I had signed up for a week-long workshop titled "The Biology of Butterflies." The event was hosted at The Nature Place, a comfortable and upbeat private educational facility nestled on 6,000 acres of ponderosa pines at an elevation of 8,600 feet in the Front Range of the Rocky Mountains of Teller County in central Colorado. (Today, the center is designated by the National Park Service as a National Environmental Study Center.) The facility is accessible from Colorado Springs and Florissant, in the distance, iconic Pikes Peak looms on the horizon.

Up to this point in my life I had had limited experience with Alpine Tundra—a high mountain, cold, and windswept ecosystem that begins above the timberline of the evergreen coniferous forest, extending up to the permanent snow line. Located on a number of high mountains in the west, the ecosystem occurs to a lesser extent in the East on Mt. Washington, New Hampshire (6,288 feet), Mt. Katahdin, Maine (5,268), and Mt. Albert, Quebec, Canada (3,786 feet)—all of which I had visited on one-day trips during my earlier career. A related ecosystem, called Arctic Tundra, is found in the far north—usually above the Arctic Circle—where the boreal coniferous forest reaches its northern growth limit. Because Arctic Tundra is defined by latitude, the ecosystem occupies much more land area than its montane counterpart. The lands are flat, waterlogged, and snowbound most of the year. It, too, is not very accessible except via air. Both Arctic and Alpine Tundra are very fragile ecosystems, primarily because of their short summer growing season. Any disturbance requires many decades to recover. Both Arctic and Alpine Tundra harbor many specialized plants and animals—including butterflies. Understandably, I had high hopes for The Nature Place.

Twenty-seven individuals from across the nation participated in the week-long program, which was directed by lepidopterists Dr. Boyce Drummond of Colorado College and Dr. Thomas Emmel of the University of Florida in Gainesville. We attended lectures, workshops, and field trips. For me the most unforgettable activity was a road trip to Horseshoe Mountain (el. 13,898 feet), ranked among the 100 highest peaks in Colorado, and located in the Mosquito Range within the Pike National Forest.

Horseshoe Mountain was a solid hour-and-a-half away. Therefore, we departed The Nature Place about eight in the morning after a hearty breakfast. First, we traveled via paved road through magnificent ponderosa pine forest (the Transition Life Zone of C.H. Merriam). We then veered onto a dirt road to begin our ascent into the Canadian and Hudsonian Life Zones, those altitudes where the mighty "Christmas trees" (dark green, needle-leaved, fir and spruce conifers) reigned. Finally, the forest began to thin, and we emerged into a rather open area studded with *krummholtz*, those dwarfed, twisted trees whose limbs appear flag-like owing to strong, directional winds. A mile or so farther on, at about 11,500 feet, we officially entered the alpine tundra, a first for me.

The road leveled a bit as we entered Leavick Valley, named after an old silver-mining town nearby. As we traveled up the narrow valley heavy low clouds settled in, engulfing, and dampening everything. Our destination was a graveled parking spot. There, we parked and were instructed to begin readying our gear. At an elevation of 12,200 feet, the temperature was in the low 40s; we felt chilled to the bone. Additionally, the pea-soup clouds prevented us from seeing any landmarks. But suddenly, the light intensified. Could the clouds be thinning? Yes! Within minutes we could see cameos of blue sky. Shortly, the remaining wisps of clouds vaporized, the Sun blazed, the thin air warmed, and the wind subsided. We now had an unobstructed view of the surrounding landscape. And it was awesome!

The parking area gave access to a rolling, treeless, and rock-strewn meadow stippled with wildflowers and persistent snowpacks. The backdrop was a classic cirque—a mountainous, three-sided, steep walled basin carved by a glacier. (Actually, the U-shaped singularity had inspired the name "Horseshoe Mountain.") Having spent most of my life in the lowlands of Louisiana, I was dumb-founded and euphoric by the high elevation and the rarified atmosphere.

CHAPTER 15: FLYING HIGH

Our leaders cautioned that although the scene was photogenic, we should not tarry. "In this high country," warned Emmel. "Hail, sleet, and even snow is possible on any given day and with little warning." With that in mind, we removed our outer layer of warm clothing and covered all exposed skin with sunscreen.

I was skeptical about observing any butterflies. I quizzed Emmel: "Where should we look?" Many diminutive plants bearing yellow and white flowers grew amid speckled granite rocks and boulders. But candidly, the display lacked the luster of those storied lupine-filled meadows in the Cascade Mountains of Washington and Oregon. The air, furthermore, seemed too cool for any insect attempting to fly.

And then it happened. As if the "Keeper of the Butterflies" had issued a silent command, dozens of yellow and orange butterflies—characteristic colors of sulphur butterflies (family Pieridae)—exploded from the low greenery. As the butterflies gained altitude, they began wheeling and reeling about, animating, and pixelating the azure sky. Some individuals descended to ground level to nectar on wildflowers. The sulphur vanguards were quickly joined by other medium-sized butterflies—basically white but with small patches of black and a pair of red and black ocelli on each hindwing—indicative markings of parnassians or apollos (primitive relatives of swallowtails, family Papilionidae). These individuals, though, fluttered near ground level in search of their diminutive host plants, stonecrop (*Sedum*), a common species around rocks, where females lay their eggs. Apollos characteristically have a lengthy-life cycle, an adaptation to the short summer season. The eggs usually remain dormant through winter, and the larvae emerge the following summer to feed on the host plant. If by chance, there is not sufficient time to complete their development due to inclement weather, individuals hibernate as older caterpillars or pupae through a second winter. The following summer, after two years—they urgently mature to emerge as adults before the temperatures drop once again.

To my amazement, I could count between thirty to forty individual butterflies on the wing at any given moment. Not wishing to waste time, and confident that I didn't have to concern myself about treading on a venomous serpent, I reflexively began to pursue a sulphur that had grazed my head. Mistake! Having lived at sea level most of my life, I was unaccustomed to the thin mountain air. After only two short sprints and two unsuccessful swings of my net, I quickly found myself terribly short-winded. I dropped to my knees exhausted. Following a short reprieve on the ground, I staggered to my feet to give chase to another butterfly. A swing, another miss, and again, I crumpled to the ground, heart pounding, chest heaving, head throbbing, and perspiration rolling down my cheeks. Not easily discouraged, I was embracing the "Joy of the wild!"

Gazing about while catching my breath, I noticed that several of my classmates, who had remained in the parking area, were pointing in my direction. I waved in embarrassment, trying to sway them to join me. No luck. The onlookers remained on the sideline laughing and yelling: "Go Tiger, go!"—a reference to the sports team of my alma mater, Louisiana State University. Infused with fresh adrenaline, and wishing to redeem myself, I was undeterred. I shed my jacket, wobbled upright, and chose another target. Another lunge, and another intimate contact with the ground. But this time was different: the specimen was in the net. Robust applause erupted from the spectators who had been watching to learn how my "cat-and-mouse" antics would play out.

This was theater—literally, "Theater in the Wild." Quirky! Whimsical! Joyous! And the butterflies were so ubiquitous throughout the meadow that the fun seemed endless. In my wildest dreams, never would I have imagined that so many individual butterflies could inhabit such a restricted habitat at such an altitude. With my lesson on how *not* to catch a butterfly in high altitudes well learned, those of us who were collecting fanned out across the polka-dot meadow, wrangling only those butterflies that could be netted with ease. Two small tarns (alpine clear, meltwater pools) nearby added to the postcard quality of the view. Participants not interested in collecting busied themselves with photography or sketching—often depicting the antics of us collectors. (The policies on conservation and collecting outlined by *The Lepidopterists' Society* were followed.)

We were captivated, entranced. When any cloud obscured the sun, the butterflies plummeted as if by sorcery. When the sun returned, the butterflies re-materialized to continue "business as usual." This synchronic up-and-down behavior continued for two hours. During our workshop that evening we hypothesized that the butterflies' ability to find protection quickly within low vegetation was probably a survival adaptation to an ecosystem where sunlight can be short lived and a shadow can portend freezing precipitation and severe wind, both potentially fatal. In addition, we concluded that the dark coloration of many of the butterflies—particularly near their thorax—coupled with long hair-like wing scales near the abdomen were also adaptations for absorbing and trapping heat from fickle sunlight in a cold environment.

© 2008 Kim Davis, Mike Stangeland, Andrew Warren

Rank and file species we collected and photographed in the alpine microcosm included: Queen Alexandra's sulphur (*Colias alexandra alexandra*), Scudder's sulphur (*Colias scudderii*), pink-edged sulphur (*Colias interior*), Mead's sulphur (*Colias meadii*), 'Rocky Mountain' parnassian (*Parnassius phoebus smintheus*), Melissa arctic (*Oeneis melissa*) and Chryxus arctic (*Oeneis chryxus*) (both, family Nymphalidae, subfamily Satyrinae). The parnassians were particularly easy to net because they flew close to the ground in search of their host plant, stonecrop. By contrast, the dark-colored arctics were sedentary, usually perched on lichen-encrusted rocks. While basking they usually held their wings closed but angled their bodies to the left or right for maximum sun exposure. (Some arctics would be so tilted that they were almost horizontal.) In such a position, the darkish, mottled coloration of the butterflies blended almost perfectly with the grainy granite rocks and the blotchy crustose lichens.

With sunny weather holding, and our psyches and bodies still pulsating with energy, we extended our collecting to a nearby talus outcrop (talus is an accumulation of rock debris fallen from the wall of a cliff). The terrain appeared perilous, composed of myriad fragments of sharply fractured pieces of sedimentary rock from the cirque—all heaped upon each other. Our targets were three specialized butterflies: 'Snow's' lustrous copper (*Lycaena cupreus snowi*) (family Lycaenidae), Magdalena alpine (*Erebia magdalena*), and Uhler's arctic (*Oeneis uhleri*). Picking our way on the loose rocks was treacherous. (In truth, most of us had one or two mishaps.) But despite the danger, our efforts were quickly rewarded when a small, brilliant coppery red butterfly, 'Snow's' lustrus copper, darted past just above the rocks. A larger solid black species, the Magdalena alpine, followed close behind. Regrettably, with our mobility severely limited, no one

succeeded in netting either of the butterflies. As we held firm to our positions in fear of accident, other similar butterflies made their appearance. Most, however, were out of reach.

Taunted, we needed a plan. Perhaps cooperation? We decided to station ourselves about fifteen to twenty feet apart so that we could command visual and physical coverage of just about the entire slope traversed by the passing butterflies; if one person missed the target, someone else might do better. The simple scheme worked. Within the hour, we each had secured a specimen or two of both the "copper" and the "alpine." (The dark Uhler's were usually stationary, content to bask in the strong sunlight. A quick plunge of the net and they were ours.)

While on the talus, we were rewarded with a bit of non-butterfly lagniappe: a pika or cony (*Ochotona princeps*)—a small feisty mammal related to rabbits. Pikas are buff/gray in color, sport short ears, and have no visible tail. On sunny days they usually perch on rocks, producing short squeaks that carry considerable distances in the thin air. An alternate name for the mammal is "haymaker" because it clips grass growing amid the talus debris, sets the greenery to dry in the sun, and then stores the cured "hay" within rock cavities for the long winter months; pikas don't hibernate and so have to feed periodically even during the winter. For me, the sighting of a pika was another "first."

With such inimitable activity, the hours raced by. About one o'clock in the afternoon we decided to return to the parking area for our box lunches. Just in time, too. The weather began to close in: a bank of dark stratus clouds began to sweep in from the southern horizon. Within thirty minutes, the entire sky was a marbled gray, temperatures dropped dramatically, and a stiff, cold wind began to blow. By the time we had redressed for winter, packed our equipment, and boarded the vans, a few large snowflakes began to fall. Thus ended another glorious adventure.

My visit to the treeless high country of Colorado reminded me that the pursuit of butterflies not only offers the prospect of observing or collecting unfamiliar species but also exposes us to new habitats—and sometimes to new countries and cultures. It is a view I've held ever since I was a nascent graduate student when I read H.B.D. Kettlewell's presidential address to the 1963 meeting of *The Lepidopterists' Society*. [Kettlewell (1907-1979) may be best remembered for his experiments with peppered moths, designed to follow up on William Bateson's pre-eminent case study in natural selection.] I, however, was inspired most by what he proclaimed in his closing remarks in 1963: *"Heaven help the scientist who, using butterflies for science alone, fails to appreciate their beauty and to take advantage of the wonderful places into which they lead us."*

[This is an integration of two of my previously published articles: "Flying High: An Adventure in the Alpine Tundra of Colorado" in *News of the Lepidopterists' Society*, Autumn 2010 (Vol. 52:3), pages 90-92 104; and "Highland Fling: Butterfly Wrangling on Colorado's Horseshoe Mountain" IN Naturalist at Large column, *Natural History*, February 2011 (Vol. 119:4), pages 12-15. Portions of texts were reprinted with permission from the publishers and with minor modifications.]

SELECTED REFERENCES

Brock, J.P., and K. Kaufman. 2003. Kaufman *Field Guide to Butterflies of North America*. Houghton Mifflin Co., New York, NY. 392 pp.

Emmel, T.C., M.C. Minno and B.A. Drummond. 1992. Florissant *Butterflies: A Guide to the Fossil and Present-Day Species of Central Colorado*. Stanford University Press, Stanford, CA. 118 pp.

Ferris, C.D., and F. M. Brown. 1981. *Butterflies of the Rocky Mountain States*. University of Oklahoma Press, Norman, OK. 442 pp.

Glassberg, J. 2001. *Butterflies through Binoculars: The West*. Oxford University Press, New York, NY. 374 pp.

Glassberg, J. 2010. *Butterflies of North America*. Fall River Press, New York, NY. 202 pp.

Kettlewell, H.B.D. 1963. Presidential address to the thirteenth annual meeting of The Lepidopterists' Society: Lepidoptera as scientific tools. *Journal of the Lepidopterists' Society* 17(3):173-177.

Merriam, C. H. and Steineger, L. 1890. *Results of a biological survey of the San Francisco mountain region and the desert of the Little Colorado, Arizona*. North American Fauna Report 3. U.S. Department of Agriculture, Division of Ornithology and Mammalia, Washington, D.C. 136 pp.

NABA. 2001. *North American Butterfly Association (NABA) Checklist & English Names of North American Butterflies*. Second Edition. North American Butterfly Association, Morristown, NJ. 60 pp.

Opler, P.A. 1999. *A Field Guide to Western Butterflies*. The Peterson Field Guide Series. Houghton Mifflin Co., New York, NY. 544 pp.

Opler, P.A. and V. Malikul. 1998. *A Field Guide to Eastern Butterflies*. The Peterson Field Guide Series. Houghton Mifflin Co., New York, NY. 488 pp.

Pyle, R.M. 1981. *The Audubon Society Field Guide to North American Butterflies*. Alfred A. Knopf, New York, NY. 917 pp.

Pyle, R.M. 2002. *The Butterflies of Cascadia: A Field Guide to All the Species of Washington, Oregon, and Surrounding Territories*. Seattle Audubon Society, Seattle, WA. 420 pp.

Scott, J.A. 1986. *Butterflies of North America: A Natural History and Field Guide*. Stanford University Press, Stanford, CA. 583 pp.

Tilden, J.W. and A.C. Smith. 1986. *A Field Guide to Western Butterflies*. The Peterson Field Guide Series. Houghton Mifflin Company, Boston, MA. 370 pp.

CHAPTER 16: AN ELUSIVE SWAMP CREATURE

In Louisiana, the rare Seminole crescent butterfly goes unseen for years, then reappears

Swamps—low-lying, normally flooded earth punctuated by stalwart trees—are dank and gloomy. Swamps usually conjure up images that, to human nature, are eerie, if not freaky. To some people, however, swamps are mysterious and beguiling.

In my home state of Louisiana, wetland acreage, which includes marshes and swamps, accounts for 32 percent of the state, although over 100,000 acres have been lost to water intrusion over the last twenty years. The major trees in swamps, bald cypress (*Taxodium distichum*) and swamp tupelo (*Nyssa aquatica*), have massive trunks supported by a swollen and fluted base—adaptations that increase support in unstable, water-logged earth. Limbs are usually short but weighted heavily with spindly festoons of the ashen-colored epiphyte known as Spanish moss (*Tillandsia usneoides*). Reflective standing water is placid and brown, due to a high concentration of tannins. Water levels are usually shallow but fluctuate depending on seasonal rainfall. During occasionally extended dry periods, the level will drop, exposing the bare earth. After heavy rains, runoff from surrounding areas can cause levels to rise two feet or so, drowning all lower vegetation. This semi-aquatic environment is home to slithering reptiles—some venomous, some gigantic with formidable teeth. And above the water, the air is menacing: sultry and buzzing with myriad biting insects, that like miniature vampires, voraciously drain your blood. Swamps are virtually inaccessible except in small boats—canoes and skiffs, for example—which may account for their mystery. And of course, Hollywood has not bypassed the opportunity to magnify and exploit this "swamp mystique." Who can forget *Creature from the Black Lagoon*, *Swamp Thing*, or *Curse of the Swamp Creature*?

For one subspecies of butterfly that normally prefers a dry habitat, the swamplands of Louisiana are an ideal home. The Seminole crescent butterfly (*Anthanassa texana seminole*) is  conventionally considered a subspecies of a common western taxon known simply as the Texan crescent (*Anthanassa texana texana*). This taxonomy is controversial: some experts think the *seminole* form should be elevated to full species category due to its singular ecological requirements. Regardless, *A. texana* belongs to the large family of lepidopterans catalogued as "brushfooted" butterflies (family Nymphalidae). "Seminoles," as they are typically referred to, are small, and—although not flamboyant in coloration—are decidedly memorable. Their signature base color is brown, overlaid with a checkerboard of white dots and extensive bright orange near the body proper. Individuals fly slowly and close to the ground with the orange of the wings flashing as a telltale beacon. [In contrast, *A. t. texana*, the western subspecies, sports wings with the orange less intense and reduced in area. This western cousin prefers open, dry, sunny fields and roadsides.] Seminoles prefer tree-filled dank wetlands usually devoid of nectar-rich flowers—habitats that are normally avoided by gossamer-winged butterflies.

Seminole crescents have always been considered rare, although they are *not* protected by the U.S. Endangered Species Act; their conservation status varies by states where they are found, but they, in general, are listed as "Vulnerable." Adults occupy only small, localized colonies scattered throughout a limited range. Most often, each colony consists of under fifty individuals. Reported haunts are restricted to the coastal geographies of the Gulf states and the eastern seaboard as far north as South Carolina. The Florida Panhandle has historically been considered the epicenter of distribution, although the species has always been uncommon regardless of geography. In Louisiana, for instance, the butterfly remained unreported until 1963, when I as a nascent graduate student at Louisiana State University, and Edward Nelson Lambremont, Jr. (1928-2017), a professor of entomology at the same institution, began researching Louisiana butterflies. The few sightings we could document all originated within the flat and low southeastern sectors of the state where wetlands are common. The species wasn't reported again until the spring of 2000 when several

CHAPTER 16: AN ELUSIVE SWAMP CREATURE

Seminoles were observed in Bluebonnet Swamp Nature Center, a popular recreational site within the city limits of Baton Rouge. For the balance of that year, and through 2001 and 2002, I tracked the species and studied its undescribed life history.

Female Seminoles are selective about the host plants on which they lay their eggs. Preferred varieties are restricted to the acanthus family (Acanthaceae), a tropical/subtropical taxon containing more than 4,000 species, most of which are touted for their showcase blooms. In Louisiana, the native host is looseflower water-willow (*Justicia lanceolata*), a low-growing pioneering species that thrives on bare soil; plants typically occur at the interface between terra firma and dependable water—a restricted zone that usually remains relatively moist. Lavender flowers occur singly and in sequence along a small spike that grows within the axis of a leaf and stem. The seeds are insignificant and inconspicuous. Reproduction is mainly through root extensions so that the plants usually form tight colonies. Consequently, females select a water-willow that is often in proximity to one that already has eggs or larvae from another female—a way of increasing success rate. A female will alight on a new leaf and curl her abdomen beneath. There, if undisturbed, she will deposit a cluster of small lime-yellow eggs within a few minutes or up to a half hour. Characteristically, the number of eggs, at best is between 110 and 125. The cluster is oval, although the shape is set by the female's ability to manipulate her abdomen while remaining stationary. After a few days of relative inactivity, she repeats the procedure. Within her life span of a month or so, she produces four to six clusters totaling 250-450 eggs.

Eggs turn pale green within a period of four to five days. After the change, they hatch synchronously into tiny larvae. The caterpillars are cylindrical in shape and translucent lime-green in color except for heads that are glossy black. Hatchlings remain within their social cluster, although they do move about to feed at night. During the day, they remain motionless. Initially, larvae consume only the lower epidermis of the leaf avoiding the tougher vascular and supporting tissues. But when that food source is depleted, the larvae relocate to the upper leaf surface, again feeding on the epidermis and the middle layer of mesophyll. Shortly, the leaf is completely skeletonized, rendering it ghostly ("lace-like") in appearance, indicative of Seminole infestation. The translucent larvae quickly become dark green due to the ingestion of chlorophyll. Their appearance at this point can be compared to that of childhood candy marketed as "gummy bears." When disturbed, a larva will exude green mucilage as it drops to the ground and feigns death while retaining a curled position. This same substance occurs in frass, or caterpillar excrement. To the human palate (candidly, I volunteered as the proverbial guinea pig), the mucilage is pungent. These compounds act as both as a physical deterrent and an antibiotic agent to prevent eruptions of disease epidemics within a quaggy home that probably is a de facto petri dish.

Caterpillar appetites are voracious. Individuals molt every few days to expand in size. Following that first molt, the larvae change color to black with tan sides, bottom, and dorsal midline and sport black, stiff, and plumose spines over their entire body. The prickles are only a bluff to spurn predation. In addition, behavioral changes occur. Caterpillars become more independent, often crawling along the ground to locate a freshwater-willow. Older larvae broaden their feeding patterns and create small holes in the leaves reminiscent of "Swiss-cheese"—another clue to Seminole herbivory.

After three weeks or so, a larva will attach its rear segment to a substantial support, usually a nearby stem in a shaded location. Once suspended, its skin splits. The resulting chrysalis (pupa) hangs motionless, resembling a dried, dead leaf. Within, the seemingly magical process of metamorphosis takes place. Cells, tissues, and organs are reorganized. After another 6-7 days, a fresh butterfly emerges to complete the insect's cycle of life. During a typical long growing season, Seminoles can produce three to five generations.

Although rainfall during summers in south Louisiana is typically abundant and dependable, droughts occasionally occur. Such was the case in 2000. For nearly six weeks, my study site in the Bluebonnet swamp received no precipitation. Evaporation within the swamp was maximized so that water levels dropped, even disappearing in several locations. This emboldened me with the rare opportunity to extend my study area. Now, with virtually no water to hinder passage, I could venture beyond the elevated boardwalks constructed through watery regions of the sanctuary so that visitors might enjoy a close encounter with a water-based ecosystem. Absent water, I had unbridled access into the deeper recesses of the virgin swamp. My only concern was to avoid crossing the path of a venomous cottonmouth.

The air was permeated with a pungent odor, musty and organic. The eeriness was heightened by numerous stalagmite-type protrusions from the cracked earth. Termed "knees," these are living, above-ground extensions of the roots of cypress trees. Height ranged from nubbins to three feet. Botanists theorize that these aerial appendages draw in atmospheric oxygen from the otherwise oxygen poor, water-logged soil—an adaptation to make up a deficiency. The curiosities reminded me of a fairy tale encampment of Lilliputians overshadowed by skyscrapers erected by a more colossal folk of yore.

I turned my attention to the adult butterflies. These proved to be rather cavalier, flying about slowly not far from their host plants, pausing frequently to rest atop a leaf where they fan their wings to adjust internal temperatures. Crescent butterflies are distinguished for being avid visitors to flowers. Indeed, their generic name, *Anthanassa*, is of Greek derivation that translates as "Flower Queen." But here in the swamp, this was not the case. In subdued light, flowering plants were few. Furthermore, the few blooms that did thrive were concentrated on ground that was relatively dry—principally along the margins of the flood zone. Yet, all flowers were neglected by Seminoles.

Day after day during the drought, I noticed a few Seminoles, mainly females, perched on cracked earth that had at one time, been covered with shallow water. Oddly, the butterflies were not easily disturbed; I could approach them. On closer inspection, I observed that the earth was overlaid by a thin bluish-green encrustation—a biofilm of cyanobacteria that was flaky with edges curling because of desiccation. Because the venue was shaded, the butterflies could not be basking. I got a clue to their activity when I noticed the proboscis of each butterfly was extended. Could this be an example of "puddling," that is, a social behavior in which males congregate at damp locations to imbibe water containing nutrients that are ultimately used in sperm and pheromone production? Yet, because most of the butterflies are females, I was inclined to dismiss that idea. Drawing on my experience with tropical butterflies, which often siphon nutrients from fermenting fruit plant tissues, fungi insect secretions, bird droppings, and carrion, I concluded that the Seminoles were undeniably feeding. Then, another question: Could biofilm be a source of food for swamp-dwelling Seminoles?

To test, I crawled close enough to touch one of the butterflies. She didn't move, an indication of the female's preoccupation with feeding. And while cyanobacteria form the basis for many food chains, only a few higher organisms have been reported to feed directly on them. I, therefore, concluded that Seminole crescents are opportunistic feeders. And to my knowledge, my observations in a Louisiana swamp in 2000 constituted a first for an adult lepidopteran.

Armageddon! In early July, the long drought ended when a torrential thunderstorm dropped three inches of rain within an equal number of hours. Runoff from nearby streets, residents, and commercial establishments raced down into the low swamp. In the aftermath, virtually all small objects from nearby sites that had not been tethered to the ground had been uprooted and washed into the swamp. Small ground dwelling creatures including Seminole larvae had been flushed away. All water-willows were either submerged or else coated with grayish silt deposited by the maelstrom. I failed to locate a single larva. I did, however, glimpse a solitary adult Seminole flitting above a submerged portion of a boardwalk, like a refugee defiantly returning to ground zero. The following day, I collected a clutch of 76 eggs covered with silt. I took these to my makeshift home lab. As suspected, no eggs hatched. Apparently, the water and silt had delivered the *coup de grace*.

During late summer and into autumn when populations of Seminoles are relatively high, individuals tend to disperse into nearby neighborhoods. Adults became more adventuresome, promiscuous. Fortunately, many residential gardens within southern Louisiana boast exotic ornamental species within the acanthus family. Examples include hummingbird plant/firecracker plant (*Dicliptera suberecta*), shrimpplant (*Justicia brandegeeana*), mohintli/Mexican honeysuckle (*Justicia spicigera*), yellow (*Jacobinia aurea*), Brazilian-plume (*Jacobinia carnea*), and Britton's wild petunia/Mexican petunia (*Ruellia caerulea*). All elicit egg-laying.

And predation? Having reared several Seminoles in a makeshift home laboratory, I knew that the body and legs of a fresh butterfly are clad with tiny, easily shed scales. Puzzling. But one day I witnessed a fresh Seminole fly into the web of an orb weaver spider—a common arthropod in southern swamps. The butterfly bounced out like a kid on a trampoline. In fact, during the entire time of my research in the Bluebonnet swamp I never witnessed an ensnared Seminole, although I did observe two other species of butterflies cocooned as silken larders. As a result, I posit that the deciduous scales clothing a fresh Seminole empowers the insect to escape entanglement.

Following my initial investigations between 2000 and 2002, I moved on to other projects, relegating the Seminole crescent as my "butterfly muse." However, John E. Hartgerink, a retired chemical engineer and nature enthusiast who was photographing life within the Bluebonnet Swamp Nature Center, continued to monitor Seminoles. His weekly (sometimes daily) observations indicated that *A. texana seminole* retained its status quo residence until 2006, after which it seemingly "disappeared." In 2008, a few individuals were again sighted. But in 2009, the number plummeted to a single individual. For the next 12 years, no Seminoles were sighted. This long absence seemed like an extirpation of *A. texana seminole* in this area.

In June 2021, the phantom reappeared. Two ornithologists on a field trip within the Atchafalaya Basin—the most extensive wetland ecosystem in the United States and exclusively within Louisiana's borders—reported a single Seminole. And in 2022, Seminoles dramatically demonstrated their resilience. As reported in *iNaturalist,* population explosions occurred not only in the Bluebonnet sanctuary, but also in six other areas, all within southeastern Louisiana, including three swamp preserves no more than twenty miles from the Bluebonnet preserve. Strangely, in no case were immature stages observed.

CHAPTER 16: AN ELUSIVE SWAMP CREATURE

Sightings lengthened into early 2023. Between July and December, the state experienced unprecedented hot and dry weather. Virtually all wetlands dried either partially or in totality. Meteorologists categorized Louisiana as officially experiencing "Extreme Drought." Previous swamplands were characterized by dry, severely cracked earth. Boardwalks originally constructed to span standing water, now rested above exposed earth. Plant species habituated to dry substrates quickly invaded—especially panic grass (*Panicum* spp.). Water-willows, although a pioneer species, were crowded to the point whereby they could not compete. My visits during the summer and fall months to most of the beleaguered areas that had only recently hosted Seminoles, were at this time, woefully unproductive.

And so, the enigmatic dynamics of the Seminole continue. I am convinced that *Anthanassa texana seminole* in Louisiana is in serious trouble. Because the taxon evolved within a wetland ecosystem, the butterfly must be accustomed to withstanding occasional environmental challenges. However, because of the current accelerating changes in climate coupled with a diminishing habitat due to urban sprawl, the species is now being assailed by inordinate pressures. Furthermore, the butterfly's host, *Justicia lanceolata*, is also struggling. Succinctly, both butterfly and host swing and sway astride an ecological tightrope without a safety net: too much or too little water is a curse. But the widespread popularity of exotic acanthus by gardeners in the Deep South, coupled with the propensity for mated females to disperse from their natural habitats, represent potential salvation. I think it realistic to imagine that long-term breeding colonies of this rare butterfly could become established and exist indefinitely in residential neighborhoods. The key would be for conservationists to educate the public about the butterfly's rarity and how community scientists can play a pivotal role in the insect's future. A challenge, but not an impossibility. Only time will tell.

Consider the following. Many species of butterfly routinely wander into urban spaces. Some citizens have even begun creating incentives to attract them (e.g., pollinator gardens). "If you plant it, they will come," is the borrowed (and adapted) line from the popular 1989 Kevin Costner film *Field of Dreams*. In virtually all cases, though, the "visitors" have not been extirpated from their breeding habitats in the wild; instead, they are exploiting new breeding grounds. For success, citizens need to be educated. Will any conservation organization step up to promote the idea and provide the information? Will landowners embrace a program that champions a small butterfly whose caterpillars munch on prize plants nurtured for beauty and food for the ever-increasing interest hummingbird husbandry? And can the Seminole crescent evolve rapidly into an urban species, either forsaking its ancestral home entirely, or in conjunction with its devastated wetland home?

Over my past two decades of research, the Seminole crescent has emerged—albeit in some years, a "no show"—as the centerpiece of the Bluebonnet Swamp Nature Center in Baton Rouge. Visitors are requested to report any sighting. While the future of this small butterfly within this metropolitan sanctuary as well as within the southeastern sector of Louisiana is tenuous, that outcome may not be fatal. I am keeping my fingers crossed for what I endearingly refer to as "my swamp muse."

[This is an integration of two previously published essays: "Swamp Muse" IN: Journal, *Audubon Magazine*, July/August 2006 (Vol. 108:4), pages 74, 76-79; and "An Elusive Swamp Creature," *Natural History*, February 2024, pages 16-23. Reprinted with permission of the publishers, and with minor editing.]

SELECTED REFERENCES

Ajilvsgi, G. 1990. *Butterfly Gardening for the South*. Taylor Publishing Company. Dallas, TX. 342 pages.

Dubois, D. 2019. Texan crescent on branched foldwing (*Dicliptera brachiata*) (Acanthus family) in Montgomery Counthy, Texas. IN: "You Are What You Eat" Column, *American Butterflies*. Winter (Vol. 27:4), pages 32-36.

Glassberg, J. 1999. *Butterflies Through Binoculars: the East*. Oxford University Press. New York, NY. 242 pages.

Opler, P.A. and G.O. Krizek. 1984. *Butterflies East of the Great Plains: an Illustrated Natural History*. John Hopkins University Press. Baltimore, MD. 294 pages.

Marks, C. 2018. *Butterflies of Louisiana: A Guide to Identification and Location*. Louisiana State University Press. Baton Rouge, LA. 462 pages.

Ross, G.N. 2002. Life History of the Seminole Crescent, *Anthanassa texana seminole* (Lepidoptera:Nymphalidae). *Holarctic Lepidoptera*, March/September, Volume 9, Number1-2, pages 1-30, frontispiece, four covers.

Ross, G.N. and J.E. Hartgerink. 2023a. Update on the Seminole Crescent in Louisiana. *News of the Lepidopterists' Society*, Winter (Vol. 65:4), pages 172-182, 200.

Ross, G.N. and J.E. Hartgerink. 2023b. Additional images of the Seminole crescent in Louisiana. *Southern Lepidopterists' News*, December (Vol.45:4), page 322.

Ross, G.N. 2024. Major habitats for Seminole crescent (*Anthanassa texana seminole*) in Louisiana. Part One. *Southern Lepidopterists' News*, March (Vol. 46:1), page 60.

Ross, G.N. 2024. Major habitats for Seminole crescent (*Anthanassa texana seminole*) in Louisiana: Part Two. *Southern Lepidopterists' News*, June (Vol. 46:2), page 90.

Ross, G.N. and B.J. Johnson. 2024. Major habitats for Seminole crescent (*Anthanassa texana seminole*) in Louisiana. Part Three. Indian Bayou National Wildlife Refuge. *Southern Lepidopterists' Society News*, December (Vol. 46:4), pages 277-280.

CHAPTER 17: THE ENIGMATIC BUTTERFLY ART OF WALTER INGLIS ANDERSON

Walking in the footsteps of an iconic Gulf Coast artist

Unless you live along the Mississippi Gulf coast, you may not have heard of Walter Inglis Anderson (1903-1965). The persona of this Ocean Springs, Mississippi artist could be characterized as ascetic, or minimalist at best. During his lifetime, critics were less kind, and critiques of his art were disparaging: "tawdry," "childlike." But Walter Inglis Anderson and his art are enjoying a renaissance. Today, he hailed by some art critics and historians as "mythmaker, mystic poet, painter, local legend, and inveterate voyager," "the South's most prolific artist," and "American's homegrown personage" alongside none other than the iconic European impressionists, Vincent van Gogh, and Paul Cezanne. Anderson's murals, in particular, have been dubbed "a festival for the senses." Art mavens point out that the so-called jaundiced nature of Anderson's sketches, watercolors, sweeping murals, and linocuts (prints made from a design cut into a mounted piece of linoleum, basically, a type of stencil) was the artist's idiosyncratic style for portraying nature's spectrum of textures, shapes, lines, patterns, and colors, i.e., the artist's language of art.

Born in New Orleans, Anderson was imbued with an unabashed passion for nature in the raw. The artist believed that human beings represented a synthesis of floral, faunal, and mineral elements—a nature-based philosophy he learned while studying in Europe from George Ivanovich (1872-1949), a Greco-Armenian mystic. Anderson believed that *Homo sapiens* could meld with nature, thereby regaining a long-lost connection. Because of that profound metaphysical belief, the artist christened himself "Fortune's Favorite Child." Nonetheless, the artist experienced a lack of appreciation in his time, and in fact, sometimes was ridiculed. But not only did Anderson persevere, he pushed the boundaries of printmaking. For example, when Anderson's linocut designs were too large for standard paper, the artist used the backs of commercial wallpaper that he purchased in rolls from local establishments. Anderson's linocut scrolls were so innovative, that in 1949 he was catapulted into the limelight by being given national exposure by the Brooklyn Museum with a new exhibit entitled *Folktales and Fantasy: Modern Scroll Prints in Color*. In 1991, to honor their local luminary, the Ocean Springs community dedicated The Walter Anderson Museum of Art (WAMA). And between March 15, 2021-January 30, 2022), the glitzy museum celebrated its 30th anniversary with a new exhibit entitled *The South's Most Elusive Artist*.

Walter Inglis Anderson ("Bob") was educated for the most part in prestigious art schools in the East. He was awarded a scholarship from the Pennsylvania Academy of Fine Arts, which provided the young Anderson with travel in France and Spain. Also, Anderson traveled to China and Costa Rica to observe people, murals in Buddhist monasteries, and orchids and butterflies in tropical rainforests. Anderson avoided the popular art centers of New York and Paris, preferring instead to remain on the rural Mississippi Gulf coast. There, he settled onto twenty-four acres of wooded water-side property named "Shearwater Estate," that his parents had purchased in 1918. In Ocean Springs (approximately 2000 residents), Anderson could concentrate on nature. And he was close to an even more pristine world, Horn Island, an uninhabited small island a few miles offshore, which functioned as the artist's "alfresco studio."

To travel to the island, Anderson fashioned a small skiff (rowboat) from the wreckage of a wooden, green-painted boat that had washed ashore. The reconstructed boat had no motor but rather was powered by Anderson himself using two wooden oars and makeshift sails improvised from a sheet and umbrella. With a combination of sailing, rowing, pulling, and pushing, he was able to traverse the water within a matter of hours. Cargo was minimal: artists' tools, a change of clothes, several cans of food. Anderson lived for weeks at a time, converting his over-turned boat into "home."

For most locals, island life would have been daunting. Consider: no communication with the mainland; sultry and windy weather during most of the year (60 inches of annual rainfall sometimes accented with violent electrical storms and devastating hurricanes), swarms of voracious blood-sucking insects, belligerent alligators, and venomous cottonmouths (one of which bite the artist but didn't deliver sufficient venom to cause more than temporary pain). But for Anderson, who always was marginalized from mainstream society, Horn Island was a halcyon refuge; he embraced every moment. When the self-imposed hermit ran out of food, for instance, he turned to whatever he could catch, or what he deemed edible from refuse washed ashore from erstwhile fishermen. Potable water was secured from a small natural seep and from the occasional rain shower. For Anderson, Horn Island was wondrous—his personal Paradise, i.e., Heaven.

What Horn lacked in amenities; it made up for in natural wonders. Ornithologists understand that the barrier islands in the Gulf of Mexico function as staging grounds in autumn for migratory birds beginning their sojourn south. In spring, the islands serve as the first landing sites for weary winged travelers returning from their winter homes in the tropics. Horn Island was a "horn of plenty," indeed.

Anderson developed a personal relationship with several "islanders" due to their curiosity and comical antics, even naming a few: "Inky" the raccoon, "Split Ear" the rabbit, "Reddy" the duck, "Bill" the lizard, and "Slimy" and "Eureka" (two frogs). All became models for the artist's pen and brush executed on standard typing paper. The daily adventures were documented in a meticulous diary that Anderson termed "logs." For historians, these detailed notes provide insight into the artist's daily activities as well as his overall psyche.

When Anderson succumbed to lung cancer in a New Orleans hospital at age sixty-two, the artist confided that his sorties to Horn Island were the "happiest times in his life." Today, Anderson's legacy is a treasure trove of thousands of works of art, many of which were sold during his lifetime at nominal prices or else given to friends or anyone who expressed the faintest interest.

CHAPTER 17: THE ENIGMATIC BUTTERFLY ART OF WALTER INGLIS ANDERSON

On a grander scale, Anderson's detailed oil-on-wood murals in his cottage at Shearwater are so outstanding that the entire room has since been reassembled in the Walter Anderson Museum of Art. In addition, the artists' massive murals on tempera that decorate the walls of the city's Community Center and the entrance walls to Ocean Springs High School have become international tourist destinations.

I was introduced to the storied Walter Inglis Anderson during late summer 2013 at an exhibit, titled *"Walter Inglis Anderson: Everything I See Is New and Strange,"* at the Louisiana State University Museum of Art (sponsored by the Smithsonian Institution). I was delighted to learn that Anderson had included lepidopterans in several of his mural paintings and individual watercolors: monarch butterfly, luna moth, cecropia moth, sphinx moth, and imaginaries. In 1941, Anderson had even begun a book on local butterflies by etching linocuts of eleven easily identifiable species, each accompanied by a brief poetic verse penned by his wife, Agnes Grinstead ("Sissy") (1909-1991). But for unknown reasons, the project was not completed.

Then the unexpected. Whereas nine of the eleven butterfly species portrayed in the original linocuts are documented by scientists as typical for southern Mississippi, two are not: zebra heliconian/longwing (*Heliconius charithonia*) and white peacock (*Anartia jatrophae*). Both are tropical/subtropical species that occur as residents in the United States only in southern Florida and Texas. Both species, especially *H. charithonia* because of its larger size and its habit of remaining aloft for greater periods of time, have been documented as "strays" in southern Mississippi and Louisiana (also, along the eastern seaboard from southern Georgia through the Carolinas). Such straying occurs usually during late summer or fall and is considered to be part of the species' evolutionary means of dispersal. But by definition, strays are not "common." Adding to the mystery, the poetic verses by Bob's wife, Sissy, indicate that the Andersons were privy to details of the insects' behavior—clues that the species were not per chance encounters.

As a New Orleans born lepidopterist, I was curious. Did Anderson observe and sketch these two colorful species in his homeland of Ocean Springs? Perhaps, Horn Island? Or, had the artist observed the butterflies during his two excursions to southern Florida? His journey to Costa Rica? And if so, had Anderson confused locations? Finally, was Anderson so enamored with the beauty of the two butterflies that his limited encounters with them, and his limited understanding of science, just didn't matter?

Now super-charged, I began my academic investigations. Records show that Anderson was quite familiar with local lepidoptera. The artist had access to *The Moth Book* and *The Butterfly Book*, two tomes by the celebrated zoologist and paleontologist, William Jacob Holland (1848-1932), chancellor of the University of Pittsburgh and director of Carnegie Museums of Pittsburgh. (Anderson had actually met Holland in Pittsburgh where Holland offered up tips on how to bait tree trunks with beer, sugar, and molasses in order to attract moths.) Additionally, the Andersons maintained at Shearwater a cabinet with drawers full of spread butterflies and moths they had collected. As evidence of Anderson's acute interest in butterflies, I cite the following from the *The Horn Island Logs of Walter Inglis Anderson* (edited by Redding S. Sugg, Jr. 1985):

CHAPTER 17: THE ENIGMATIC BUTTERFLY ART OF WALTER INGLIS ANDERSON

Wednesday October 21, 1959:

"…flocks of Monarch butterflies are sheltering out of the wind everywhere."

And for Tuesday, November 3, 1959:

"Beautiful butterflies on the way. Thorny Ash in bloom, little bright orange wild tomatoes (also in flower), fritillaries, monarchs, large and small sulphurs, a Grapta (personal note: this is the earlier generic name for what is now *Polygonia interrogationis*, the question mark butterfly), buckeyes."

Too, the newly married Andersons had experiences with butterflies in southern Florida during their 1933-1934 road trip. In Fortune's *Favorite Child: The Uneasy Life of Walter Anderson* by Christopher Maurer (2003) the author states: "They [Andersons] chased butterflies across the elegant lawns of Miami and Coral Gables." Continuing with a quote by the young Walter: "This trip has added to my already great admiration for the young lady [Sissy]. If you could have seen her pursuing butterflies in the face of the Miami tribe, completely indifferent [to them] with her shirt tails flying in the breeze!"

Such clues were too poignant to ignore. By the fall of 2015, I committed to a 150-mile road trip to Ocean Springs to investigate what I deemed "My Walter Anderson Butterfly Mystery."

October 12, 2015. Shearwater, the original Anderson property, remains intact within the quaint Ocean Springs community of 17,225 (2020 census). The grounds are bordered on the south by a shallow bay of the Gulf of Mexico, Anderson's gateway to Horn Island. The slightly rolling terrain of Shearwater is dominated by stately live oaks, southern magnolias, and long-leaf pine trees. The estate is currently the home of "Shearwater Pottery," founded by Bob and his two brothers, Peter (older) and James "Mac" (younger). Peter was the master potter responsible for designing and creating. Bob and Mac decorated all with distinctive glazes and designs that focused on flora, fauna, people, and geometric shapes.

Shearwater had been impacted severely by Hurricane Katrina, a Category 5 storm that slammed directly into the Mississippi coast in late August 2005. High winds accompanied by a twelve-foot surge of salt water destroyed most buildings. But after the maelstrom, many of the structures were restored, and much of the historic artwork—including pottery molds and linocuts—restored. [NOTE: Prior to Katrina, many of the smaller linocuts were photographically converted into typical stencils for future screen printings that could be marketed to a burgeoning tourist industry.]

My exploration of the grounds at Shearwater revealed that two of the host plants (*Passiflora incarnata* and *P. lutea*) for the zebra heliconian, and one of the hosts, frogfruit (*Phyla nodiflora*), for the white peacock, are common along trails and roads on the property. I observed no larvae and no adult butterflies, regrettably. But bush lantana, a favorite nectar plant for many butterflies, was common along the borders of wooded areas; several plants were even thriving directly outside the window of the pottery barn. I shared photos of the two "mystery" butterflies with the resident potters, James Anderson (son of Walter's brother, Peter), and his son, Peter Wade Anderson. They had no reaction. Disappointed, I had but one option: a boat trip to Horn Island. Perhaps the milder temperatures due to the encircling waters dictate a more favorable microhabitat for subtropical butterflies? A trip was a priority—definitely!

Horn Island is one of several small elongate islands that parallel the coasts of Mississippi, Alabama, and Florida. All are barrier islands, that is, they separate the open waters of the Gulf of Mexico from the calmer water of what is labeled, Mississippi Sound; each island is between seven and thirteen miles by boat from the coast. The orientation is strategic: natural buffers to the not infrequent tropical storms and hurricanes from the south. In 1971, seven of these barrier islands were selected to comprise the Gulf Islands National Seashore (GINS). The landmark is administered by the National Park Service (NPS). Since 1978, Horn Island and its immediate smaller eastern neighbor, Petit Bois Island, have each been designated as a National Wilderness Area, a special status that guarantees federal protection; even airplanes are banned from flying over to protect from sound pollution. Visitation is encouraged, but all animals, plants, sea life, and natural formations are not to be disturbed. The NPS motto, "Leave No Trace," is strictly enforced.

The first stop in my quest to solicit travel to Horn Island is GINS headquarters. Although the chief biologist is interested in my project, and a ranger visits the island on occasion, I am afforded no assistance for travel to the island. I am advised to visit the Ocean Springs Small Craft Harbor nearby. There, I engage with the Harbor Master, Danny Jalanivich. The middle-aged, amicable gentleman suggests that he and his adult son would be eager to take a day off to fish near the island—something they had not done in many months They could drop me off for the day, fish off the Gulf side of the island, and, at a designated time, retrieve me. If interested, an agreement to purchase motor fuel would seal the deal. I extend my right hand—no hesitation at all.

October 15. The weather is clear, windless—perfect for a boat trip. Our vessel is a 21-foot Key West Bay Boat equipped with a 225 hp outboard motor that allows us to cruise at a modest 30-35 mph on the placid water. En route we are treated to the antics of several small pods of Atlantic bottlenose dolphins (*Tursiops truncatus*), a common sea mammal in the Gulf that can attain a weight of 1,400 pounds. My mind tries—but is unable—to imagine what such travel must have been like for Anderson in his small skiff, a journey of seven to ten miles (depending on launch site) undertaken time and time again across decades. Such Herculean, mind-numbing efforts are testament to Anderson's passion for the natural world. As our boat speeds along, my respect for the artist grows stronger and stronger. I am convinced the artist was a superhuman.

CHAPTER 17: THE ENIGMATIC BUTTERFLY ART OF WALTER INGLIS ANDERSON

Within 15 minutes, a sliver of white land capped with dark green pine trees appears on the horizon. Captain Jalanivich matter-of-factly states: "signature for Horn." I am exuberant! But for the seafaring Anderson in his small rowboat, the sight of terra firma must have been the awaited beacon that would rejuvenate both body and psyche. After another 10 minutes, we are in the shallow glassy water off the northern Sound side of Horn. There is a modern wooden dock, but it is proprietary for NPS, not for use by the public. I quickly disembarked into the ankle-deep water near the shoreline. We agree that four o'clock should be the hour for my pickup; my hosts quickly depart to fish in the open Gulf on the island's southern side.

Horn Island is nearly 13 miles in length and 0.5 miles wide at its center—a total area of 4.247 square miles; the high point is a mere seven feet above sea level. There, NPS has constructed a radio tower and hurricane-proof building for personnel. While most of the island is made up of sand dunes, there are several sizable tracks of slash pine trees (*Pinus elliotti*) as well as shallow brackish water ponds surrounded by marsh. Red-winged blackbirds (*Agelaius phoeniceus*) rest on reeds, filling the air with their high-pitched songs. I, however, have been cautioned by a NPS biologist to be wary of the ponds on the island because of high populations of surly alligators (*Alligator mississippiensis*) and venomous cottonmouths (*Agkistrodon piscivorus*), abundant due to fish washed in from the Gulf during periodic high tides.

This beach bordering the Sound is broad, sandy, and sugary white, punctuated by clusters of charismatic sea oats (*Uniola paniculata*). Tree stumps, dead pine trees, and assorted driftwood are everywhere as evidence of past devastating hurricanes. And even though NPS conducts periodic beach clean-ups, human litter is everywhere. Anderson's once-upon-a-time paradise is no longer picture-postcard. Nonetheless, I am euphoric to be able to walk in the footsteps of my muse, my eyes no doubt feasting on some of the same images that captivated Anderson. Candidly, I feel honored to be on "hallowed ground."

Near the water's edge, sea gulls, terns, and several small shore birds are ubiquitous. Ghost crabs—small translucent beach dwellers—scurry along on dainty pointed feet before disappearing into small holes in the sand. At one point, I come across a sole Atlantic horseshoe crab (*Limulus polyphemus*), a so-called "living fossil" because of its ancient heritage. The crab is motionless. I pick it up. It is alive! I realize, though, I should quickly return it to its original position since the island is known to be a breeding site for the species. Overhead, a large, long-necked bird flaps its snowy wings in a steady cadence—an animated, dramatic silhouette against the expansive azure sky. Eventually, light reflecting from the sand and water becomes painful for my eyes, causing me to move inland onto vegetated dunes.

CHAPTER 17: THE ENIGMATIC BUTTERFLY ART OF WALTER INGLIS ANDERSON

Many dunes are carpeted with xerophytic vegetation: opuntia cacti, saw palmetto, baccharis, and yaupon holly. The hollies sometimes form impenetrable thickets—many ablaze with small, glossy red berries, a bonanza food source for browsing wildlife. In several venues, woody goldenrod (*Chrysoma pauciflosculosa*) and coastplain honeycombhead (*Balduina angustifolia*) are in thick stands and in full bloom; their blossoms attract a variety of insect pollinators, including several species of common butterflies. Occasionally there are lone tall dead pine trees, several crowned by a massive nest of twigs—a previous home to a family of ospreys (*Pandion haliaetus*).

Because the island is narrow, I can navigate easily across to the Gulf side. There, water is indigo in hue, and the surf is a bit rougher than that of the Sound. Too, the beach is more limited, but pleasingly cleaner—a clue that erosion is impacting this south-side of the island more than its northern counterpart. The beach morning glory vine (*Ipomoea stolonifera*), a global species important for anchoring sand grains, is abundant, spreading its serpentine tendrils across the nutrient-poor sandscape; moon-like flowers are attracting bumblebees, but no butterflies. After a half-hour or so, I retrace my footsteps to the more picturesque Sound.

At lunch time, I sit on a large water-logged tree trunk that rests in the sugary sand. My protein bar and sports drink are like "manna from heaven." In deep contemplation, Andersen's life penetrates my memory. Did the artist, too, commandeer beech debris for use as a bench or table for his makeshift meals? What thoughts might have run through the artist's head during down time such as this? Did Anderson ever regret spending such time on the island? Lots of questions, but no answers. It doesn't take me long to understand why an artist such as Walter Inglis Anderson, a loner in a lonely place, would portray his subjects as mystical, wistful, and capricious—surreal.

And butterflies? I observe eleven species. One of these is the monarch (*Danaus plexippus*), a species known to migrate in large numbers each fall along the Gulf coast to overwintering grounds in central Mexico. Individuals are common and particularly attracted to the blossoms of the woody goldenrod and coastplain honeycombhead. But zebra heliconian and white peacock? They and their host plants are "no shows" anywhere.

At the appointed hour, I am awaiting pickup on the white sandy beach of the Sound. My face tingles from the day-long exposure to the strong light; and both face and hands itch from numerous insect bites. I view the discomforts as a small price for my "rite of passage" into the inimitable world of Walter Inglis Anderson. When the boat returns, Captain Jalanivich displays the catch for the day: nine edible-size fish; he is very much satisfied. For the next two days I drove about the coastal highway—from Ship Island in the west to Dauphin Island, Alabama in the east. Now, after a decade since Hurricane Katrina, the landscapes still bear scars of a major catastrophe. Seemingly, many landowners initially cleared rubble and then listed their property for sale. But sales were few. With much open land, wildflowers have hastened to re-establish. Maybe an attempt at redemption by Mother Nature? Maybe. I document at least a dozen lepidopterans nectaring mainly on hairy beggarticks (*Bidens pilosa*) and lantana; but again, my winged quarries are absent.

October 24. Before departing the Gulf coast, I gave my contact information to the potters at Shearwater in case they observed either of the two butterflies in question. For years, I heard nothing. That changed on September 11, 2020, when Peter W. Anderson forwarded me an electronic note stating that he has been observing for a week or so a zebra heliconian on the lantana growing outside the pottery shed. The young Anderson even included a photo for validation. Furthermore, I had learned in several recent scientific periodicals that the same species was observed during late summer and fall in southeast Louisiana and in multiple venues in South and North Carolina. During that same period around 2020, both Gulf and Atlantic coasts were impacted with an unprecedented twelve named tropical cyclones. Coincidence? I think not.

Reflecting on my scientific adventure that spanned seven years, I concluded that neither *H. charithonia* nor *A. jatrophe* are current, or were, past residents of the Mississippi (or Louisiana) Gulf coast. Nevertheless, both species are common, even abundant, throughout most of southern Florida. Anderson surely must have encountered the two butterflies in southern Florida. There, he would have been able to collect specimens for future sketching. Sissy, too, would have had the opportunity to observe the butterflies' behaviors to compose the verses that accompany Bob's sketches. At Shearwater, if the Andersons ever sighted either of the species, which may have been transported by hurricanes and that the artists had admired in Florida, the artists could have believed—and understandably so—that the butterflies were tell-tale residents of Mississippi, too. Such a conclusion, although is not definitive; it is, though, substantively credible.

My theory is personally edifying. Some lepidopterists might argue that Anderson's inclusion of *H. charithonia* and *A. jatrophe* as "common butterflies" in southern Mississippi is disconcerting and misleading. From a scientific perspective, I agree, of course. Nonetheless for a mid-twenty-century artist, whose unconventional and transcendental life kept him on the edge of society as well as the art community, and whose close encounters with the primal world were visceral, the charisma of the two butterfly species, whether "common/uncommon," "native/stray," simply superseded conventional science—and Merriam-Webster, too.

And the future? With global climates in rapid flux—more hurricanes, more erratic weather patterns, and warmer winters—I am convinced that both *Heliconius charithonia* and *Anartia jatrophae* are poised to establish permanent breeding populations in coastal Mississippi. Louisiana, and Alabama. After all, the regions already accommodate established host plants. Candidly, data from the early 2020s by lepidopterists such as myself as well as several local citizen scientists indicate that such scenarios are already in progress. After all, animal populations are dynamic—just depends on the time scale. But that will be a tale of a future lepidopterist.

[This is an integration of two of my previously published illustrated articles: "Walter Inglis Anderson and the Case of the Linoleum-Wood Block Butterfly Prints" in *Southern Lepidopterists' News,* March 31, 2016 (Vol. 38:1), pages 17-31; and "The Enigmatic Nature of Walter Inglis Anderson and His Art" in *Natural History,* July-August 2021 (Vol. 129:8), pages 26-33. Portions of texts were reprinted with permission from the publishers and with minor modifications.]

SELECTED REFERENCES

Anderson, J.G. 2024. *The Bicycle Logs of Walter Anderson.* Institute for Southern Storytelling at Mississippi College. Clinton, MS. 304 pages.

Bass, H. & E.B. Lewis. 2009. *The Secret World of Walter Anderson.* Candlewick Press, Somerville, MA. 48 pages.

Brock, J.P., and K. Kaufman. 2003. Kaufmann *Field Guide to Butterflies of North America.* Houghton Mifflin Company, New York, NY. 391 pages.

Brou, V.A., Jr., M. T. Lefort, & K.J. Cunningham. 2008. *Anartia jatrophae guantanamo* Munroe in Louisiana. *Southern Lepidopterists' News,* Vol. 30:3, pages 100-101.

Editors. 2004. Zone 9: News *of the Lepidopterists' Society.* 2003 Season Summary, Southeast: Louisiana. Pages 69-70.

Editors. 2013. Art Talk. LSU Museum of Art News. Summer. LSU Museum of Art. "Walter Inglis Anderson: Everything I See Is New and Strange." August 2-October 13. Baton Rouge, LA. 15 pages.

Glassberg, J. 1999. *Butterflies through Binoculars: The East.* Oxford University Press, New York, NY. 242 pages.

Holland, W.J. 1931. Original copyright 1893. *The Butterfly Book*. Revised Edition. Doubleday & Company, Inc., Garden City, NY. 424 pages, 77 plates.

Holland, W.J. 1941. Original copyright 1903. *The Moth Book*. Doubleday, Doran, & Company. New York, NY. 479 pages, 48 plates.

King, A.R. 1999. *Walls of Light: The Murals of Walter Anderson*. University Press of Mississippi, Jackson, MS. and Walter Anderson Museum of Art, Jackson, MS. 117 pages.

Klots, A.B. 1951. *A Field Guide to the Butterflies of North America, East of the Great Plains*. The Peterson Field Guide Series. Houghton Mifflin Company, Boston, MA. 349 pages.

Lambremont, E.N. 1954. The Butterflies and Skippers of Louisiana. *Tulane Studies in Zoology*, Vol. 1:10, pages 127-164. Tulane University, New Orleans, LA.

Lambremont, E.N. & G.N. Ross. 1965. New state records and annotated field data for Louisiana butterflies and skippers. *Journal of the Lepidopterists' Society*, Vol. 19:1, pages 47-52.

Marks, C.W. 2007. The butterflies of Acadiana. *Southern Lepidopterists' News*, Vol. 29:4, pages 140-144.

Marks, C.W. 2015. September on the Gulf Coast. *Southern Lepidopterists' News*, Vol. 37:4, pages 165-168.

Marks, C.W. 2018. *Butterflies of Louisiana: A Guide to Identification and Location*. Louisiana State University Press. Baton Rouge, LA. 462 pages.

Mather, B. & K. Mather. 1958. The butterflies of Mississippi. *Tulane Studies in Zoology*, Vol. 6, No. 2, pages 63-109. Tulane University, New Orleans, LA.

Mather, B. & K. Mather. 1959. The butterflies of Mississippi. Supplement No. 1. *Journal of the Lepidopterists' Society*, Vol. 13:2, pages 71-72.

Mather, B. & K. Mather. 1976. The butterflies of Mississippi. Supplement No. 2. *Journal of the Lepidopterists' Society*, Vol. 30:3, pages 197-200.

Mather, G. & K. Mather. 1985. The butterflies of Mississippi. Supplement No. 3. *Journal of the Lepidopterists' Society*, Vol. 39:2, pages 134-138.

Maurer, C. 2003. *Fortune's Favorite Child: The Uneasy Life of Walter Anderson*. University Press of Mississippi, Jackson, MS. 367 pages.

Maurer, C. 2010. *Dreaming in Clay on the Coast of Mississippi*. Paperback Edition. University Press of Mississippi, Jackson, MS. 357 pages.

Newlin, A. 2005. *Horn of Plenty: Seasons in an Island Wilderness*. University Press of Mississippi, Jackson, MS. 249 pages.

Opler, P.A. & V. Malikul. 1992. *A Field Guide to Eastern Butterflies*. The Peterson Field Guide Series. Houghton Mifflin Company, Boston, MA. 486 pages.

Pickard, M. A. & P. Pinson with C. Maurer. 2007. *Form and Fantasy: The Block Prints of Walter Anderson*. University Press of Mississippi, Jackson, MS. 127 pages.

Ross, G.N. & E.N. Lambremont: 1963. An annotated supplement to the state list of Louisiana butterflies and skippers. *Journal of the Lepidopterists' Society*, Vol. 17:3, pages 148-158.

Ross, G.N. 2008. What kills tropical butterflies in marginal temperate zones? *Butterfly Gardener*, Fall (Vol. 13:3), pages 4-5, 7.

Ross, G.N. 2016. Notes on October butterflies along the Mississippi-Alabama Gulf Coasts. *Southern Lepidopterists' News*, June 30 (Vol. 38:2), pages 92-109.

Ross, G.N. 2022. Update to sightings of *Heliconius charithonia* and new sightings of *Anartia jatrophae* on the Gulf Coast in 2020, 2021, and early 2022. *News of the Lepidopterists' Society*, Summer (Vol. 64:2), pages 96-99.

Scott, J.A. 1986. *The Butterflies of North America: A Natural History and Field Guide*. Stanford University Press, Stanford, CA. 583 pages.

Sugg, Jr., R.S. 1985. Revised Edition. *The Horn Island Logs of Walter Inglis Anderson*. University Press of Mississippi, Jackson, MS. 240 pages.

CHAPTER 18: THE BUG IN THE RUG

An ancient Mexican dye recipe produces red hues that are responsible for the world's finest butterfly tapestries

In the southern state of Oaxaca, Mexico's three main mountain systems converge to form one of the most convoluted and geologically unstable areas on the entire North American continent. There, in the winter of 1982, my Dodge pickup inched along what could have been the trail of an enormous serpent lost in the series of high ridges and deep gorges. At times, the curves and switchbacks were so sinuous and extreme that I had to slow barely to five miles per hour. Jumbled by frequent earth tremors, green, pink, and orange rocks shared the landscape with oversized cactuses and dwarfed trees with red bark that flaked away. There were four of us sandwiched in the vehicle. I was a forty-two-year-old American ethnobiologist who had returned to Oaxaca during a sabbatical from my university to further document the use of a scale insect, cochineal, as the basis for a traditional red dye still prepared by a handful of Zapotec Indian artisans. My guide was Isaac Vásquez Garcia., a forty-seven-year-old pure blooded Zapotec master weaver from Teotitlán del Valle, a highland village distinguished for its production of textiles and natural dyes. A teenager (the son of a missionary/linguist family headquartered in Mitla, Oaxaca), who had volunteered to compensate for my faltering Spanish, along with a thirty-plus-year-old hitchhiking Mexican merchant, rounded out the uncceremonious passenger list.

Our destination was the Pacific lowlands of the Isthmus of Tehuantepec. The route was historic. For centuries, Zapotec Indians (ancestors of the Vásquez family) from the mile-high Oaxacan Plateau had braved trekking from this mountain bulwark to the lowlands bordering the Pacific Ocean, to obtain the leaves of the *tejute*, or *hoja lisa*, tree (*Miconia argentea*), an essential ingredient used in the preparation of their opulent cochineal dye. Distinguished as creative textile artisans and astute merchants, the Zapotecs held a monopoly as suppliers of quality fabrics in pre-Columbian Mesoamerica, where numerous laws and customs regulated attire. On all occasions, from workaday labors to formal settings and on battlefields, everyone wore fabrics that signaled his or her social status. Dress was identity itself, and dyestuffs were the principal basis of this hierarchy of clothing. And when it came to dyes, the Zapotecs reigned supreme.

Human runners transported the treasures of *tejute* leaves along with processed indigo bushes (blue dye), and processed murex snails (purple dye)—all from Oaxaca's Pacific lowlands. The biological products were later processed to color hand-woven fabrics. To this day, these dyestuffs produce the most esteemed and long-lasting colors known to humankind.

That well-trodden footpath provided the foundation for the current serpentine ribbon of asphalt identified as the iconic Pan American Highway that now guided my pickup from the plateau toward lower elevations near the Pacific coast. After several hours, the undulations ceased as the road straightened onto a rolling plain of pasturelands. Then, a few additional miles of relatively straight road, Isaac shouted: *"Tejute!"* I slowed the truck, pulling onto the shoulder of the road. We exited and crossed a barbed wire fence into a pasture. Turns out, *Tejute* is a small bushy tree with an umbrella canopy and large, coarse leaves that are whitish and heavily veined, and common. Within but an hour, we had gathered enough leaves from only three trees to fill six sacks, which Don Isaac contended would be enough for a full year of cochineal dyeing. With our mission completed, and after a pause for refreshments and to cool down from the sultry air, we began our arduous backtrack to the more pleasant climate of the plateau.

The genesis of my interest in cochineal dates to 1977. When visiting an upscale gift boutique in San Antonio, Texas, I was impressed with the wall-hangings (several with butterfly themes) that were created by a Mexican master weaver. The shop proprietor informed me that the extraordinary tapestries were from Teotitlán del Valle ("Valley Home of the Gods"), a rural Zapotec village located about twenty miles south of the City of Oaxaca in southern Mexico. Whereas most of the men in this community of more than 5,000 were weavers, and the village itself renowned across Mexico and among connoisseurs worldwide for fine hand-loomed tapestries and rugs, one artist stood out: Isaac Vásquez Garcia. And so, after purchasing a sample of the artist's work featuring a butterfly, I vowed to travel to Oaxaca, Mexico as soon as my schedule permitted.

That opportunity came one year later, 1978, when I had been awarded a six-month medical leave from my teaching position at Southern University in Baton Rouge. The leave was for recuperation from recent abdominal surgery. My goal? To meet Isaac Vásquez Garcia in Teotitlán del Valle, and to learn the history behind his fame. I traveled from Baton Rouge to Oaxaca City, Oaxaca via air. There, I was met by friends associated with a missionary-linguistic organization titled the Summer Institute of Linguistics/Wycliffe Bible Translators—an international organization with a focus on understanding unwritten indigenous languages followed by translating Christian scriptures into the newly written native tongue. Although the primary headquarters for the group was in Mexico City, the group maintained a sizable field office in Mitla, a Zapotec community an hour's drive on the Pan American highway southeast from Oaxaca City. My hosts, who I had come to know during my 1962-1967 butterfly research in the Popolucan stronghold in Los Tuxtlas, Veracruz, Mexico, graciously provided me with living quarters for my entire stay. And Teotitlán del Valle, the venue of my quest, was but a few miles distant and accessible each day by local second-class bus. "Lady Luck" was certainly smiling on me!

CHAPTER 18: THE BUG IN THE RUG

Upon entering the Vásquez showroom on my first visit, I was greeted with open arms and a broad smile from an individual who radiated confidence and dignity. "Don Isaac," the honorific I endearingly bestowed upon the artist, spoke slowly in Spanish, his second fluent language, to enable me to comprehend every word due to *my* poor language skills. As my eyes glanced along the walls that were adorned with the artists' work, I was overwhelmed with the kaleidoscopic colors before me. Don Isaac sensed my flood of emotions: "These tones can be achieved only with natural dyes. I and my younger cousin, Alberto Vásquez Jiménez., my protege here in Teotitlán, are the only artists here in the village willing to take the time to prepare a dye bath as our ancestors did long ago." He smiled even wider, adding: "The natural reds are particularly beautiful when used to accent the favorite subject in my *tepetes* (tapestries): *las mariposa*s (butterflies) from pre-Columbian Mexico."

As my admiration continued, my eyes concentrated on the profusion of red nuances—crimson, scarlet, maroon, mauve, coral, pink, and even lavender—all displaying a subtle finesse like nothing I had seen elsewhere. Isaac noticed my wonderment. "Yes," he exclaimed, "the reds are my favorites, too." Then, he questioned: "Did you know that we Zapotecs cultivated the dye-producing

173

bug, the cochineal insect, long before the arrival of the Spaniards?" I had to admit my ignorance. The master walked to a small table, picked up a jar of what looked like small, gray seeds, and handed it to me. The seeds proved to be the dried bodies of thousands of tiny cactus-feeding insects. Isaac explained that the dye is relatively simple to prepare. He explained: "The dried, brittle bugs are ground into a powder on a stone grinder and then boiled in a water solution with lime juice and certain dried leaves."

During the next three years, I researched cochineal dye as well as the mythology of pre-Columbian butterfly motifs, in my spare time. From past studies in which I visited several Indigenous cultures in Mexico, I was already aware that butterflies usually have a symbolic, literal, and spiritual connection with humankind, and have done so throughout the ages, regardless of geography. To understand the Mexican Native peoples' preoccupation with butterfly motifs, one must backtrack to pre-Columbian Mexico. Then, much of that geography was dominated by Teotihuacán culture (100 BCE-550 CE), Toltec culture (900-1168), and finally, Aztec culture (1240-1519) culture. All inhabited the extensive Central Plateau of Mexico, all embraced a pantheon of deities, and all relied on psychoactive plants to enhance their sacred rituals.

Although little is known about the Teotihuacános and Toltecs, Aztec civilization was at its apogee; as such, much of Aztec life is legend. When it comes to divination, Aztecs embraced a consciousness that was unequivocally butterfly centric. There were specific words for a butterfly, butterfly eggs, butterfly caterpillars, and even a "Mother Goddess" (*Xochiquetzalpapálotl*), represented in the mortal world by the two-tailed swallowtail butterfly (*Papilio multicaudata*), a relatively common species in the uplands. The Goddess reigned over aesthetics, love, flowers/vegetation, domestic laborers, fire, and spirits of the dead. She accompanied warriors into battle, making love to them while holding a butterfly between her lips. (At death, the warrior's spirit was transformed into a butterfly before being escorted into the paradisaical afterlife.) Additionally, the Goddess was the mother of *Quetzalcóatl* ("feathered serpent"), the God of Life and the Lord of Dawn who gave birth to humankind. By one account, warriors at death joined with the sun as companion with the reborn *Quetzalcóatl*, and after four years were transformed into either hummingbirds or butterflies. A third Goddess, *Itzpapálotl* (the "Obsidian Butterfly Goddess") was illustrated holding four knives, and recognized in the real world as the large saturniid moth, *Rothschildia orizaba*). This Goddess represented movement/travel, the hunt, human sacrifice, war, and the celestial Venus, Earth, and Moon; she also was the patron of women who died in childbirth. Most of these deities were associated with the transformative nature, aka metamorphosis, of lepidoptera, a trait that patently would be difficult to overlook.

Deities were often portrayed as a God-butterfly hybrid—a mythological avatar. This nexus is theorized as a bridge between the ethereal world of the spirits and earth-bound man. Also, images of single butterflies were rife—particularly in clay stamps, painted murals, and ceramics. It is this treasure trove of artifacts that was inspiring Zapotec weavers. such as Isaac Vásquez G. in Teotitlán del Valle. to create their unique *objets d'art*.

CHAPTER 18: THE BUG IN THE RUG

Meanwhile, my previous knowledge of cochineal insects proved very limited. I soon learned that entomologists classify the dye insect in the order Hemiptera (formerly Homoptera)—sap sucking plant parasites such as leafhoppers and relatives that are akin to true bugs. For clarity, the cochineal bug is a type of scale insect that can plague many house and garden plants. The species name of the bug (labeled *Dactylopius coccus*) has varied considerably throughout its illustrious past, primarily because there are two distinct forms. A small, wild cochineal lives on prickly pear and similar cactuses, which can be found from Florida to Arizona and New Mexico, and south into the

drier parts of Mexico and Central and South America. The slightly larger form, the cultivated, or domesticated type, depends on human care for seasonal protection from the cold; it thrives specifically on cactuses of the genus *Nopalea*, called nopal in Mexico. Both forms of the insect produce a brilliant red dye, although the domesticated variety is generally preferred because it is larger and is the only one commercially available.

The uncommon natural histories of the two forms of the insects are virtually identical. Males undergo several metamorphoses as they develop into winged adults and fly about searching for a mate. By contrast, females remain in a prolonged larval stage on a cactus pad, never changing into winged adults to fly off, but nonetheless, still become sexually mature.

Young females settle near their mother in groups of from four to ten and secrete from their abdomens a white, weblike material, which accumulates and becomes a cottony puff. This wax-based secretion is an effective barrier against desiccation in the semiarid climate and a camouflage against potential predators such as birds, small rodents, and insect parasites. When mature, each female becomes a silvery, purplish black balloon about one-quarter inch long, similar to a fully engorged tick parasite.

Females are the source of the dye: a deep maroon pigment pervades all their body fluids and tissues. The maroon pigment, chemically identified in 1910 as carminic acid, is bitter and astringent to the taste and probably acts as a repellent to those few animals attempting to feast on the insects themselves or on their prickly cactus homes. It constitutes about ten percent of the total dry weight of the insects, a high proportion compared with other insect pigments.

While the pigment may be repulsive to the palate it is a feast for the eyes. There is, perhaps, an evolutionary basis for the color's fascination: red pervades the biological world as a color to warn and gain attention, and it is the color of human blood. Since paleolithic times, humans have sought out and used red pigments, beginning with such ready-to-use substances as ocher, a natural iron ore. With further experimentation they developed pigments that required some form of processing. Historians posit that cochineal ranks second to indigo, a plant-based pigment, as the oldest processed natural coloring material.

Cochineal cultivation seems to have originated with either the Zapotecs or the Mixtecs—the latter. A Native culture centered also in the Oaxacan mountains. The husbandry was extensive and intensive in both these ancient cultures by the time the Aztecs first recorded its practice in the thirteenth century. The war-mongering Aztecs, who were constantly trying to broaden their sphere of control, did not always enslave or annihilate their captives. When the captured could provide a valuable profit, they were simply exploited by extracting a periodic tribute from them. Early Spanish chronicles indicate that the tribute exacted from the Oaxacan highland peoples by the Aztecs consisted of cochineal, other dyestuffs such as indigo, and finely woven textiles.

The arrival of the Spaniards in 1519 signaled a new era of cochineal production. The plundering foreigners had been exposed only to fabrics dyed red either from the roots of the madder plant or from the bodies of kermes, lac, or Saint John's blood, all insects that are related to each other and to the cochineal bug, but which produce less brilliant, more purplish shades of red. The Spaniards were instantly mesmerized by the intense scarlet cochineal dye, although they did not immediately recognize its origin as dried insects. Rather, they mistook the semi-spherical bodies for seeds, which they appropriately termed *grana*, the Spanish word for seed (the scientific family name for the insect, Coccidae, also translates as seed). *Grana* was shipped from Mexico to Spain, where it met with instant success, becoming the rage of Europe. Next to gold, cochineal became the most desired commodity imported from New Spain, and in the seventeenth and eighteenth centuries, more was being produced in Mexico—principally in Oaxaca—than before the Spanish conquest. (A three-ship fleet that sank off Louisiana in 1766 is supposed to have been carrying 599,522 pounds of cochineal.)

But Spain could not maintain her monopoly on carmine dye for long. In 1777, a French naturalist managed to enter Mexico secretly, travel on foot to Oaxaca (itself a miracle), collect several cactus pads with their insects intact, and finally return to the coast and smuggle this living booty to Haiti. There, in that French protectorate, cultivation flourished, producing lucrative commerce for merchants in Paris.

Throughout the next few years, through legitimate trade, or by acts of subterfuge, other countries secured cochineal stocks and appropriate cactus hosts. Soon, cultivation was taken up in Nicaragua, Colombia, Ecuador, Peru, Brazil, Portugal, the Canary Island, and India. Because the international market for cochineal dyes collapsed following the invention of the first synthetic dyes in 1856, only Peru and the Canary Islands currently produce the dyestuff in sufficient quantities to sustain dye production in today's markets.

As the preeminent natural red dye, cochineal has had a varied but limited use in the food, cosmetic, and pharmaceutical industries, also. Earlier in the twentieth century, the dye colored such diverse commodities as pork sausage, pies, dried fish and shrimp, jams, jellies, ice cream, canned fruit, soft drinks, candies, cider, vinegar, medicinal pills, experimental laboratory stains, lipstick and rouge, and the famed maraschino cherry. Later, with the advent and spread of inexpensive synthetic coloring agents, cochineal gradually was replaced. But the major red substitutes—red dye no. 2 and red dye no. 40—have not been problem free. Practically all such coal-tar dyes have been linked to one or more forms of cancer in laboratory animals and are suspect for humans as well. Alarmed by this determination, many manufacturers have again turned their attention to the biological world for safe color additives. Cochineal, already approved by the Food and Drug Administration in the United States due to its time-proven safety, is now being reconsidered for more extensive use.

Embedded in this biogeographical odyssey is an ironic anecdote. Although cochineal production was common in southern Mexico, little or no knowledge of the insect and its aesthetic and economic potential reached the Indigenous peoples of what is the present-day American Southwest. By the early sixteenth century both the Pueblo and Navaho Indians had developed a sophisticated weaving culture. They did not possess a strong red dye, relying instead on whatever reddish pigments they could draw from various barks, roots, and soils.

The Spanish, who moved north from Mexico in the early 1800s into what is now Arizona and New Mexico, brought with them colorful blankets from Spain, which they valued for themselves and their horses. The blankets were made of *bayeta*, a commercially manufactured English flannel, colored by cochineal dye from the New World. These textiles fascinated the local Native peoples, who quickly parlayed and traded whatever they could to secure the items. These early Americans, principally Navajos, then unraveled the blankets, re-spun the threads, and rewove them into their own distinctive textiles, many of which have become important historic artifacts in today's native cultures as well as in museum and private collections. Quite a turnaround!

Imbued with this background regarding the cochineal insect and dye, in 1982—on sabbatical from my teaching position—I returned to Oaxaca, cochineal's ancient home. Don Isaac wasted no time with "getting down to business." The day after my arrival we undertook the arduous drive to the coastal lowlands as described earlier. Upon our return to the village, and while the *tejute* leaves we had collected dried in the sun for several days, my host acquainted me with the history behind his artistry and growing fame.

"When I was twelve years old," Don Issac began, "I was very curious about the dyeing methods of my ancestors—my heritage. Spurred on by my father, I gradually persuaded several of the older men to explain the process which had been abandoned in the early 1900s when the more vibrant and less troublesome synthetic, or aniline, dyes became available from Europe." He described how, after a short period of practice, he was able to prepare a dye bath that produced the desired result. "With a bit of additional experimentation," he added, "I was able to create shades that varied through the entire range of red."

After honing his skill, the visionary lad tried to interest his fellow weavers in natural dyeing. The colors were sumptuous, opulent. By contrast, fabrics colored with synthetic dyes always seemed to be a flamboyant, flashy—a few viewers might even say, "gaudy." But after attempts to interest his fellow weavers in returning to historic dyes, no one wanted to spend extra time preparing natural dye baths. Thus, enthusiasm quickly waned. Except for his younger cousin, Alberto Vásquez Jiménez, all artisans reverted for convenience to the packaged aniline dyes with their simple cookbook recipes.

In addition, the young Isaac was inspired not only by the cultural importance of using natural dyes. "Unlike the colors from the European dyes, the cochineal hues are virtually permanent. Naturals resist fading from light and repeated washings; synthetic dyes do not," Don Isaac boasted.

The artist walked over to a cabinet against a far wall in his showroom. He returned with a casually folded piece of woolen cloth. "Here is a skirt that has been in my family over three hundred years," he said, unfolding the piece, which no doubt, had been scrubbed and beaten on rocks with harsh detergents and exposed to the intense tropical sun immeasurable times. Handing the piece to me, he exclaimed, "Look at the brightness. It is almost as fresh as newly dyed wool. This is the advantage of cochineal." The cloth was remarkably vibrant, although a small number of threads were torn. Noting my admiration, Don Isaac smiled: "I think you are ready for cochineal. Let's dye!"

Most activities in a Zapotec household are concentrated in the central, open-air patio; the Vásquez residence was no exception. Within the family's patio, one small area in a shaded spot and protected by the overhang of a tile roof, was reserved for dyeing. There, a fifteen-gallon aluminum pot rested on a simple tripod of rocks. Stacked nearby was wood, gathered from the mountains above the village. First, the pot had to be filled with well water and the fire kindled to bring the contents to a boil. About two hours of heating were required, during which time Don Isaac and his wife, Maria, prepared the wool and ingredients for the eventual dye bath.

The artist selected three skeins of his wife's handspun tan colored woolen thread, about two pounds, and immersed them to soak in a tub of clear, cool water. As soon as the dye pot started

steaming, three to four handfuls of the dried, crumbed *tejute* leaves were added. I suspect the leaves contain oxalic acid, as do the leaves of many other members of the plant's family, Melastomatacae. This acid is recognized in professional dye literature as a color intensifier and mordant for cochineal. (A mordant is a substance, such as a metallic salt, which combines with an organic dye to form an insoluble colored compound or "lake," in the fiber of the fabric.)

As the water heated, my host plucked approximately eighty fresh limes from a tree that grew conveniently in the middle of his patio, squeezing out the juice. I looked puzzled; I knew that the citrus family of plants is considered a native of the Old World, having first entered Mexico during the early colonial period. So, I made my point, thinking I had stumped my local historian. "You are correct," Isaac responded with a broad smile. "The Zapotec use of lime, crucial for the intense red color, dates only to the sixteenth century. Before, some alternative plant or soil acid must have been used. He sighed, adding: "But my investigations have uncovered no written or spoken records; the secret remains in a world we have lost."

Don Isaac was confident that there had to be an earlier intensifier, because he had seen samples of cochineal dye that survive in thirteenth-century Aztec manuscripts. The shades of red on such texts could not have been produced by dyeing with anything other than cochineal insects and *tejute* leaves. His most recent ancestors (those whom he had questioned) had apparently experimented with lime trees, which can be easily cultivated near home sites. As they welcomed the new acid into their repertoire, the original intensifier must have faded into obscurity.

While the master squeezed the lime, Maria prepared the cochineal insects for the dye. Since the supply in Mexico at the time was limited, the weavers were purchasing their dried insects from Peru for about forty-seven dollars a pound, approximately 70,000 insects—a bargain since each bug must be tediously handpicked, swiftly killed by immersion in boiling water, which also dissolves its wax coating, and then dried in the sun for several weeks. As an emergency reserve, the Vásquez family maintains a small colony of the insects on a grove of nopal cactus cultivated in the backyard.

Maria placed a *metate*, or "grinding stone," in front of her on the earthen patio floor, and using a stone rolling pin, ground the dried bugs in much the same way she would grind corn for tortillas. Within thirty minutes, she had transformed one-half pound of the drab grayish bugs into a red-colored powder. The grinding complete, Maria removed the powder and rinsed the *metate* with a cup of water, carefully collecting the runoff; cochineal is too valuable to waste.

When the water was boiling, the master added the powder and the salvaged dregs, causing the solution to become a dark, rich red. He stirred the dye for a few minutes with a stick bearing the tenacious stains of past dye pots; he then added the lime juice. Instantly, the water turned a brilliant red. Finally, the three skeins of wet woolen threads were lowered into the boiling cauldron, and the solution was kept simmering for one to one and one-half hours longer.

The acrid odor permeated the air. My eyes watered as Don Isaac invited me to stir the pot. However, within only a few minutes, my tears signaled my host to relieve me. With a smile he said: "My father told me that when he was a boy our entire village reeked of this odor. Practically everyone prepared the cochineal dye several times each week." His smile faded as he reflected: "Today, only a few recognize the source of the smell. What a tragedy." I agreed as I shifted my eyes downward.

According to my host, the final color depends on many factors, such as: (1) the wool's raw color, which ranges from white through various shades of gray, brown, and black; (2) the length of time the wool is in the dye bath; (3) the amount of powdered cochineal used; and (4) the amount and type of lime used (fresh or dried). By manipulating these factors, a wide repertoire of hues within the red spectrum can be created. Because the precise conditions are never recorded, only years of experience and perceptive eye endow Isaac with an understanding and control of these natural colors, a sensitivity that can be admired and even envied, but never copied.

When Don Isaac gauged the wool to be the appropriate color, he removed the skeins of thread from the dye bath, shook them vigorously to dislodge the fragment of *tejute* leaves and limes, and then hung them on a nearby tree limb to cool and dry overnight. The dye bath, now exhausted, was emptied onto the bare ground of the patio. If a relatively muted pastel color is desired, the master weaver will reuse the solution immediately for dyeing additional woolen skeins. Moreover, an exhausted dye solution may be employed for over-dyeing, i.e., a process in which threads previously dyed with one color are redyed with a second to achieve an uncommon hue. The variety of possible hues is almost endless, a tangible testament to the creativity of the artist.

The following day we packed the pungent threads into my pickup and traveled three miles of rocky road above the village to a small trickling stream. There, Don Isaac washed the threads in a bucket of sudsy water ("FAB" is the product of choice) and rinsed them thoroughly in the flowing stream. The *tejute* leaves had fulfilled their mission once again; the threads retained their intense red color. Back in the village, the skeins were suspended from a tree limb for two to three days of final drying before being painstakingly transformed on a large European design four-poster or treadle loom into celebrated *objets d'art*. (Prior to European contact, weaving in the New World by indigenes was undertaken on what is commonly termed "backstrap loom"—a portable implement operated by someone in a seated position with one end of the loom strapped around the weaver's waste and the other end anchored to a nearby post.) With my enlightenment into wool dyeing completed, I understood why Isaac Vásquez Garcia is an internationally esteemed master of his craft. In the end, I departed Oaxaca, blissful and thankful that I had the opportunity to learn from such an imaginative and skillful an artist.

As an aside, the recuperation from my surgery was a grand success!

EPILOGUE: Today the Zapotec *tepetes* from Teotitlán del Valle, Oaxaca, Mexico, can be viewed not only on a grand and timeless scale, but as ambassadors for promulgating a deep respect for the art, mythology, and spirituality (including butterfly veneration) of historic Mexico. Another upshot is that what once was a bucolic Indigenous village off the beaten track, is today reputed to be a modern tourist-friendly destination that boasts the highest standard of living of any Indigenous community within the Western Hemisphere, if not the entire world. For examples: Teotitlán del Valle is currently serviced by an all-weather, cobble-stone roadway linking it to the Pan American Highway, a central water/sewer system, a fully staffed medical clinic supervised by Don Isaac's oldest son, Jerónimo, who has a medical degree, modern factories for processing raw wool into thread, a modern/clean cafe, and indoor tourist facilities—even a cozy Bed & Breakfast featuring authentic Zapotec cuisine. In addition, the village is included in most package tourist circuits highlighting Oaxaca City and environs; each day, groups of international tourists disembark from first-class tour buses to experience the *pièces de résistance* of modern Zapotec textile artisans using ancient techniques. Visitors are always in for a treat: a live demonstration of wool preparation, dye-bath preparation, dying, and the opportunity to view tapestries colored with the plushest of hues, and of the finest quality. Understandably, sales are usually high. On a personal note, the Isaac Vásquez Garcia family now showcases the family's art in a new, modern, vibrant showroom/studio they have proudly named "*The Bug in the Rug*," in English, and as a tribute to my 1986 story in

CHAPTER 18: THE BUG IN THE RUG

Natural History magazine that had contributed to the family's fame. Both Isaac Vásquez Garcia and Alberto Vásquez Jiménez have now passed away: Isaac, December 2022, Alberto, several years earlier. Nonetheless, the Vásquez studio—"*The Bug in the Rug*"—continues to flourish under the direction of Don Isaac's youngest son, "Isaac Junior Vásquez," in time, the new "Don Isaac."

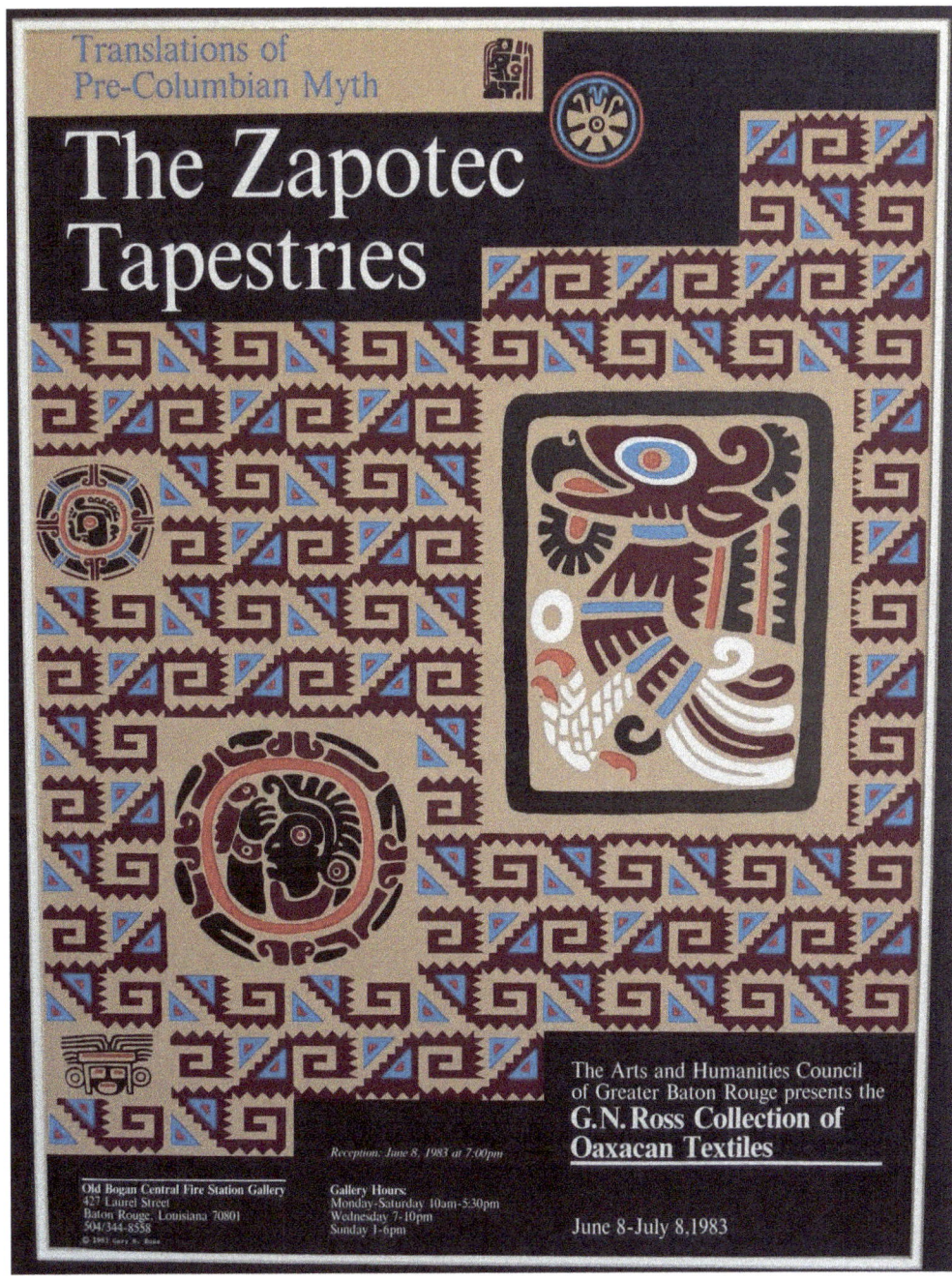

To pay homage to Mexico's heritage of textile artistry and butterfly worship, I orchestrated an ambitious exhibit of Zapotec fabrics in the gallery of the Arts and Humanities Council of Greater Baton Rouge between June 8 and July 8, 1983. Titled "The Zapotec Tapestries: Translations of Pre-Columbian Myth," the exhibit showcased sixty-two textiles and several hundred photographs from Teotitlán del Valle. During the first two weeks, Don Isaac Vásquez G. was present to interact with visitors throughout workshops and gallery tours. The artist proved himself a gifted ambassador for his craft, his culture, and his country. At closing, the exhibit ranked as the largest single gallery opening in the history of Baton Rouge. Later in 2004, I arranged a two-year (2004-2006) exhibit titled "Zapotec Tapestries" to inaugurate the McGuire Center for Lepidoptera and Biodiversity, Florida Museum of Natural History, University of Florida (Gainesville). The display presented thirteen tapestries woven by the illustrious Vásquez cousins.

[This is excerpted from two of my previously published articles: "The Bug in the Rug," *Natural History*, March 1986 (Vol 95:3) pages 66-73; and "Insects in Mythology and Religion," 2024, Chapter 5, pages 95-117. IN: *A Cultural History of Insects in the Modern Age*. Volume 6, 217 pages. Edited by Robert K.D. Peterson. IN: *A Cultural History of Insects (*Volumes 1-6*)*. 2024, General Editor: Gene Kritsky. Bloomsbury Academic. London, UK. Texts used with permission of the editors/publishers and with minor edits.]

SELECTED REFERENCES

Beutelspacher, C.R. 1999. *Las Mariposas Entre Los Antiguos Mexicanos* (Tezontle). Fondo de Cultura Económica. México D.F., México. 103 pages.

De la Maza Ramírez, R. 1987. *Mariposas Mexicanos*. Fondo de Cultura Económica, S.A. de C.V. México D.F., México. 302 pages.

Enciso, J. 1953. *Design Motifs of Ancient Mexico*. Dover Publications, Inc. New York, NY. 153 pages.

Enciso, J. 1971. *Designs from Pre-Columbian* Mexico. Dover Publications, Inc. New York, NY. 105 pages.

Field, F.V. 1974. *Pre-Hispanic Stamp Designs*. Dover Publications, Inc. New York, NY. 208 pages.

Manos-Jones, M. 2000. *The Spirit of Butterflies: Myth, Magic, and Art*. Harry N. Abrams, Inc. New York, NY 144 pages.

Ross, G.N. 1988. Threads of tradition. *Americas*, July-August (Vol. 40:4), pages 16-21.

Ross, G.N. 1990. Cochineal—The Bug in the Rug. IN: Dyes from Nature. Plants & Gardens. *Brooklyn Botanic Garden Record*. Summer (Vol. 46:2), pages 6-9.

Ross, G.N. 1997. Goddesses fly again: Butterfly images in Mexican myth and textiles. *American Butterflies*, Winter (Vol 5:4), pages 14-18.

Ross, G.N. 2005. McGuire Center: Butterfly tapestries depict Mexico's rich cultural heritage. *Natural History* (special issue for The Florida Museum of Natural History), November (Vol.114:9), pages 76-77.

Ross, G.N. 2012a. Threads of tradition: the butterfly motif in Mexico's Zapotec tapestries. *News of the Lepidopterists' Society*, Fall (Vol. 54:3), pages 98-103.

Ross, G.N. 2012b. Zapotec butterfly tapestries: a legacy of Pre-Columbian mythology. *News of the Lepidopterists' Society*, Winter (Vol. 34:4), pages 197-214.

Ross, G.N. 2015. My experiences with butterfly imagery in contemporary indigenous cultures. Part 1: Mesoamerica. *Southern Lepidopterists' News*, March 31 (Vol. 37:1), pages 5-15.

Rothschild, M. 1991. *Butterfly Cooing Like a Dove*. Doubleday. New York, NY. 215 pages.

Selcraig, B. 2003. Dream weavers. *Smithsonian*, November (Vol. 14:8), pages 72-78.

Stanton, A.F. 1999. Zapotec Weavers of Teotitlan. *Museum of New Mexico Press*. Santa Fe, NM. 114 pages.

Whitecotton, J.W. 1977. *The Zapotecs: Princes, Priests, and Peasants*. University of Oklahoma Press. The Civilization of the American Indian Series. Norman, OK. 338 pages.

CREDITS FOR PHOTOGRAPHS

The majority of photographs contained within were taken by yours truly. Because of the year, most were shot on Kodachrome 25 or 64 slide film for 35 mm cameras; these were digitized for publication. However, several photographs (or artwork) were graciously supplied by others, who are listed below. I am exceedingly appreciative; my deepest THANKS!

Robert F. Andrle (deceased), (Buffalo, NY): Frontispiece

Bruce Howard (Mandeville, LA): page 111 (bottom)

Deborah Matthews (University of Florida, Gainesville, FL), two images: page 33

Anupama Priyadarshini (University of Florida, Gainesville, FL), two images: page 33

Sarah Rayner (Baton Rouge, LA): page 12

Andalyne Tofflemire in iNaturalist.org: page 34

Andrew D. Warren in Butterfliesofamerica.com, two images: pages 31, 148 (bottom)

Andrew D. Warren, Kim Davis, Mike Strangeland in Butterfliesofamerica.com, five images, pages 24, 147

Walter Anderson Museum of Art (WAMA), (Ocean Springs, MS), two pieces of art, page 162

www.ingramcontent.com/pod-product-compliance
Lightning Source LLC
Chambersburg PA
CBHW040928240426
43667CB00026B/2988